TO SPEAK AS A JUDGE

To Speak as a Judge

Difference, voice and power

SANDRA BERNS
Professor and Dean of Law
Griffith University

Ashgate

DARTMOUTH

Aldershot • Brookfield USA • Singapore • Sydney

Published by
Ashgate Publishing Ltd
Gower House
Croft Road
Aldershot
Hants GU11 3HR
England

Ashgate Publishing Company
Old Post Road
Brookfield
Vermont 05036
USA

British Library Cataloguing in Publication Data
Berns, Sandra
    To speak as a judge : difference, voice and power. -
(Applied legal philosophy)
    1. Women judges 2. Judgments
    I. Title
    347'.077

Library of Congress Cataloging-in-Publication Data
Berns, Sandra.
    To speak as a judge : difference, voice and power / Sandra
Berns.
        p. cm.
    Includes bibliographical references and index.
    ISBN 1-84014-742-3 (hc.)
    1. Feminist jurisprudence. 2. Women judges. 3. Judicial process.
I. Title.
    K349 .B47 1999
    347'.014'082--dc21   98-46596
                                                                          CIP

ISBN 1 84014 742 3
Printed and bound in Great Britain by MPG Books Ltd, Bodmin, Cornwall

Contents

Preface   *vi*
Acknowledgments   *viii*

1   Speaking and Judging   1

2   Authority and the Voice of the Other   21

3   Speaking Law and Rendering Judgment   37

4   The Subversive Moment   51

5   Free Will and the Judge as Subject   83

6   From Polyvocality to Narrative Coherence   102

7   Texts, Authority and the Force of Law   128

8   Judgment as Rhetoric   157

9   To Speak as a Judge/Woman: A Different Voice?   193

10   Justice, Finally   214

Bibliography   *232*
Index   *238*

Preface

To Speak as a Judge was born out of my disquiet with conventional accounts of adjudication and with their understanding of what it might mean to speak as a judge. Over and over, the image of the rule of law towered above our understandings of judgment, until it often seemed that there was no room for judgment within adjudication. Notions of constructive interpretation, and the relationship such notions posited between the judge and an expanded conception of law did little to relieve this disquiet.

Against this background, my first encounter with Robert Cover's work was a revelation. His understanding of the violence of judgment, of the degree to which the judge was, inevitably, implicated in law's violence, however desperately she might seek to avoid it, has had a profound and lasting influence on my work. For me, at that time and even more today, its rightness is beyond question. This rightness inevitably led me to further and more difficult questions, questions about the relationship between the judge and authority and about the gendering of law and of authority and about the speech of those women who, like their male counterparts, deal in pain and death on a daily basis.

Other influences, chief among them Stanley Cavell, have shaped the context within which I work. Professor Cavell introduced me to philosophy in my undergraduate days at Berkeley and has had a lasting and profound influence on my intellectual development. I can truly say that he helped me begin to find my voice in philosophy. It was at Berkeley during those years that I began to make sense of the scars left by Cartesian scepticism upon our expectations of knowledge and understanding. Those scars form a very important part of the context of this work.

More recently, my engagment with the work of Robin West has helped in the development of my own understandings. All of the ways in which I have, gradually, come to disagree with her bear witness to the influence her work has had and to my ongoing engagement with it.

This book has been a long time in the writing, longer than I might have wished, but its form has been shaped by the events that have prolonged its gestation. If, when I began writing it, my understandings of authority and of the ways in which I, as a woman, might or might not speak with authority were for the most part academic, during the last few years I have become intimately acquainted with the uneasy relationship between authority, voice and difference.

During the writing of To Speak as a Judge I have have amassed many intellectual debts. To all of those – especially Paula Baron, Michael Tilbury, Ian Duncanson, Shaun McVeigh and Helen Stacy – who struggled through earlier drafts and offered encouragement, I am deeply grateful. Without your encouragement, this work would not have come to fruition.

Finally, on a more intimate level, I want to dedicate this work to my partner, Mort and to our Siberian Husky, Arwen Evenstar. The struggle to achieve more than one ever thought possible is always made easier by the knowledge of a safe harbour.

Sandra Berns
Griffith University
Brisbane, Queensland
July 1998

Acknowledgments

The author gratefully acknowledges permission to reprint previously published material here. An earlier version of a portion of chapters 1, 3, 4, and 5 originally appeared as chapter 3, 'Constituting a Nation: Adjudication as Constitutive Rhetoric' in sampford & Preston, eds, *Interpreting Constitutions*, Sydney, Federation Press, 1996, 84-120 [ISBN 1 86287 241 4].

1 Speaking and Judging

Introduction

I do not want to ask questions about the nature of law as if law were a thing that could, perhaps must, have a nature in something of the same way that dogs or people or even rivers or oceans are thought to have natures. Those questions seem nothing more than endless rehearsals for a reaffirmation of the status quo, another purported discovery legitimating business as usual. I have other fish to fry, other questions to ask. I am interested, not simply in the nature of law, but in the speech of judges, in all those different things judges do with words that go to make up the performance we call judgment. Judgment let us say as theatre. And by performance I mean total performance, beginning to end, from the moment the case appears on the docket to the moment at which judgment is final and cannot be called back. I am interested in questions of voice, of presence and absence, of the possibility of the feminine in or as judgment.

I take as the beginning law and power, law as force, the judge enforcing the law. I do not see how law can exist without a kind of force, at least for us, in our cultures. Once force is admitted, even insisted upon, the question of authority is posed. Force demands authority, for authority alone can legitimate its use, and without a certain kind of authority (or authorisation), force becomes illegitimate violence. One of the questions from which I cannot escape is whether the requirement for authority negates the possibility of a voice for the feminine. In even wishing to speak of a voice for the feminine, I am conscious at once of voices accusing me of some form of essentialism, and of other voices asking how it is that a negation can speak at all. Some might say she cannot speak and speak the law, that to speak a law which denies her voice, which insists that her speech is, ultimately not just impossible but somehow not law.

Perhaps, at least as we confront the law, I/she/we are caught in what Lyotard has named an *ethical tort*. Either we cannot speak of the wrongs done us because they are wrongs which do not 'match up' to the assessment of the law (and the speech of judges), or when at last we find our voices the law tells us that because we can speak of what has happened

1

we have not been harmed.[1] In law it often seems that where our voices ought to be there is only silence or denial. Are we, therefore, also excluded from speaking as judges? If, for us as women, the history of the law is nothing more than an *ethical tort*, how dare we speak it without becoming spoken by it and losing our own voices, such as they are?[2]

And what kind of speech anyway is judicial speech? Our cultural myths insist that the judge speaks the law, that her speech is not and cannot be her own in the way, say, a story or a poem or even a conversation could be said to be her own.[3] On the other hand, because her judgment cannot be other than her own, cannot be remitted to someone else, her speech must be her own in the fullest possible sense. In saying this, I am also suggesting that it is wrongheaded and misleading to insist that responsibility for a decision lies elsewhere – with the rules, or the legal history and traditions of a particular community. No judge, today anyway, can get off that easily. The responsibility lies where it must, on the one who speaks judgment even if she or he might wish it lay elsewhere.

At the least, then, a tangled web,[4] a sense of simultaneous (and equally necessary) presence and absence. She is present at once as woman and as judge, as if there were no contradiction between the two, judgment lying with her alone. She is simultaneously absent as woman to the precise extent she is present as judge, because to be present as judge is to be present as the law.[5] The problem has been posed. The elements in the ritual scenario are clear enough in their way – force, absence, presence, authority, power, and among all of these, that which Irigaray has named this sex which is not one. Where does that which exists most completely as a negation fit in? How can she admit, concede at once to being a negation, to being not male, and yet claim to speak as a judge, to speak not only with authority but also with power, to speak the law? What does it mean, to us, now, to speak in this way?

I want to say at the outset that the sense that I have is **not** of being captured by the law, at least not in the sense of being somehow its victim, but of something else. I have a sense of what it might mean to make myself real through the law in something of the same way a mushroom or toadstool heaves open the earth and makes itself real in the world. If this is not perhaps a pretty image, it is one that I see as powerful and maybe a little subversive. There is something subterranean about it that appeals. Perhaps I should be thinking about why in a book which is to be about the possibility of a 'different voice' in judging my mind turns to the subterranean, to dampness, fungus, decay, and a wonderful kind of blind growth – and why I believe that if the feminine is to be truly spoken this must be so.

Another question as well, a question that is also difficult and tangled. If the problem of the subject remains central, we need to look at what happens to subjectivity when the subject is a judge. Not only must the question of the subject be revisited, reopened, but also the possibility of contextualisation must be acknowledged. It is not simply subjectivity that is at stake, but what happens to subjectivity when the subject becomes a vehicle through which the law is expressed. The question is not simply whether it is possible to simultaneously speak as a judge and speak the feminine, but whether it is ever possible to speak fully as a subject and speak as a judge. We might even ask whether it is possible to speak as a judge and yet remain a subject, as subject is conventionally understood. And this is, of course, a bow in the direction of the freely choosing subject beloved of traditional philosophy, a subject who has, from time to time at least, found her way into jurisprudence and even into judge's chambers. Yet, the judge as subject is somehow determined or spoken by the law even as the law is spoken, reimagined by the judge. Again, these are allusions, a bow in the direction of law, language and ideology, and the tangle these create. In merely sketching the problem at this stage, I do not mean to belittle or dismiss it. It and the implications that flow from it are enormous. I simply wish to flag my concern regarding what it means/might mean to be a subject and to perceive oneself compelled to speak with a voice that may be repugnant.[6]

Obviously I have introduced questions here that it will be difficult to address in these introductory pages, sketched an outline of something messy and open-ended. This is not going to be a saga of law triumphant, still less of law's empire and the judge as its crown prince.[7] I said at the outset that law was not my topic, even less law's empire. What it might mean to be a woman and to speak as a judge, and to speak as a judge and as a woman in a world in which woman remains a negation – now that is a topic worth pursuing. Yet even here, I must register a further and more profound concern. If to speak as a judge can be, at times, to speak in a voice one finds repugnant, and if at some point the judge finds that she must deny the feminine if she is to speak as a judge, how does she (do I) speak at all if by our speech we have accepted that we exist, at best, as the never-to-be of justice? Can one, perhaps, write oneself out of existence with one's own words?

Leaving Behind Some Bad Habits

I want to begin by making a number of distinctions and trying to sketch a little of what it is I am trying to do. We legal academics (especially those of us in jurisprudence) have fallen into a number of bad habits. One of them is the almost irresistible tendency to believe that the 'judicial text', and particularly the appellate judicial text, is **the** unique subject of jurisprudential investigation as it sometimes seems of legal investigation. It is significant, and terrifying, that it is as written text that the law summons its greatest authority and power. I cannot help wondering if, given our bondage to a metaphysical tradition which privileges speech over writing, it is not of **un**-speakable importance that law and the written text (from Moses onwards) are synonymous. It, somehow, has come to represent 'law'. That this should be so is, of course, a fascinating story, and a very important one, on its own.[8] This tendency is particularly marked in those theories which focus upon the interpretation of the judicial text – speak, for example, of 'imposing meaning', or of constructive interpretation – as if the text had a life of its own.[9] I find this tendency a little scary, almost a flight from reality. The text, and in particular the written text, becomes, in the end, more real than the events leading to its creation.[10]

There are, of course, good reasons for this emphasis. The entire panoply of authority in the common law tradition, the hierarchy of courts, the doctrine of precedent, the designation of decisions as authoritative, or merely persuasive, or as *per incuriam*, or even as a mistake, encourages us in this particular folly. Even the traditional insistence that the proper subject of jurisprudence is the 'nature of law' lures us away from real people and into a shadow world of readers and texts.

I would like to try to pull us back out of this house of mirrors, abandon the 'literary' for the 'social', at least at the beginning. I am interested in judicial decision making, in the giving of judgment, and not for the moment in the production and reproduction of texts. Although texts are inevitably woven through decision making, part of the web of which I spoke earlier, they are only one part of a complex social event. Because I am interested in judicial decision making as a social as well as a legal process, I am interested in how stories make their way into the law.[11]   I could have used 'narratives' rather than 'stories', but narratives are, it seems to me, very different from stories. Narrative suggests a kind of coherence which is not always there at the beginning, particularly when the 'beginning' is in a lawyer's office and when the story is spoken by an ordinary man or woman, one without legal training. It is, I think, central to what happens (and does not happen) that these stories are often spoken by those who are not, in that setting at least, authoritative. At the beginning then, hierarchy is introduced, hierarchy of a very particular kind. The background images include the old canard of the 'learned professions', of the lawyer as holding the key to obtaining a 'legal remedy' or as providing the only avenue through which the 'rightness' of one's position can be affirmed. This kind of hierarchy relates both to the lawyer's possession of a particular body of knowledge and to the fact that this body of knowledge imposes certain kinds of narratives upon very much more ordinary stories. (And now I know why I wanted to call them stories, because part of the process of bringing them before the law is translating ordinary stories told in ordinary language into legal narratives.) There is another kind of hierarchy involved here as well. The lawyer assumes control of story telling, governs the presentation of the story, rehearses what will and will not be said. The intrusion of control, even at this very early stage, is also significant. Whether claiming legal rights is, as is sometimes suggested, unambiguously empowering, or whether the process can also become profoundly disempowering, one in which ordinary people are progressively deprived of their authority over their own stories, seems relevant here. It is another avenue to be explored in this investigation of voices and texts. That the 'laws of evidence' loom large among the avenues through which this occurs goes without saying. We might wish to consider –

> the way in which the laws of evidence frame the discourse of law: what matters with regard to the photofit/graph is inside both a physical and a legal frame, constructed to form the narrative of visual evidence. Whatever it is which is outside the frame is excluded, it cannot be inside what Michel Foucault calls the "order of things".[12]

Here, what Mari Matsuda has called the 'soul killing tyranny of inside-outside thinking' comes unbidden to my mind. Is law, perhaps, a narrative of partial stories, the home of inside-outside thinking, beyond redemption?[13]

If you, as I, have a sense of drowning in complexities, of floating down through level after level, I must apologise. Everything in my background and training, in law, in philosophy, even in the social sciences, demands simplification. I hear dark mutterings of 'Occam's razor' in the background. Everything I know of the law, of legal speech, of ordinary people and their stories, and of the possibilities for authoritative speech by ordinary people warns me against simplification. Each time we simplify, we silence, write some stories (and those who must live them) out of existence. We must confront and deal with the complexities if we are to get it right, find out which ideas are fundamental and which are merely allusions (or is it illusions?) woven around a few core ideas.

Before going on I want to say a little more about claiming legal rights, and about the process of translation involved. Yes, claiming legal rights can be empowering, more so, perhaps, when the right is asserted against the government or its agents, but very often, far from being empowering, this experience is brutally disempowering. The kinds of authority involved, the loss of meaning and self-authority which often accompanies a forced translation of events and meanings into a language not always apt for the purpose, the jurispathic function of the courts (even of the law itself), are potentially destructive.[14] Yes, sometimes they can and do enable those who are victims to reclaim authority for their own lives, pursue claims of right against those who would oppress them. All too often, something very different happens. In the process of claiming rights, too often people lose their control of and their faith in their own experiences, their own perspectives. They become, in a frightening and perhaps frightened sense, isolated from what has happened to them and what it means. What begins as a struggle for empowerment can end as a struggle to survive as an individual, to reclaim one's own meanings. This is not simply a sociological plaint concerning the cost of justice (although that can be very great and dehumanising). It reflects a very real concern about whether those who understand themselves as other can find their own voices in the law. We need to consider people's stories long before they become legal narratives, when they are simply stories, encounters (at least in the ordinary private law case) between individuals.

Yet, even my sense that we must keep our foothold in the ordinary may be problematical. After all, and this insight should serve as a warning against hasty generalisation, these embryonic legal stories are stories which owe their existence, at least in part, to 'law', in precisely the sense I said at the beginning I did not want to talk about it. Put another way, those stories, and the sense of being wronged that accompanies them, owe much of their form and structure to the 'law', to the fact that our culture identifies particular kinds of disputes as being 'legal disputes'.[15] How do ordinary people, particularly in a country such as Australia where legal advertising is relatively new and contingency fees are only beginning to emerge, identify a dispute as a 'legal dispute'? They not only can, they do, and some are prepared to pursue their interests unremittingly. I am not saying that this is a bad thing – far from it. I am simply, and for the moment, insisting upon the role of law in our perception of being wronged and the role of law in our failure to recognise certain other happenings as 'wrongs'.[16] Something very interesting has happened to a culture in which right and wrong have become questions of law,[17] and in the next chapter I shall begin to consider why I have this perception and what it means.

So, ordinary stories told by ordinary people, but a special kind of ordinariness that leads them and us more or less irresistibly to law. 'Alternative dispute resolution' is just that, alternative![18] There is another element as well. If some seek out the law to gain redress for a real or imagined wrong, many more are brought before it involuntarily. Having said at the beginning that I wanted to avoid reifying 'the law', here I am doing much the same thing. At the least, I am talking about why some kinds of stories wind up in lawyer's offices and about the role of 'the law' in all that. I flag my own annoyance with myself at allowing my argument to be dragged off its course so quickly. Still, I cannot help thinking that the role of law in shaping the kinds of stories that find their way into lawyer's offices is important. Just where it fits in I am not certain, but I do have a sense that even this far back the force of law, of legality, if you will, has an influence, that it both creates and forecloses possibilities. One of the things I want to say here is that we have yet to get the possibilities right.

Voices

Once within the courtroom even the simplest story is the product of at least four voices. As the performance unfolds, other voices are added – those of witnesses, for example, and, from time to time, even the voice of the judge. Again, these voices become so much a part of the story that is being created, the legal narrative, that it does not exist without them. That is, I think, important. The relationship between the courtroom performance by lawyers, witnesses, parties and, inevitably, the judge and the eventual outcome of the case, the answer, right or otherwise, is at least as significant as the amplitude we give the concept of law. Our account would be much simpler, and the way could be seen much more clearly if this were not the case. Something else is important as well. At some point the legal narrative must attain narrative coherence, must seem to dictate outcomes, to become unambiguously clear and certain. I am interested in precisely how a polyvocal story, one that unfolds through the voices of numerous participants, is transformed into a 'seamless web' and becomes a narrative that depends for its force as law upon its apparent inevitability.[19]

At this very early stage in my account, it is important to be very clear about what I am doing. I am not listing sources of potential bias. Indeed, I am not suggesting that this inherent polyvocality has anything at all to do with bias. Bias is a separate, and, I suspect, rather unimportant issue in the big picture. Rather, I am insisting that who in particular the lawyers, the witnesses, the parties, and even the judge are matters. It matters for the kind of story that is ultimately told, and for the way that story reaches the law and the law reaches that story. Gender matters, race matters, and class matters. These things matter, not as potential sources of bias, but as a necessary and inevitable part of the story which is unfolding. If we do not like the fact that these things matter, or do not like the particular way they matter, if we find our inability to attain neutrality and objectivity frightening, we might want to think long and hard about why this is so and what it suggests about our beliefs about the law and our expectations of it. Why, for example, is it still suggested that, in some matters at least, a black judge or a woman judge would be somehow biased while a white male judge would be impartial and neutral? What does this suggest about our language and culture? Impartiality and power form an unspoken and unspeakable subtext here. We might, I suspect, want to ask just what it is about occupying a position of power 'as of right' that ensures that one is impartial. What can im*partial* mean in this context? What might it mean to be *partial*, or worse still, to be permanently and inevitably *partial* because of an 'accident' of race, or chromosomes, or ethnicity, or sexuality?[20] Up to this point, I have not even begun to specify the ways in which I think these things matter, or how they might alter what happens in the courtroom. For similar reasons, I have not hinted at the further complexities of the appellate jurisdiction. As we all know, it must address the law, not the facts, as if it were going to be easy or even possible to keep them separate and apart. I cannot even begin to speak of something called 'the law' without seeing a parade of facts, a collage of fact clusters which have become part of the law just as ivy becomes part of a brick wall. All I have been doing is sketching some of the things that may be relevant to what judges do, without even suggesting how that relevance might make itself felt.

The written decision, even more the reported decision, with all the freighting of authoritativeness that suggests, may be the final product but it is not the entire performance. Despite the emphasis in legal culture upon the giving of reasons, the insistent demand that every decision, every exercise of judgment be accounted for, a reason given, it is wrong to let the written judgment dominate our notions of legality. As is the case with any written text, it is produced, not as a kind of accidental adjunct to the decision making process, but as a document designed to serve certain specific functions. First, of course, it makes the giving of reasons wholly public, celebrates this aspect of legality.[21] No reasons could be more public, more accessible, and therefore more 'proper' in this context than those contained in a formal written judgment, or better still a reported judgment which is also the authorised text.[22] I want to emphasise the way in which writing, reporting, and finally authorisation contribute to the mystique of legality. Second, and even more important, particularly if the decision is one at first instance, or one where, for some reason, the law appears to be uncertain is the persuasive function of the written judgment. The act of judgment, the speech act in which a decision is handed down[23] affects the parties to the case. It also affects the various functionaries entrusted with carrying out the mechanics of the decision, and those others that are present in the courtroom or read a report of the case in their daily paper. The written decision, on the other hand, the formal published document, may extend its influence both through space and through time, reach those half a continent or half a century away. The rhetorical freight carried (although often unacknowledged) by the written decision is immense and our legal traditions and machinery inadvertently conspire to magnify it. Should it fail to persuade, it fails altogether.

While our legal traditions try to insist that this persuasive function is incidental to the purer process of giving reasons, accounting for a particular decision, I suspect, is much more significant than this would suggest. Let me explain. A judge, who in particular she is does not for the moment matter, has reached a decision. For whatever reason, it has not been an easy case.[24] Perhaps 'the law' seemed ambiguous and confused, perhaps the witnesses were not all that might have been wished, perhaps the judge is simply unhappy with the decision she believed herself compelled to make. The written judgment (if there is one)[25] serves both to persuade others, to speak directly to those who might also doubt its appropriateness or correctness, and to quiet the doubts of the judge herself.[26] If, on the other hand, while the case has not been an easy case, the judge has reached the decision she believes was 'just' the need for persuasion becomes even clearer. Here, above all, it becomes essential to portray the case as one in which 'the law'[27] dictated the outcome. The persuasive element, the demand inherent in the production of reasons for judgment, that these reasons be such as to persuade others, dictates the form and shape of the judgment. I am not suggesting that this is improper or illegitimate. Indeed, I suspect that the need for rhetoric, for the extension of the art of persuasion through space and time, is fundamental to whatever claim to legitimacy that our legal system has. What I do want to insist upon is the idea that an artefact constructed to persuade bears the scars of **that** purpose. The persuasive purpose is intrinsic to the narrative, not incidental to its form and structure.

I believe that the persuasive aspect of the judgment, the way it addresses its audience (be that an appellate tribunal, a subsequent court, or an audience of academics or students) has far greater significance than is ordinarily thought. When Richard Weisberg observed that *Brown v Board of Education* gave its narrative heart to social scientists,[28] he was remarking upon a failure of persuasion, not a legal failure. For a moment, perhaps, law and justice came closer than is often the case, but the social science narrative lacked the capacity to sustain the connection.

Despite the undoubted importance of the written decision, and the ethical pull of the demand for the giving of reasons,[29] it is wrong to focus upon the written judgment as the epitome of legality and of judicial decision making. To do so is to reify law. If each act of judgment must (at least potentially) end in persuasion and in rhetoric, its beginnings are very different and even more significant. At the beginning, the task of persuasion lies elsewhere, not with the judge, but with the parties to the dispute and their lawyers. To them belongs the use of rhetoric, of all the persuasive tools of speech. In some cases at least, the judge is confronted by two plausible stories, two attempts at persuasion, pulling, inevitably, in different directions.[30] How she deals with this, how she constructs a seamless web out of the tangled web[31] of the courtroom narrative is one of the stories that needs telling.

Adjudication begins from uncertainty, from ideas, images and even, perhaps, more or less unthought intuitive responses, responses drawing upon beliefs and convictions lying so far below the surface of character that they are often unacknowledged. Again, I want to make it clear that I am not talking about potential sources of bias,[32] rather I am suggesting that what is necessarily in play here is the character of the judge. We surely neither could nor would wish our judges to be devoid of character, featureless functionaries on a legal stage. At least some of these responses may, in certain sorts of cases anyway, suggest that one outcome rather than another would be just, and note that here justice is being spoken of, not merely legality. Just where these perceptions about justice come from is another question. Some of them, undoubtedly, come from the law, from legal traditions and legal texts. Duncan Kennedy spoke of these traditions as the 'voices of the ancients'.[33] Some come from the character of the judge, from the kind of person she is and the kind of social order she believes is worth having. Some of them come from the stories told to her, from her ability to empathise with one party or another, one story or another.

The judge must attend simultaneously to the stories being told in the courtroom and to the stories being told by the law and to recognise as well that these may at any point in time pull in different directions. How she is to do this, how she is to reconcile the tension between these possibilities is very much what this is about, about the struggle to reach a decision which must then be handed down and justified. At least three separate strands then, the struggle to reach a decision, the moment at which it is handed down, made a part of the world, and, in the end, its justification.

Women's Voices

Beneath the tangle sketched above, lies the question. Can the voice of the other make a difference? Woman, other, this sex that is not one, the marked term in linguistics, the subordinate to the male superordinate, make a difference? In judging? In law? Immediately I want to say, don't be silly. How can a toadstool make a difference? Something subterranean, forcing its way into the light might, perhaps, occasion comment, as indeed the possibility of women as judges once did (and not too long ago), the threat being of lowered standards. But make a difference? Over the centuries, the law has survived bad judges, even the odd corrupt judge. Surely, we are not to believe that the voice of the other could, actually, make a difference. What kind of difference anyway? More precisely, how different? On the one hand, we have the 'different voice' of Carol Gilligan,[34] the suggestion of an ethic of care and responsibility to balance the ethic of rights and rules characteristic of law and of justice talk. Somewhere here as well we find talk of empathy, of an act of power that is loving. On the other hand, we find suggestions that the different voice of which Gilligan speaks is simply the voice of the oppressed, the voice of one barely able to speak at all let alone speak in a voice which is truly her own. Does the bare act of questioning whether, and how, women's voices can make a difference, whether it is possible both to speak the feminine and to speak as a judge, suggest a kind of essentialism, a tacit acceptance of either the law as unmovable and unchangeable or of the feminine as, finally, mute, so accustomed to silence that speech remains foreign?

I have a whole range of concerns here. First, and critically, I have problems finding my own voice when I try to interrogate these texts. I am simply not sure that rights and responsibility are as far apart as Gilligan and, sometimes, Robin West,[35] make them seem. A lot depends upon how we look at rights claims. I find that I do like to make such claims but I hope I do not simply assert rights, but assert them within a context in which I accept ultimate responsibility for the manner and purpose of their exercise. That is, I would like to think that I demand certain rights precisely because, without them, I cannot accept responsibility for my own life in certain areas.[36] My demand for rights carries with it my ultimate responsibility for the manner and form of their exercise. Despite this, I believe the demand for rights to be fundamental, a bottom line we dare not abandon. Rights give me the space to make choices and claim ends as my own, and as a woman I find I need that kind of space.

Second, while on the one hand I have an understanding of law which suggests that being ground down by it is a real possibility, on the other I think that there are spaces within which it is possible to move, points of looseness and flux, where the toadstool can make her way up into the light.[37] One of the great advantages of an understanding of law which insists that it is a tangled rather than a seamless web is the untidiness of the image and therefore the possibility of gaps, of spaces where movement can occur. To the extent that law is socially constructed (to use a kind of shorthand), it has been constructed by something which it is in the process of reconstructing and which is, in turn, in the process of reconstructing it. The relationship between the law and the social order is too complex for any unitary understanding – the act of using the law changes the social (at least a little bit) and that changed scene, in turn, influences the law. If at times I seem to suggest that there is no room for women's voices in law, that to speak as a judge requires that the feminine be banished or denied, at other times I want to say something just a little different. Perhaps it is not only speaking as a judge that ought to be called into question, but also speaking as a woman. The whole idea of a different voice may be part of the problem, an image seducing me away from what is actually going on. Maybe what we need to do is try to understand what happens to us, as women, when we claim our right to participate authoritatively within an interpretive community which has, for most of its existence, been unproblematically male. In identifying that particular interpretive community as unproblematically male, I am attempting to shift the location of the unmarked term, attempting to problematise the maleness of our understandings of law and of adjudication. In particular, I think it is important to problematise the maleness of the interpretive community as such, the extent to which it proceeds while remaining blissfully unaware of its maleness. If we insist upon the maleness of those understandings and that interpretive community, if that becomes problematical, then the question is no longer whether one can speak simultaneously as a judge and a woman. Rather, we are likely to wonder how all those men came to believe that they were speaking as judges in some universal and objective sense when they were simply speaking as men.[38]

My concern here is with the idea of judicial speech, with the extent to which the judge may, legitimately, speak in her own voice, and that to which she is spoken by the law and must speak it. The question here is not simply whether there is room in the law for women's voices, but whether the law allows room for any voice that has not been woven into its fabric. Can one who speaks the law do anything but speak the law? Again, reluctantly, I note, but do not pursue, that cultural insistence I wish to resist. I am prematurely invited back into an exploration of the nature of law – rather like the exploration of a fine example of the art of taxidermy. One of the dangers in any study of 'the law' is that its subject is not the living law, but the shadowy world of texts and their interpreters. If not, if to be a judge is simply to speak the law, so that who in particular the judge is neither can nor does matter, the whole messy question of responsibility resurfaces. The judge cannot be a freely choosing subject as we understand that idea, because the judge has no choice.[39] Then why can't we simply substitute a calculating machine, indeed why shouldn't we? At the very least results would be more consistent; calculations once made could be replicated indefinitely. But a calculating machine is responsible for nothing. It simply churns out data. Do we really want an image of judging in which people are processed like data, decisions made, power exercised, the whole creaky machinery of the law stirred into action without any sense of human agency. Is that not truly terrifying, an ultimate image of power without authority?

Other issues emerge as well. One of the most significant of these lies in a vague and ill-defined sense I have of 'institutional culture', or even the institutional culture of a particular court at a particular time. I want to ask whether there is something special about the interpretive community constituted by particular courts, the Australian High Court, the United States Supreme Court, and the Canadian Supreme Court for example. Are these courts somehow unique – or, at least, do they at particular moments and for particular cases generate an institutional mystique, an institutional persona which shapes the voices of individual judges? We need to look at what happens to the possibility of voice when people become judges, not as an empirical question that might be resolved by an appropriate social scientific methodology, but as a question of epistemology, of moral philosophy. Even more, we need to look at what happens to voice when not only does the judge speak the law, but also speaks a law she wishes were other than it is. All of this has enormous implications for that whole question which I touched upon earlier, the question of what it means to be a subject. I wonder whether the whole question of subjectivity is somehow more problematical when the subject is, or becomes, a judge. It is against this background that the question of whether one can simultaneously speak as a judge and as a woman carries real weight, begins to haunt the mindscape. Submerged in this question, another, the question of what judging demands, of the space it leaves for individuality.

Do these questions arise for men as well, or can they be forced when we insist that men cannot claim forever linguistic privilege? If we insist that the masculinity of the judge matters, that he speaks with a 'different voice' for that reason (and there was no reason why Carol Gilligan should have felt compelled to characterise the voice of a woman as a **different voice**)[40] we acknowledge, at the least, that there is nothing natural, inevitable about all this.

I have not even begun to touch upon where justice fits into all of this. The word has scarcely been spoken. It is, I think, best to admit at the beginning that there is no necessary connection between law and justice, and probably no unnecessary connection either. It is simply that we would like to believe that there is some connection, whether this is an act of self-deception or not. Even if we let justice talk in, suggest that it is permissible to compare the legal with some other standard or standards, acknowledge that our interpretive communities are nested and that there is some interpenetration, another way of making room for openness and flux, the problem will not have necessarily been resolved. Justice talk is not noted for its openness to women's voices either. All too often, the possibility of the feminine gets lost in its fake universality.[41] We forget that all that we are likely to find behind John Rawls' 'veil of ignorance' is an infinite replication of John Rawls himself. Each of us might find herself there but then the theory would be very different, and *that* difference would not have any necessary implications for justice or for law or for anything else. Despite this, I do think we need to look at where justice fits in. We need to look at the relationship between justice and legality and the implications of this relationship particularly when we are talking about the possibilities for women's voices in law. Even raising these possibilities suggests that women's voices might make a difference. Yet, even if this is true, and even if, as a woman, I am said to speak in a 'different voice', I do not know where that difference ultimately is to be found. Perhaps I should let others theorise my difference; indeed, as I noted above, I suspect it exists primarily in their eyes. Even if we begin by talking about judging and judgment, perhaps we must end in talking about justice. If we cannot bear to speak of justice directly, we must speak about the relationship between what judges do and justice, between law and justice, between what goes on every day in our courts and justice. In the end we must seek the connection between the voices in which we speak, and justice. Our search is made more difficult because we know of justice only by what she is not.[42]

Notes

1   A little rougher than usual handling, all reasonable women know that men sometimes behave that way, she led him on, a 'precocious' five year old girl who somehow seduced an eighteen year old male babysitter. See, among others, *The Queen v Stanbrook* Unreported, 16 March, 1993, Supreme Court of Victoria; *R v David Norman Jones*, Unreported, August 26 1992, Supreme Court of South Australia; *Hall, Oliver & Reid v Sheiban* (1988) EOC 92-227.

2   See Douzinas, C & R Warrington, '"A Well-Founded Fear of Justice": Law and Ethics in Postmodernity', (1991) 2 *Law & Critique* 115, 130.

3   And even then they are both her own and owned by culture and context and the inevitability of both of these. If the author is not dead, she is inevitably situated. Both the erasure of individual identity and the challenge posed by difference are further explored in chapter 9.

4   And this tangle I insist upon – not seamless, not unitary and of a piece, but tangled, overwoven, even knotted. The web part is true enough, but somehow more akin to a spider's web than anything else. Cf Dworkin, RM, *Taking Rights Seriously*, London, Duckworth, 1981 in which Hercules is to strive to make of the law a 'seamless web'.

5   And behind the text I write, 'the law', in precisely the sense I insisted at the outset that I did not wish to talk about it.

6   In speaking of the way, prior to the United States Civil War, pro-abolition judges ruthlessly enforced the fugitive slave acts, Robert Cover said: '*The judicial conscience is an artful dodger, and rightfully so.*' Cover, R, *Justice Accused*, New Haven, Yale University Press, 1975, 201.

7   Dworkin, RM, *Law's Empire*, Cambridge, The Belknap Press, 1986, 407.

8   See the very interesting discussion of this and related issues in Schlag, P, 'Clerks in the Maze' in Campos, PF, P Schlag & SD Smith, eds, *Against the Law*, Durham & London, Duke University Press, 1996, 218. As Schlag notes,

>Indeed, the obvious dissonance between the "law" of the academy and the law practiced by lawyers has nothing in particular to do with the embrace of "theory" or the abandonment of "doctrine" in the academy. It has everything to do with the fact that lawyers understand the violent, instrumental, and performative potentials of any given law while legal academics strive mightily – whether they are doing "theory" or "doctrine" – to avoid such recognition. A lawyer looks at doctrine and sees a tool, a vehicle, an opportunity, a threat, a guarantee. A legal academic typically sees only a propositional statement.

And yet, as Haldar reminds us, within the 'frame' imposed by the laws of evidence, the written text is, emphatically, 'best evidence'! Only when the written text comes into question does oral evidence attain prominence. See Haldar, P, 'The Evidencer's Eye: Representations of Truth in the Laws of Evidence' (1991) 2 *Law & Critique* 171-186.

9   The violence in this image is also worth noting. The judge subdues the texts, imposes meaning upon them, makes them the best possible examples of the legal genre they can be. Yet, simultaneously, the judge is constrained by the text, must not violate the law to attain (what she believes to be) justice. A little 'rougher than usual handling' is permissible but rape is naughty. For those of us who cannot tell the difference it becomes a little puzzling.

10 Certainly this is true of 'landmark' decisions. The fate of the individual men and women involved becomes vastly less significant than are the subsequent legal ramifications of the decision, a fact which is both interesting and frightening.

11 As I write this, I am conscious of building in another source of incompleteness – excluding all those matters that are settled before they ever reach the courts. I am conscious as well of other matters, often involving women, which are dumped by police and by prosecutors into the too hard basket, of mediation, conciliation and other forms of alternative dispute resolution. I can only insist that I set out to talk about speaking as a judge – and one has to stop somewhere.

12 Haldar, 'The Evidencer's Eye', 181.

13 See Matsuda, MJ, 'Voices of America: Accent, Anti-Discrimination Law, and a Jurisprudence for the Last Reconstruction', 100 *Yale LJ* 1334, 1405 (1991).

14 And here I want to say that while I understand why Richard Delgado insisted that those who have been oppressed will want rules and rights rather than community, and while I as well would much rather place my faith in rights and rules than in a community in which I exist if at all as other, the sword can also crush those who would grasp it. Delgado, R, 'Critical Legal Studies and the Realities of Race – Does the Fundamental Contradiction have a Corollary' 23 *Harv CR-CL LR* 407 (1988).

15 This introduces a worrying note. We begin with stories, but many of them are stories which would never have been told were it not for the background of legal culture. Sexual harassment, after all, did not exist until it was given a legal name. In some sense, up to that point some stories were simply disappeared. I can't help recalling here being 'sexually harassed' by a class-mate at the age of eleven or so. Having no formal remedy, I selected an informal one and was enough of a fighter to pull it off during lunch and behind the sheds. My success and his black eyes gave me great pleasure! On the other hand ten or eleven years later when the same thing happened in my first real job neither a legal remedy nor an informal one was available. I had lost the physical advantage and needed the job. Today, should it happen again, a legal remedy exists, but it is probably both less effective and less empowering than the informal one I availed myself of at eleven.

16 What has been termed 'date rape' is a particularly contentious contemporary problem. It has been propelled to the forefront through powerful academic arguments and writings, yet many people still cannot accept the existence of compulsion without the indicia of brutal force. The kind of rape which occurs because 'no' is understood as 'maybe', and moderate force is confused with persuasion, and the woman ceases to be a person because he is certain of her consent remains unintelligible to many people (men?).

17 And here I foreshadow a meditation in chapter 4 upon the distinction between promise and contract, and, in particular, upon the difference between being answerable for a promise, a relationship, a whole way of being between individuals and having a contractual obligation, an obligation whose *gravitas* comes from its en*force*ability.

18 And in saying alternative dispute resolution remains just that, I am not diminishing it or its importance. I am simply signalling that it is thereby marked, that it stands as an alternative to coming 'before the law'. It, as well, is other.

19 And in this particular transformation, the rules of evidence are of critical importance.

> Evidence is thus concerned with the notion of guarantees of authenticity, of delivery, of verisimilitude, of presence. Such guarantees are essentially visual or oral in their perceptual form, and are privileged over the written, scriptural forms of communication.

Haldar, 'The Evidencer's Eye', 182.

20   To have one's identity transformed into a source of bias, of partiality is to be excluded, not only from the judiciary but from all forms of normal human intercourse. The silencing inherent in such claims is, it seems to me, a casting out, a sense of thrownness, an absolute exclusion from even the possibility of being authoritative.

21   It is extremely significant that an intrinsically private act, writing, becomes in the context of judgment, supremely public. I write alone, in my study, perhaps with my clerk. I speak judgment in an open court, in public, as 'judge' – and here I am wigged and gowned – depersonalised, deprived of identity. And no, I would not have it otherwise. Were it not so, the responsibility would be too great for any individual to survive – at least any individual whom one might trust with the act of judgment.

22   In an increasingly visual culture, one in which the dominant art form is the 'sound bite' perhaps the textuality of law signals an archaism, a link with iconic texts such as the Bible and the Koran, texts in which the 'before' of 'before the law' led to an altar in a desert. In our culture, if we truly wished to make the giving of reasons wholly public we would rely to a far greater extent than we do upon the visual media – signalling our return to altars in the desert.

23   The imagery is important.

24   No, I would not deny that easy cases exist. They are inevitable, if only because in some areas the shared understandings of ordinary men and women are so closely woven as to be impenetrable. That today's 'easy case' may become tomorrow's 'hard case' goes without saying.

25   In this light, it is immensely significant that the great majority of cases are never reported. At most, they live in a shadowy half life of transcripts and tapes.

26   The experience of writing, arguing, is also often a way in which one can argue with oneself – write the case one believes one must ultimately make, but with oneself in opposition.

27   And, in referring to 'the law' I do not mean in any way to imply a narrow reading of law. I am, after all, no positivist, and even Dworkinian 'rights and principles' may not capture all, which I would term: 'the law'.

28   Weisberg, R, *Poethics and Other Strategies of Law and Literature*, New York, Columbia Univ. Press, 1984, 46.

29   Nothing I have said, or shall say in this text in the future ought to be read as diminishing this 'ethical pull'. Once either we as individuals or our legal system fail to answer to that ethical pull, fail to be dragged back on course by the demand for reasons, we have lost all there is worth preserving in our culture and traditions. Reasons can always be challenged; silence is a dead weight upon the impulse to justice.

30   That is, after all, is what the common law, as opposed to the civil law, system is all about.

31   And it is perhaps appropriate that the judgment of Athena upon Arachne is revisited upon the judge herself.

32   The persistent perception, on my part, of a need to explain, to argue for the possibility
     of individuality and character and beliefs in an individual judge, seems at war here
     with a tradition which suggests that these things somehow prejudice impartiality and
     fairness. I am reminded here of the report in an Australian newspaper that some
     members of the New South Wales judiciary believed that continuing legal education
     for judges concerning, for example, gender bias, would compromise their indepen-
     dence. Where education in respect of a potential source of bias is thought instead to be
     a potent source of bias, arguments that who in particular judges are has a profound
     bearing upon the decisions they reach are likely to suggest compromise and bias. Such
     reasoning, and the fears which motivate it, I find profoundly sad.
33   Kennedy, D, 'Freedom and Constraint in Adjudication: A Critical Phenomenology' 36
     J Legal Education 518, 562 (1986).
34   Gilligan, C, *In a Different Voice: Psychological Theory and Women's Development*,
     Cambridge, Harv Univ Press, 1982.
35   West, RL, *Caring For Justice*, New York, New York Univ Press, 1997 is the latest in a
     line of works pursuing this theme.
36   I find this reasoning particularly compelling when I am considering such things as
     whether women ought to have a right to an abortion when necessary. Where this is
     denied, particularly where the woman seeking an abortion is a victim of incest, or rape,
     or other forms of coercion (or perhaps even of contraceptive failure), what is being
     denied is also her right to assume responsibility for the decision of whether or not to
     bear a child at a particular point in time. I don't see it as the right of the woman
     somehow in competition with the right of the foetus, but as a question of whether
     women are to be allowed to assume responsibility for their own sexuality and its
     consequences. If one has no choice, one cannot be responsible. I will set the alternative
     out bluntly. I am raped and become pregnant. In my view, if I do not have the choice
     to abort, I am not responsible for my pregnancy or for the child that may result.
     Responsibility and choice are linked.
37   And this perception is an acknowledgment of my recognition that I am a white,
     professional (lawyer), middle-class female. I can be ground down by the law, but, on
     the other hand, if there are gaps and movement I should be able to find them.
38   I might, somewhat prankishly, and with a bow towards Freud (and Lacan) suggest that
     once again having the penis was confused with having the phallus. As usual, they
     believed that they had the phallus. No wonder the **Word** turned out to be just words.
39   And yet, of course, in a very important sense she has no choice – she must decide – but
     what she decides is another matter entirely.
40   If she bought the normativity of the male, who am I to resist, but resist I shall. Perhaps
     Lawrence Kohlberg exercised too great a spell. My voice is mine, authentic, I hope
     authoritative, and female. If it is a 'different voice', its difference lies, not in my
     speech, but in your hearing! And again, I want to shift the location of the marked term.
     I am not 'different'. You have imposed your normativity upon me. I will not
     understand myself as *your* 'different voice'.
41   In saying this, perhaps I go too far. I can, at least, find myself behind Rawl's veil of
     ignorance, I may be uncomfortable there, but the door is not labelled 'men only'. See
     Rawls, J, *A Theory of Justice*, Oxford, Oxford Univ Press, 1972. Were we to go back
     but a little, to Hobbes, to Locke, to Rousseau and Kant, or worse still, to Aquinas or

Aristotle, I would have been told something very different. Not only was the door labelled 'men only', women had not yet made it to being persons.

42   And perhaps, hidden behind all of this, is my sense that my commitment to the idea of justice follows in some almost unspeakable way from the ways in which justice herself is other, not law, not politics, not here, not ever to be.

2   Authority and the Voice of the Other

Introduction

The particular kind of authority accorded judges and the decisions of courts in the common law tradition is remarkable. On the one hand, the legal system has come to symbolise a particular kind of impartiality, a special kind of fairness standing outside the grubby reality of politics.[1] On the other hand, lawyers are frequently disrespected, even despised. While the mystique of the courts has been challenged from time to time, the courts (and the decisions of judges) do occupy a unique role in our understandings of what it means to live under the rule of law. Even those of us who are sharply critical of contemporary legal and political institutions acknowledge the authority of law and work within the spaces it makes available. One of the things I want to begin to do in this chapter is to look at the kind of authority the law has in our cultures, and where this authority comes from. We see the law as unique, and the role of the judge as special, and I want to look at the ways in which that uniqueness and that specialness have been constructed.

The Idea of Authority

Within contemporary Western cultures, the ideas of authority and legality are linked in a number of very particular ways. This is particularly true within those predominantly English speaking cultures which affirm the ideal of the rule of law with all the connections with social contract theory and the liberal tradition that particular ideal suggests. The law plays a very special role in our understandings of authority. I think it is important that we look very carefully at what makes speech authoritative, at those who speak with authority, and at those whose recognition is essential to the acceptance of speech as authoritative.[2] Certain speech acts are clothed with the authority of the law. We need to understand what happens to the law

21

and to those who speak it when this speech is also that of an outsider, whether because of gender, or race or ethnicity. Because of the cultural position occupied by the law, and by legality, it seems to me that it is simply not possible for an individual to be understood as other and partake fully of the authority essential to law.[3] It is important to be very clear here about what I mean. I am not suggesting that women, and indigenous people and Afro-Americans, cannot participate authoritatively as judges and as lawyers. They both can and do. My concern is with a very different and more critical question. Can the knowledges born of their self-understanding as other illuminate their exercise of authority or are those knowledges inevitably forced back below the surface, repressed? I am hinting, I cannot do more, at a relationship between being other and being authoritative, at a possibility that the balance of power may shift (just a little), at the possibility of an authority which is uniquely other.[4]

The possibility of authoritative speech[5] from one who is a woman, and thus by virtue of her very otherness, the antithesis of authority, leads to further complications. For us, in our cultures, the judge occupies the role once reserved for the high priest. As de Tocqueville noted:

> The French Lawyer is only a scholar; but the English or American man of law resembles in a way the priests of Egypt; like them, he is the unique interpreter of an occult science.[6]

Legality has become *the* central cultural myth. Legal texts have replaced religious texts as uniquely authoritative cultural texts, and in the process have become as inaccessible to ordinary people as religious texts once were. I am tempted to use the term 'the laity' rather than 'ordinary people'. Ordinary people and their concerns do occupy the same position in regard to the law and the doings of judges (and lawyers) that the laity occupied with regard to the clergy in, say, pre-Reformation Europe. I could extend this further back to priests and priestly castes... but I'm not certain I want to. I want to capture a very peculiar kind of relationship, a particular mystique – and I'm thinking here specifically of the sale of indulgences.[7] The language of the law has a great deal in common with the language of religion. I think in particular of the language of religion as it functioned when much of its mystery and authority stemmed from the fact that the language of the church was not the language of the people, not the vernacular. Ordinary language, the language of the people, lacked authority, lacked power, could not bridge the gulf between god and man and guarantee redemption. Just as priests mediated between god and man, lawyers and, ultimately, judges mediate between women, men, and 'the law'. It is crucial both to this connection and to our understanding of legality that the speech of priests mediated between the written text[8] and the laity in the same way the speech of lawyers mediates between ordinary stories and the world of legal texts (and judges). Through legal proceedings, through the process of coming (or being brought) before the law, ordinary stories told by ordinary men and women become legal texts. This is a process of translation, yes, but also a process by which these stories are transformed into authoritative texts, texts that are somehow determinative of future events. This process also detaches these texts from the events that sparked them. Part of what happens when texts become part of the legal canon is that they come to exist, not as ordinary stories involving ordinary men and women, but as authoritative texts which prescribe (or purport to prescribe) particular outcomes. Abstraction, the power of the text, the effacement of individual voices and the substitution of plaintiffs and defendants, accuseds and their victims, are central to law's singular authority. Were it otherwise, were we to allow ourselves the luxury of remaining ordinary women and men even before the law, were the judge to speak in her own voice, were ordinary stories to be told, law would be much too close to us, much too much a part of our everyday lives. Its power (such as it is) would be greatly diminished and this we simply cannot afford.[9] Law depends for a large part of its authority upon its singularity, upon its distance, upon the absence of real men and women and the presence of a stock group of legal characters.[10] One of the possibilities here is that otherness doubles upon itself. If I, as a woman am irrevocably other, all of us, men and women alike, become other when we are brought before the law – other even to our own understandings of who we are and what it means to be a person.

The illicit congress between speech and writing is critical. Douzinas, Warrington and McVeigh suggest that the common law courts are, fundamentally,

> places where discourse is spoken about writing. Writing insidiously inserts itself into the spoken process and becomes always already there before the speaking starts. In the common law process, an oral tradition is turned into written records, as court proceedings become reported, and legal arguments, precedent, becomes simply the rereading of the already written... The effect of this is that law is now also a matter of writing. It is transformed from the

oracular, where there can be no doubt as to the truth, via the spoken where the possibility of endless discussion promises, at least in the socratic tradition, the possibility of the truth, to the written where the fact that the writer's true intentions might not be properly expressed, might be never known, might be dubious or duplicitous (and so on) guarantees if not the certainty of mis-understanding, the endless paralysing fear that the truth might be missed. In recognising this danger, the trial process tries to keep at bay the dangerous supplement of writing. Trials are still conducted orally and potentially, endlessly, until all spoken argument is finished. It is only in modern times that the Court of Appeal has taken written submissions, and when it does so it is clearly with fear and trepidation.[11]

An endless chain: from speech to writing to speech to writing to... Our bondage to the orality of the trial process is signalled by the jurisprudential insistence upon the application of 'certain written rules' or the more recent insistence upon 'right answers' which are not only undiscoverable in practice but vary from judge to judge. Law as seamless web attempts to signal clôture, a return to the oracular, a discrete and finite end to argument as if the oracle had spoken.[12]

If the images here threaten to become oppressive, perhaps it is time to step back a little, tease out some of the threads of the web that is weaving itself around me as I write.[13] My subject in this chapter is authority. There are many different kinds of authority. The authority of the lawyers and their translations begin the transition from ordinary story to authoritative legal narrative. Then there is the authority of the judge, who at once authors a new text and authorises certain actions and events. Ultimately the ways in which the authority of legal texts extends through time and space set their stamp upon legality. I see this authority as a uniquely powerful and pervasive cultural force. I am interested in the ways in which it is constructed and the spaces, if any, which remain open when we come (or are brought) before the law.[14]

We have already glimpsed the outlines of one of the ways this authority is constructed and sustained. Through the power of abstraction, the substitution of stock characters for real people, the replacement of ordinary stories by legal narratives, the law invents its own authority. It continually creates its own myths and enforces those myths upon the bodies of its subjects. While these myths operate most urgently upon those who are brought before the law, they are truly pervasive. Legal scholarship perpetuates them, adding the grace notes of purported legitimation (although it is central to my understanding of law that legitimation is entirely superfluous). Our daily lives are lived in their shadow, the law being always and forever present as possibility. Given the power of law, its unique cultural role and the way this role both constitutes the authority of the courts, and is constituted by virtue of their authority, the parallel Samuel Weber has drawn between deconstructive texts and the role of the judiciary is striking. Weber notes:

> Like the Anglo-American lawyers described, deconstruction concerns itself more with "the opinions", or more accurately, with the writings "of others", than with ideas of its own. Indeed, deconstruction turns out to share at least *two* of the *three* traits through which de Tocqueville defines the judiciary: it comes only when called, and its concern, or occasion, is always tied to the particulars of that call: particular texts, questions, conflicts. In its manner of intervention, however, it distinguishes itself from that of the courts, and in particular from the Anglo-American legal tradition described by de Tocqueville. For if deconstruction responds to conflictual appeals, it is not with a view of arriving at a definitive verdict. In this sense, deconstruction does not arbitrate, nor set precedents... To a society whose "constitution" depends in no small measure upon the rereading of a written text, in order for its authority to be reaffirmed in the face of ever-changing conditions, deconstruction cannot but be both familiar and uncanny. As de Tocqueville remarked:
> 'It is surprising to observe the power (puissance) of opinion accorded by men to the decisions of the courts. This power is so great that it remains attached to the judicial form even after its substance has ceased to exist; it gives body to a shadow.'
> In its peculiar way, deconstruction is called upon to address precisely the *power* to give "body to a shadow", and in so doing it raises the question of whether the two – body and shadow – can always be told apart.15

In claiming a central role for authority, emphasising the authority of the judge and the process by which authoritative texts are generated, I am also, *sotto voce*, signalling disinterest in the question of whether we, as citizens, have an obligation to obey the law or whether it is simply that we are obliged to do so. The text, if it is truly authoritative, generates its own obligation. Nothing more is required.16 That is the point of the whole exercise. To the extent that this fails, to the extent that the (written) text is challenged and its obligatory force questioned, we are dealing less with obligations than with textual decay. We are dealing with the breakdown of certain connections between ourselves as subjects and a canonical text and with attempts to foreshadow a new order. Talk of obligations, of whether we (really) have an obligation to obey the law or are (merely) obliged to do so is talk which belongs to a discourse whose irrelevance is becoming increasingly apparent. In saying this I am also (and more significantly) consigning an entire theory of the subject to irrelevance. Questions about whether or not we have an obligation to obey the law (and all the associated questions about the nature of the responsibility of an individual judge) gain their meaning from a tradition which understands the individual as a potentially chaotic subjectivity which must be constrained – hemmed in by the written text. In emphasising the written text and the peculiar authority with which it surrounds itself, a web of authority, I allude to the insistence that this text and that tradition bind the speech of the judge, subordinate her speech and her individual identity to... To what? To law, as if law had a formal existence, to a set of cultural conventions, to power – but I cannot escape the sense of absolute necessity underscoring this subordination to text. It is, perhaps, a mark of my own otherness that I want both to insist that to be a judge she must subordinate her speech and her individual identity to the law and to its authority and to insist that to whatever degree she subordinates herself and her identity to the law she remains responsible for the decisions she authors and for the violence those decisions authorise. While she remains a judge, there is no exit.[17]

I do not like what I have written above – frankly, I find it terrifying. I do not understand myself (or you dear reader) as a 'potentially chaotic subjectivity'. The written text and its peculiar authority are things from which I cannot escape – at least if I wish to remain within the law. To speak the law is to subordinate myself to the texts of the law (and perhaps to the law of the text) but in so doing I do not negate (or escape, or obliterate) my own responsibility both for the texts I author and for the violence authorised thereby. In using the word 'thereby' am I trying desperately to distance myself from responsibility? Is it possible in this way to authorise violence and yet to be devoid of responsibility for the violence which one has authorised? These are word games, mechanisms of self-enchantment. If they are successful, I may delude myself into thinking that by acknowledging my bondage to text I shed my responsibility for the way in which I exercise power, almost as a snake sheds its skin.[18] Yet at some level that is how it works – to the extent that I am simultaneously the prisoner and the author of the text I am both responsible – the decision is mine and mine alone – and nonetheless devoid of responsibility. I have decided 'according to law' and therefore stand absolved.

Writing this, the *act* of writing, is forcing me to think much more carefully than I might otherwise about the relationship between text and author and between text and reader. Ultimately, we must all confront the relationship between legal texts and those who, knowingly or otherwise, are bound by them. The authority of the text, its weight, its coherence or lack thereof, is at once inseparable from the authority of its author and uniquely textual – a function of the text and not the individual. It is also a function of the fact that it is a particular kind of text, a text whose weight, whose gravitational force must be visited anew at each moment of judgment. Behind or within all of this we can glimpse the entire hierarchy of courts, the panoply of judging. The shadow of the courts falls upon the text. The written text cannot be understood at all except to the extent that it is understood as a integral part of the machinery of power and in full knowledge of what interpretation becomes within such a context.

The relationship between textuality and power makes it critical for us to try to isolate the act of judgment from the written judgment. To the extent that we allow ourselves to be seduced into treating them as one and the same, we miss everything that is really important, miss the fault lines between interpretation and power. We must force ourselves to explore and understand the difference between judgment as speech act and judgment as text. Why am I being forced into these patterns? I want to say, not that the spoken judgment (and in adjudication, uniquely, speech inscribes itself upon the bodies of those who come before the law) is privileged, truer, more immediate, but that it acts in a different way. It is functionally distinct from the written text. *They are not and cannot be the same* – the spoken word commands, the written text persuades. The authority of the former comes from the force that lies barely concealed behind the ritual gestures of the courts, the theatrics of judgment. The authority of the latter lies in the interface between rhetoric and reason. So I have restored with one word the 'rational subject' but lately exorcised from my text. I can, it seems, no more escape my bondage to reason than my otherness. Two problems now, not one. First, how can I simultaneously speak as a woman and inscribe[19] the spoken text upon the bodies of those who come, not before a woman, but before the law.[20] Second, can I simultaneously understand my self as other and create a text whose authority depends upon its ability to persuade. For it to be persuasive, it must bear the marks of having been generated simultaneously by 'the law' and by a 'rational human subject'. As Derrida reminds us, the human subject, that subject which is the measure of justice, is also 'paradigmatically the adult male, rather than the woman, child, or animal'.[21] For the other to raise herself to view, to burst, like the toadstool, through the soil and into the light of day, she must fuse otherness and reason – remain other and inscribe[22] that otherness within a rational text, a text which bears its reason and its persuasiveness on its face.

Judgment as Speech

To speak as a judge, and here it is imperative to privilege the act of speaking as a judge, is at once to pronounce judgment, to command, and to bring to a conclusion. Judgment inscribes within itself inevitability and choice.[23] She believes herself to have been compelled to decide as she has, and for that reason, her decision carries within itself the shadow of the inevitable. Nonetheless, she has chosen. The decision could have been other than it is, and therefore she is free even as she is enslaved by the imperative of decision. To pronounce judgment is to command, to compel others to act in particular ways and to have the authority to do so. Judgment is a form of clôture, the thread[24] is cut, the possibility of justice relinquished yet again. Despite this finality, this pushing back of justice, judgment is not simply clôture. The act of judgment brings to an end, severs the thread and marks a new beginning, sets a chain of events into motion.

The act of judgment climaxes in the spoken word.[25] Speech is both the privileged precursor to violence and the ultimate act of creation in a phallogocentric legal order. The link between the spoken word and the machinery of the law reminds us that the word becomes both flesh and law. Again, the parallels between religion and law haunt my text. Jurisprudence often bewitches us into a vision of law and of adjudication as rational, as the supreme act of obedience to text. What is forgotten in this enchanted garden of texts and Herculean judges is law's power to obliterate, to erase stories and replace them with legal narratives, to erase people and replace them with plaintiffs and defendants. When we focus, not upon the process by which a decision is reached, not upon the authoritative written text which may be generated as a consequence of that process, but upon the speech act by which judgment both cuts and binds, the picture is very different. This insistence compels the double gesture by which I acknowledge the unique power of speech (and was not Adam called upon to *name* the animals?).[26] I also acknowledge those who insist that the impulse to privilege speech over writing is further evidence of our bondage to the traditions of Western metaphysics. Perhaps it is, perhaps this bondage is itself signified by the fact that judgment is spoken. We do not simply send the parties a letter, even in civil matters. If the possibility of sending the parties a letter seems absurd, why should this be the case? Other matters, even matters of immense significance, are routinely conducted by post, or fax, or... Adjudication demands that the ritual be performed and concluded, that judgment is pronounced.[27] The orality of the process is critical to the process itself. Atropos must play her role; the thread must be cut. The act of clôture, the actual handing down of judgment, marks a critical break. The tangled web is finished, the last thread tied off and cut. Only after the tangled web is finally complete, laid to rest, can work resume on the law, on another kind of weaving. In the shift from tangled web to seamless web, from Arachne and Atropos to Hercules, ordinary stories, ordinary people cease to matter. They are not relevant. What is relevant is the seamlessness, necessity and majesty of law, of law as persuasion (as rhetoric). The authority of the text, and here the written text necessarily and inevitably comes to the fore, is uniquely privileged above speech. It cannot be isolated from its rhetorical structure, from its capacity to move its reader from disbelief to belief to recognition of the absolute necessity of the judgment, as it stands, every word. So long as that necessity holds, does not falter, authority and enforceability remain intact. Should it falter, its force dissipate, all that remains is words on paper, nothing more.

Otherness/Différance

Our gaze must now shift from the spoken judgment to the one who speaks it, from the written text (as text) to she who both authors and authorises it. Can her voice be at once the voice of a judge and a different voice – does space remain for a different voice in judgment? Others have given you Hercules[28] and Hermes[29] and I, what have I to give you? Female images of justice abound but then of course justice has little if anything to do with law. 'Law as integrity' offers at best a cursory bow in her direction before scurrying off in pursuit of coherence via fairness and procedural due process.[30] *I want to say here that the grammatical relationship between law and justice is precisely the same as the grammatical relationship between man and woman.* Justice is always other to the force of law, what did not happen when law has had its way. I am simply trying to understand the grammar of legality, judgment as the speech of judges. I am also speculating aloud about otherness, about justice as *not law*, about woman as *not man*. Thus, when I ask what space remains for a different voice in judgment, I am asking what happens to the grammar of law when that grammar makes room for the voice of the other. At once unmarked, as only law can be, and marked, branded, always the site of investigation. And for these meanings to be given full weight another question arises, one that must be answered first.

In our culture, a great deal is made of the ritual mystique of law. The judge is invested with robe and, until recently, in Australia, with wig, the ritual accoutrements of office. (And we might well ask where in time and space she is thereby placed.) Individual identity is symbolically eradicated.[31] The entire panoply of legality is invoked to maintain the pretence that as the judge speaks the law it is the law which speaks – who in particular the judge is does not matter. But every lawyer knows, and knows to her core, that who in particular the judge is matters profoundly. For any submission to be made blindly, made without acknowledgment of who in particular the judge is, would be at once an act of the most profound faith and an act of utter folly. It would be the act, not of a lawyer but of a madman or a holy fool.

Yet, even acknowledging that particularity is critical raises further questions. Earlier a picture of adjudication began to emerge. In it we saw a process of thought tending now this way now that, responding first to one argument then another, until the tangled web was complete and the thread severed by the act of judgment. Only when at last this process had reached its conclusion – the inevitable having been acknowledged, could attention be turned to the seamless web, the web, not of reason, but of rhetoric, the art of persuasion. How and where in this process can we factor in the particularity of the judge, capture a sense of what it might mean to speak at once as a woman and as a judge? I said earlier that talk of a different voice, at least in the ways implied by Gilligan, unsettles me. So, and for many of the same reasons, does talk of an act of power which is loving. I cannot shake other, harsher (and older) images, of the thread being cut as judgment is given, of the (spoken) word being made flesh, inscribed on the bodies of those before the law. That is it, I think, at least for me. This talk of responsibility, of care, of nurturing, of an act of power that is loving and empathetic domesticates law, and, worse still, purports to domesticate justice. Here I want desperately to say that as women it is not our purity, our responsibility, our care or our love we have to offer law, but our difference. Our difference is none of these – these are merely what men have hoped to find in us, the things they have wanted us to be for them. It is not like that at all. Choices must be made. The thread must be cut.

It is with these images in the forefront of my mind that I try to understand what kind of difference we might want women's voices (or indigenous voices, or Afro-American voices for that matter) to make in judging. Suggestions that women's moral development is somehow different leave me unmoved. While making a conscious decision to shift between the abstractions of legal thought and concrete experiences of oppression can become essential in some circumstances,[32] nothing in the experience of oppression is, in and of itself, likely to produce moral insight. What most of us gain from oppression is not wisdom or even compassion and understanding, but anger, bitterness, a loss of any sense of self-worth, and, ultimately, hatred, both of self and of others. Any 'different voice' forged by these emotions is unlikely to be one of which we should be proud. So it is not the experience of oppression that is needed but something else, enhanced recognition of what is lost by abstraction and by our failure to recognise, and perhaps even insist, that judges bring what they are to adjudication. One thing those of us who are other simply cannot pretend is that we represent the norm – our difference is written in our lives and we are continually reminded of it. We know our experiences are not universal. They are a function of class and of gender and of ethnicity and of the complex interaction between these. By this, I mean that gender is experienced differently according to where one is located in terms of class and ethnicity. Class and ethnicity are also experienced in profoundly gendered ways. Judges bring to their work their experiences of gender, of class, of racial or ethnic background and the understandings (both positive and negative) which they have gained from these experiences. This should be no more surprising to any of us than it is to say that they bring the totality of their education, their training, and their participation in a particular professional community with particular conventions and understandings to their work. We might hope for an awareness of these 'darker images', an awareness which confronts them and acknowledges that in the cutting of the thread and the giving of the word the judge must be, if not free, responsible. An act of power which is loving is not essential, and may not even be desirable. An act of power which is truthful, which acknowledges itself for what it is, and accepts the attendant responsibility without pleasure but with necessity and understanding, is.

Power brings its own imperatives, although all too often these remain unspoken and unacknowledged. I wonder, sometimes, if my concern, and the concern of many of my colleagues with responsibility, with power, and with the connection between these and the violence which lies at the heart of our (and every) legal system stems from our perception of our own powerlessness. We do not have such responsibilities. At most we sit on tenure committees or blackball the odd student. It is minor and very petty. I cannot help wondering whether, ultimately, those *'princes of law's empire'*[33] of whom I speak have come to power so gradually and naturally that it sits lightly upon them as a familiar cloak, leaving them unaware of the terror behind the cutting of the thread and the giving of the word. Perhaps it is this naturalness, this sense of entitlement that we might hope that a sense of otherness could unspeak, disestablish. At the least, it might offer the possibility of a heightened sensitivity to subordinated perspectives, to the actual stories told (and untold), to the ways in which the law itself shapes stories.

Authority and Differance

One of my real concerns here lies in gaining some understanding of the extent, if any, to which authority and differance are capable of coexisting. I have a sense, in what I write, of treading on eggs, of a need to move slowly and carefully. The judge herself, fully contextualised, located, as is Arachne, at the centre of a web of bureaucratic structures, epitomises the power of law to cut and to bind. Hemmed in by texts and by the ritual drama of the trial though she is, she goes clothed in authority:

> Judges write on a field of pain and death. So do many others who have power over human beings. This reality is itself painful. We do not like to confront that we are, in fact, hurting others, and that the pain we inflict is a matter of

choice; it could have been otherwise. And so we make our action compelled, as though we could have done no other.[34]

The authoritative thrives upon distance, distance from self and from responsibility. One of the ways (and of this I *am* sure) of sustaining this distance lies in cloaking the steps to authority with a kind of naturalness. This naturalness in turn depends upon the sense of many of those who have assumed these positions that they have done so by right, by entitlement. To the extent that the facade of naturalness collapses, to the extent that those who have come to power cannot pretend that they have come to their positions by right, distance from self and from responsibility also diminishes. This diminished distance from self and from responsibility not only magnifies the demands upon the individual judge but also diminishes her authority – both in her own eyes and in the eyes of others. In this sense, to wish for a voice for otherness in adjudication represents a move in a profoundly dangerous game. Power does not rest lightly upon outsiders, at least to the extent that they remain aware that however much they may appear to be part of the charmed circle they remain outside it. Authority exacts its price, both personally and institutionally. Distance cannot be sustained, the exercise of power seems unlikely to be perceived, either by self or by others, as uncomplicated in quite the way that it normally would be. Because the exercise of power cannot ever be natural in the same way, those who are other are marked by their otherness. The legitimacy of their choices is always open to question. Let me explain. Because she is linguistically marked, she can do nothing that will not become, potentially at least, a site of investigation. Either she violates expectations, or she confirms them.[35] If the former, she is in danger of being seen as a brotherly sister, one who has so mastered/been mastered by the prevailing rhetoric that the potential difference of her voice has been eradicated. If the later, her difference is always, potentially at least, lawless, not lawful. On the personal level, therefore, the legitimacy of her actions is permanently in question. Distance collapses. Responsibility is magnified. The greater her potential power, the more powerless she is likely, at any moment, to become.

On the institutional level, to the extent she is seen as other, the legitimacy of her decisions is forever open to question – in a word, questionable. Her difference, in particular the fact that she cannot be seen to be in the position she occupies as of right, diminishes her institutional authority. To the extent that she remains other, brings to her institutional role the knowledges that come from exclusion, otherness, oppression, her decisions deny universality, neutrality. She has violated the ethics of adjudication, serves as proof of the diminished moral and ethical character of the other. She cannot speak universally. She is not male. It is her very otherness, of course, that enables her to understand that the realm of the universal and objective to which she has aspired is a fake. Far from being a realm of integrity and coherence which can legitimate decision making and foreshadow an enhanced political process, it is a mirror in which the brothers see themselves reflected, not as they are, but as they believe themselves to be.

Notes

1   And here the cultural archetype is the figure of 'blind justice', of whom more later.
2   I will also be looking at related concepts, at the connection between ideas of authority and the whole idea of an author, and, ultimately, of the word.
3   Within the academy it is increasingly possible to simultaneously speak with authority and speak as an outsider although, of course, very real questions arise as to the degree to which one's oppositional stance is invalidated by one's complicity in the very set of institutional structures which one is attacking.
4   And perhaps the image of an authority which is uniquely other can be linked to my sense that justice is herself other!
5   There are a whole range of issues here, questions about what makes speech authoritative, about whether it is possible to isolate the authority of the spoken word from the perceived authority of the speaker, even about the possibility that authority can somehow 'rub off' on one who might otherwise lack it.
6   de Tocqueville, A, *de la democratie en Amerique* 167 (1981) cited in and translated by Weber, S 'In the Name of the Law' in Cornell, D, M Rosenfeld, DG Carlson, eds, *Deconstruction and the Possibility of Justice*, London, Routledge, 1992, 232, 237-238.
7   This very 'inaccessibility' is critical to preserving the mystique of law. Despite the enormous cultural pressures towards plain English drafting (the ordinary language movement in law) something about legality wants to maintain the ritual.
8   The parallel between the 'word of god' and the 'word(s) of judges and parliaments' is, of course, intended.
9   And if it here seems that I am closer to Thomas Hobbes than to Robin West, so be it. As Robert Cover said, 'often the balance of terror ... is just as I would wish it'. Cover, R, 'Violence and the Word' in Minow, M, M Ryan & A Sarat, eds, *Narrative, Violence and the Law*, Ann Arbor, Univ of Michigan Press, 1992, 203, 211. That we must try to keep the balance of terror in place is central to our understandings of law and legality. We have nothing to replace it, nothing at all, not rules, not love, not faith. I do not, I might add, believe we ever will. As Arthur Leff reminded us, 'if all men are brothers, the ruling model is Cain and Abel'. See Leff, AA, 'Unspeakable Ethics, Unnatural Law' (1979) *Duke LJ* 1229, 1249.

10 This, in turn, is probably why the lingering suspicion remains that the various forms of alternative dispute resolution, particularly mediation and conciliation, are second class 'justice' for second class citizens.

11 Douzinas, C, R Warrington & S McVeigh, *Postmodern Jurisprudence: The Law of Text in the Texts of Law*, London, Routledge, 1991, 156. And yet the United States Supreme Court has, for years, accepted extensive written pleadings, the Brandeis briefs marshalling not only legal argument but also sociological documentation etc.

12 Dworkin's Hercules is a modernist oracle, a last ditch liberal attempt to ensure that the walls of liberalism are not breached and chaos admitted. 'Law as integrity' enables Hercules to (pretend to) neutralise the 'dangerous supplement' by transforming it into a 'seamless web', a speech surrogate proclaimed to be as 'oracular', as beyond question, as the outcome of a trial by battle. Unfortunately, trials are conducted in courts, before what are, in the end, ordinary women and men, and Hercules remains silent on Olympus, speaking only when summoned by Dworkin. See Dworkin, *Law's Empire*.

13 And it may be significant that originally the sentence read, 'tease out some of the threads of the web that is weaving itself around me as I **speak**'. The act of writing is simultaneously a speech act – so that I speak through my text and my text speaks to me.

14 And it is critical that in all of this justice remains both unspeakable and unspoken.

15 Weber, S, 'In the Name of the Law', 238.

16 This follows upon the development first of writing and subsequently of printing and the printed word. (And I do not even want to reflect upon the impact of the electronic media.) These developments made it possible for the text to attain a life of its own, to be severed from all (human) agency. I really think that this is terribly important – whereas speech and the spoken word are necessarily agentic – the written text (and above all the written legal text) are at once enormously powerful and devoid of human agency.

17 The doubling back to the Sartrean text and all it implies is intended.

18 And here I think of the biblical Abraham – and of the kind of obedience to text that the story of Abraham and Isaac signifies. (And note it is the *Biblical* Abraham – not Kierkegaard's.) Only that kind of obedience to text suffices for absolution.

19 To inscribe is to do more than catalogue or list, it is to cut, to carve the flesh.

20 When the word becomes flesh it is inscribed in and upon body, not mind. Kafka had it aright when he imagined both the law and the sentence as tattooed upon the bodies of those who came before it. See Kafka, F, 'In the Penal Colony' in *The Transformation and Other Stories: Works Published during Kafka's Lifetime*, translated from the German and edited by Malcolm Pasley, London, Penguin, 1992.

21 Derrida, J, 'Force of Law: The "Mystical Foundation of Authority"' in Cornell, D, M Rosenfeld & DG Carlson, eds, *Deconstruction and the Possibility of Justice*, London, Routledge, 1992, 3, 19.

22 And again the image of cutting.

23 Even here, at the moment when judgment crystallises into force, the web is tangled, the judge both its creator and its victim, the spider and the fly.

24   And the allusion here, quite deliberately and fittingly, is to the fates, and to Atropos in particular. Arachne's thread is fine indeed, her webs endless in their complexity, but she weaves endlessly.

25   In the beginning was the Word...

26   The act of naming remains, I believe, the ultimate speech act, that act which, uniquely and conclusively establishes identity.

27   And what does it say about the status of family law that, at least in some jurisdictions, a divorce can be obtained by post, without any hearing at all?

28   Notable not only for his wisdom but for his brutality – murderer and rapist as well as superlative judge. And perhaps the connection is more appropriate than might at first appear.

29   We meet Hermes in his role as an exponent of the authorial intent theory of statutory interpretation in Dworkin, *Law's Empire*, 317-337. Hermes, the androgynous messenger boy of the gods, was, Dworkin tells us, a failed Hercules. Or, perhaps, it was simply that Hermes was one of the 'fairies at the bottom of the closet', unable and unwilling to come out until outed by Dworkin in a last ditch effort to affirm the authority of a phallogocentric model of legality. For this marvellous image, as for so much else, I owe thanks to Michael Dobber. It is rare, and marvellous to encounter a student who pushes one to the limit, knows it, and becomes a colleague in a marvellous intellectual adventure!

30   Dworkin, *Law's Empire*, 404-407.

31   And is it true to say that this is another kind of repression, of burial, and that this symbolic eradication of individual identity is critical to our understanding of what it is to be a judge?

32   Matsuda, MJ, 'When the First Quail Calls: Multiple Consciousness as Jurisprudential Method', 11 *Women's Rights LR* 7 (1989).

33   Dworkin, *Law's Empire*, 407. And it is significant that, in the vast majority of cases they remain just that, *princes* of law's empire.

34   Delgado, R, 'Norms and Normal Science: Towards a Critique of Normativity in Legal Thought' 139 *Univ Penn LR* 933, 942 (1991).

35   It goes both ways. If her decisions are seen as ordinary, conventional, mainstream, owing nothing to the presence of otherness, she can, all too easily, come to be seen as rejecting her status as other, as assimilating, trying to be simply one of the boys. If her decisions reveal the mark of the other (and I here think, irresistibly, of Demian) she will at once confirm her position as other, as grammatically marked and critically destabilise the legitimacy of her role in decision making. See Hesse, H, *Demian, The Story of Emil Sinclair's Life*, trans. by M. Roloff & M. Lebeck, Harper & Row, New York, 1965.

3 Speaking Law and Rendering Judgment

Introduction

In this chapter, I want to canvass the gap between process and persuasion, a gap that mirrors that between law and justice. Process, persuasion, the idea of a gap, the image, introduced in the last chapter, of justice as other, as not law, the overwhelming conceptual freight embodied in these terms threatens to swamp what set out to be a simple introduction. Process, ambiguous at best, means, in this context, the way in which the judge reaches a decision, the interaction between what happens and doesn't happen in the courtroom, the legal materials[1] and the mind and heart of the individual judge.[2] The gap between process and persuasion is marked, on one level, by the act of judgment, the concrete moment in which judgment is (orally) handed down in the courtroom. On another, very different, level it is marked by the experiential shift from being (almost by definition) open to persuasion to being (at some level) irrevocably committed to the persuasion of others. And just who these others are is necessarily ambiguous, context laden. A single judge sitting at first instance may seek to persuade a potential appellate tribunal, justify her decision to a more or less diffuse professional community. In some ways, the act of producing a written judgment signifies that the case was out of the ordinary. The formal written judgment is no longer the norm, particularly at first instance. An appeal judge has further and weightier reasons for producing a written judgment, whether she, on the facts, upholds the judgment at first instance or overrules it. Where the appellate judge sits on an intermediary tribunal, it seems to me that the written judgment must face two ways at once. It must justify the decision of the appellate court to the parties and to the judge at first instance. It must also extend persuasion to the future, to a further appellate court, perhaps, or to another court sitting on another matter in the future. Where the written judgment is crafted, not by the judge herself, but by her clerk (or one of her clerks) persuasion becomes more complex still. Here, I believe, it is linked with another question, that

37

of authority. By whose authority and by what warrant does one without authority, save only that which might be delegated by another, seek to persuade and of what, of his own thoughts or those of another? Douzinas, Warrington, and McVeigh offer an account that is, at least in some respects, parallel.

> Let us return to the story of the trial. The authority of the judge is the opposite of that of the storyteller. It is a function of institutional structure and power, rather than of the tactics of seduction. The judge as narrator assumes rather than negotiates his authority. However, as the narratee of the stories of the participants in the trial, he is as open to seduction as any other. Finally, as the narrator of legal theory and doctrine, the judge becomes the hero of Herculean deeds and the storyteller of grand narratives.

Their image for the process of judgment, for the interaction of the judge with the trial itself and everything that transpires therein, an image of seduction, seems to me both evocative and ambiguous. To the extent, the judge is 'as open to seduction as any other' she is at once an agent and object. In this double gesture, this turning back upon itself, the gap between process and persuasion marks the point at which 'law' is affirmed and justice again repressed and denied.

> The task of the pragmatics of narrative is to address the complicated relations between the narrator and the narratee, the narrator and the narrated, finally the narratee and the narrated [while acknowledging that] as all seduction, storytelling is duplicitous.[3]

The image of seduction calls up a striking and strikingly arcane image. As narratee, the judge is the innocent maiden of melodrama. She is putty in the hands of duplicitous counsel. They appeal to her desires (for example the desire to further her life's project as a 'liberal activist judge')[4] while striving to realise their own projects. As narrator, however, she does more than assume her authority rather than negotiate it, she em*bodies* authority. She is the *body of authority* (although the extent to which the body of authority can also be the body of a woman remains in doubt). How this authority can be reconciled with the seduced maiden of the trial and the brazen seductress of the process of persuasion, she who can legitimate her own seduction only by seducing others becomes the narrative of jurisprudence. Liberal modernist apologists with Herculean ambitions seek to freeze the oscillation between narrator and narratee and imprison the text within a prison house of right answers. As chain novels replace the play of narrative, and the pornographer's art that of the storyteller, pragmatics replace possibilities.[5] Our dreams of justice once again lose out.

The Sign of Law

If the sign of law marks any act, in our culture, it is the handing down of judgment.[6] At the moment of judgment all ambivalence and ambiguity must be repressed. The shift from reason to power is complete. If it does not always figure in scholarly texts, in accounts of the nature of law, it dominates the understandings of law which are woven into popular culture. It is visible, audible, and, most of all, active and authoritative. Even if the judge simply speaks, declares judgment, her speech is speech which is immediately embodied in action.[7]

My paradigm is, for the present, that of a single judge sitting at first instance. I have chosen to begin in this way for a number of reasons. It is at first instance that the 'tangled web' is woven, that the voices of the parties are given legal form, that the legal narrative is at its most unequivocally polyvocal. While, even at first instance, the judge must have recourse to authoritative texts, those texts are but a part of the story and it may be and often is, that they are a relatively small part. It is also at first instance that we cannot but recognise law's bondage to evidence and to the laws of evidence. It is, as Haldar suggests:

> evidence which connects the law court to the outside world, an internal world of codes to the (sic) external world of chaos, where an event as violation has occurred... What constitutes the truth in law? And how does it prove knowledge? In other words, if the truth in evidence constitutes information about the event as violation then evidence 'represents' a theory of knowledge – an epistemology of normative, legal facts. Evidence is the law of how that information is to be received by the court.[8]

However, evidence does not merely connect the court to an external world of chaos, it also becomes an aporia, that which will not allow passage. The laws of evidence determine what stories will be told, what images will be received. In a rape trial, the laws of evidence represent/re-present/ the victim to the jury. How the court receives her becomes the law of law. Evidence inscribes the victim as madonna or whore, determines whether the jury will witness the recreation of an act of violation or the exposure of an act of seduction. The theory of knowledge that is the law of evidence knows not the ethical tort of Lyotard. The laws of evidence demand that the testifying phrase of the victim be devoid of authority. Either the harm, the rape, never took place (rape is a charge easy to make and difficult to disprove), or the victim was not truly harmed. That she survived and is capable of speech, transforms her speech once again into a lie. She was, after all, unconscious and therefore was not traumatised as she would have been had she been conscious. In the end, she was not, truly raped, for to be raped one must be conscious of violation. It is of the essence of rape, I believe, that the laws of evidence reconstruct the external world to ensure that 'the injury suffered by the victim is accompanied by a deprivation of the means to prove it'.9 As victim, the victim is the creature of the laws of evidence.10

The elements that make up the social practice we call adjudication are sharpest and most clearly delineated at first instance. As the trial begins, the judge is institutionally and necessarily open to persuasion by others. At its conclusion, the judge is equally institutionally and necessarily committed to the persuasion of others. At its core lies the instantiation of institutionalised violence *we* call the act of judgment. In all that precedes the act of judgment, violence is untenable, outside the limits. No one is *persuaded* by violence or by the threat of violence. I would not deny that violence might, and often does, seek to foreclose the necessity for persuasion. What it does not do and can never do is acknowledge that it is right and proper that the matter be left to the judgment of another, to a choice which in the end must depend upon argument and upon the giving of reasons. Once judgment has been handed down, the giving of reasons attains even greater urgency. If judgment is to stand, not only in respect of the matter before the court, but for the future, the reasons given must have the capacity to persuade others who may be a continent or a generation away. Violence may coerce, compel a choice this way or that and that choice may well stand for the moment. It can never convince others, whether a continent or a generation away, that a particular course of action is right, proper and just. It is devoid of rhetorical force. In its direct connection with violence, its institutionally mandated bondage to power, the act of judgment stands radically apart from everything which has preceded it and from everything which will follow it. Robert Cover spoke of the judge sitting atop a *pyramid of* violence, dealing.[11] The act of judgment is the apex of that *pyramid.* Its base is anchored, not in reason, but in power.

Earlier in this chapter, in an aside, I intimated my overall agreement with Duncan Kennedy's phenomenology of adjudication.[12] As an account of how legal reasoning[13] feels from the inside, it is both accurate and perceptive.[14] As an account of adjudication, it is curiously sanitised. It seems carefully distanced from the realities of courtrooms and parties and power and, ultimately, socially and culturally legitimated violence. Kennedy's work confronts us with the paradox of a self-styled 'phenomenological account' which begins and ends in judge's chambers, in the recesses of Kennedy's mind. I find this headlong retreat into introspection profoundly disturbing. In his focus upon the subjective experience of legal reasoning and the experience of simultaneous freedom and constraint which, for Kennedy, is an inherent part of legal reasoning, he constructs an account which seems as divorced from reality as those he critiques.[15] To the extent that it involves characters other than Kennedy himself, they are no less unreal than those in conventional casebooks. If not quite as stylised as A and B, heroic workers and greedy bosses seem no more contextualised, no more real. Kennedy acknowledges having structured his hypothetical to highlight the politics of adjudication. In particular, he wants to emphasise the political or ideological dimension which may become central if there is a conflict between a judge's understanding of what 'the law' requires and her intuitions about justice, 'How-I-want-it-to-come-out', in other words. The proceedings he imagines involve an *ex parte* application for an interlocutory injunction, the applicant bus company seeking to enjoin striking workers from repeating lie-in tactics which have disrupted service. As a substitute for parties and context we are given 'workers', 'bosses' and a struggle over the control of the means of production (affectionately known as 'mop').[16]

Kennedy's account carries with it not a suggestion of courtroom encounter, of parties and pleadings, of the necessity to hand down judgment, to confront the violence of adjudication at first hand. Not for him the pull of context, of narrative, of a ritual in which the play of voices becomes part of the web. Even the interior dialogue[17] he envisions is limited to the interplay between the mind and character of the judge, the legal materials (and I include under the rubric 'legal materials' Kennedy's 'voices of the ancients') and various sets of role expectations. His sketched factual scenario is played out in stylised terms.[18] It is as if, for Kennedy, the context which is relevant to decision making is to be found, not in what happens, and doesn't happen, in the courtroom, but in what happens and doesn't happen within his own mind. The characters in his hypothetical are caricatures, a mockery of his insistence upon the need to start with some imagined situation.[19] His hypothetical eliminates all of the complexities that are woven into what I have called the 'tangled web'. In compressing everything that precedes the act of judgment into a self-conscious monologue, Kennedy magnifies the importance of *this* process (and establishes thereby the supremacy of reason). While he insists that the judge must *work* to achieve an outcome, in his single minded focus upon the process of reaching that outcome he seems blind to the importance and the nature of the outcome itself. In a very real sense, the most important part of the outcome (at least for Kennedy) appears to be its overall contribution to his 'life project of being a liberal activist judge'.[20] Legal decision making becomes an intellectualised game, a game that is far removed from the immediacy of the courtroom. Despite the emphasis upon legal reasoning as a form of ethical/moral reasoning, it seems devoid of any authentic acknowledgment of ethical considerations.[21] Kennedy collapses a complex three-stage process into an interior monologue, which is as isolated from considerations of power and persuasion as that of any hypothetical Hercules (Hyporcules). We are left, in the end, with pure thought, radicalism without reality and without any real understanding of the dynamics of power and violence marking the moment of judgment.

Within any actual courtroom, on the other hand, the immediacy of the shift, the seamlessness of the translation from speech to action, from decision to realisation, emphasises that the moment of judgment is on some level, complete in itself. What has gone before, the balancing of narratives within the courtroom, the interplay between courtroom narrative and legal text, and the ways in which the subjectivity of the judge figures both (and is figured in both) vanishes. Whatever the concrete content of the process of judgment, when judgment is handed down the act of judgment is complete within itself, is the only act which matters. It marks the critical transition from being in some sense open to persuasion (whether by the narratives of the courtroom or by the legal texts) to being obligated to attempt to persuade others. The importance of this transition must not be underestimated. Phenomenologically, the necessity for persuasion, in short for rhetoric, is the ultimate judicial obligation. Without rhetoric, without the attempt through the giving of reasons to persuade others of both the rightness[22] and inevitability of judgment as rendered, no judgment is properly judicial. Every great judge has recognised the unspoken (but nonetheless irresistible) demand for rhetoric that is inherent in the requirement that she give reasons for her decision. In an era of *deus absconditus,* it is fitting that, more than ever, judgment hangs upon rhetoric, upon persuasion. Without fixed stars to guide us, it is surely better to rely upon reasoned persuasion than upon any of the alternatives that present themselves.[23]

Rhetoric is not sufficient on its own, of course. Rhetoric reaches out to the future, builds a bridge to other courts, other judges, through the attempt to justify in the first instance, an act of power, and second, the role of the judge in that act. Behind the balancing of courtroom narratives, the attempt to integrate narrative and text, we might hope that the judge has attempted to trace a connection between law and justice. Culturally, we need to believe that an intuition about justice, and about what would be just in the circumstances is relevant to her decision.[24]

The parties to a legal dispute expect the judge both to decide 'according to law' and to give them 'justice', as if the two were (or at least could or should be) synonymous. This belief is both deeply embedded and fundamental to ordinary understandings of the rule of law. Perhaps, for ordinary people an accord between law and justice remains thinkable. Thomas Hobbes, after all, claimed that justice was nothing more or less than deciding according to the rules.[25] Many of us would like to take refuge in something similar but remain uncomfortably aware that this kind of certainty (I might even suggest faith) is no longer available to us.[26] The events of this century have left us with a sense of loss, a recognition that the face of evil can as surely inhere in the following of rules as in their disregard.[27] If we do not have anything which can truly be called a shared morality, we can trace the figure left by its absence.[28] Worse yet, and this is, perhaps, still more a matter of academic culture than popular culture, we no longer have the faith that we once did in the idea of rules as followable in any straightforward sense. In an age when computers assert expertise in 'fuzzy logic', it has become clear that following rules is ambiguous at best, and a connection between rule application and justice unthinkable. Despite this loss of or lack of faith, even the most bitterly sceptical among us expect that somehow our judges will seek justice. What we have lost is the belief that they will be able to make good their commitment to her pursuit.

The gap between process and persuasion holds out the possibility that, just as a photographic negative contains the 'absent figure' of the developed print, the 'absent figure' of justice is present as trace within the written judgment. It is this trace whose meaning awaits interpretation by other courts and other judges.

This chapter is about power as power is realised in the act of judgment. It is about what happens and what does not happen when judgment is handed down, about the gap when the work of reason has been completed and what remains is power, authority and obedience. It is, in short, about what happens when the weaving of the tangled web is complete and the thread must be cut.[29]

The Act of Judgment

Robert Cover recognised the centrality of the separation of interpretation and judgment. As he wrote:

> We have done something strange in our system. We have rigidly separated the act of interpretation – of understanding what ought to be done – from the carrying out of this "ought to be done" through violence. At the same time we have, at least in the criminal law, rigidly linked the carrying out of judicial orders to the act of judicial interpretation by relatively inflexible hierarchies of judicial utterances and firm obligations on the part of penal officials to heed them. Judges are both separated from, and inextricably linked to, the acts they authorize.[30]

No judge acts alone. Both the violence which lies at the heart of the act of judgment and the inevitability of the 'agentic roles' through which that violence manifests itself bear witness to the implication of the judge in our social practices of institutionalised violence. What is remarkable is not the embeddedness of the judge, her entrapment within the institutional threads binding her to the violence authorised by her decision. Rather, what is truly remarkable is that both this violence and its role in constructing the social meaning of law have largely escaped the notice of works on the nature of law.

I want to figure the act of judgment in isolation. There are several reasons for this. Most important, perhaps, its orality sets it apart. In the act of judgment, it is right and proper that the judge speaks. Her speech is authorised, even compelled, part of the meaning of judgment. Until and unless she speaks, judgment, as such, does not exist. Conclusions may have been drawn, decisions made, but until these become public, and are spoken as judgment, they are devoid of institutional role, devoid, in short, of force. They occasion nothing.[31] The act of judgment, that moment when the outcomes become public and enforcement is possible is also, in our culture, the founding moment, the moment at which the problem of justice is deferred yet again.[32] The moment of judgment marks the oscillation between our aspirations towards justice and our bondage to force and, in particular, to the force of law, to the moment of violence. Stanley Fish has written, in a critique of HLA Hart which, I believe, can serve as a metaphor for the trial process,

> Could it not be said that procedure rather than doing away with force merely masks it by attenuating it, by placing it behind a screen or series of screens? After all, the crucial question, which returns the original problem to center stage, still has to be asked: Who gets to make the rules? And once that questions is answered, another question (it is really the same) waits behind it, who gets to say who gets to make the rules?... [If]... "the law... is what the courts say it is"...[i]f this is indeed the case, then the rule of law or, more precisely, the law of rule becomes an illusion, for the rule as a constraint, as a safeguard against casual violence, falls to the daily acts of violence committed by judges who call the tune as they happen to see (and desire) it... If it is the business of law to protect the individual from coercion that is random, unpredictable, and arbitrary, then the individual is no less at risk when he is at the mercy of an interpreting court than when he is at the mercy of an armed assailant.[33]

Yet, of course, it is precisely to the point that the violence committed by judges has never been and could never be 'casual'. If, as a matter of procedure, it is attenuated, screened from view and remaindered to agents, it is nonetheless deliberate. The judge assumes, **as she must**, that there will be officials to ensure that her word becomes flesh, that it will be en**forced** as **law**. Every official assumes that judgment is legitimate, that their role will be absolved because it is wholly institutional, agentic, depersonalised, because, in short, they were only following orders.[34]

Despite this, even now there are times when judges step outside the confines of their roles, when they refuse to permit their judgments to become vehicles for this kind of deliberate institutional violence. A recent and, I believe, significant, example may be found in the judgment of Her

Honour, Justice Margaret White in Queensland. In sentencing a 17-year-old Aboriginal youth convicted of the manslaughter of a local publican, she refused to order a term of imprisonment. She insisted that the conditions in the fringe camp in which he lived meant, in essence, that he was already serving a life sentence. This sentence was imposed upon him, not for any wrongdoing, but by the conditions of his birth and origins. The decision is, of course, being appealed, and one expects that, in the end, her judgment will be vacated. Even so, her refusal is, I think, worthy of note, a statement of limits even more powerful because so seldom invoked.[35]

In discussing a somewhat parallel refusal by His Honour, Justice Harold Stern, sitting as judge in the United States Court for Berlin to hand down a custodial sentence, Cover notes:

> Harold Stern's remarkable sentence is not simply an effective, moving plea for judicial independence, [i]t reveals the necessity of a latent role structure to render the judicial utterance morally intelligible. And it proclaims the moral unintelligibility of routine judicial utterance when the structure is no longer there.[36]

In an extended footnote, Cover continues:

> Judge Stern confronted an unusual situation – no independent system of courts, and no *explicit* denial by those in control of official violence that their power was constitutionally limited. In a sense the situation was one of *de jure* lawlessness. But Stern's reasoning reaches beyond the case at hand; it may be extended to include, for example, the *de facto* state of lawlessness that attends life in many United States prisons. Institutional reform litigation – whether applied to prisons, schools, or hospitals – entails complex questions of judicial remedial power... But Stern's decision in *Tiede* pursues a different path. A judge may or may not be able to change the deeds of official violence, but she may always withhold the justification for this violence. She may or may not be able to bring a good prison into being, but she can refrain from sentencing anyone to a[n]... inadequate one.[37]

Margaret White assuredly lacked the power to alter the conditions in the fringe camp in which the defendant lived. She did not even have the power, had she chosen to sentence the defendant to a custodial term, to ensure that he did not die in custody as have so many others. She did the one thing she could, on her own. She refused to authorise a custodial term. She withheld justification for further violence. She said, in effect, 'Thus far and no further'. By her decision she acknowledged that she sat 'atop a pyramid of violence...dealing' and refused to accede to the demand that she behave as if she must simultaneously 'exercise judgment [and] have no choice'.[38] She accepted the responsibility of judgment and insisted that, ultimately, if judgment is to be judicial there must always be choice.

Notes

1   I am deliberately leaving that term vague and ambiguous, apt to include precedent, legislation, and... I am indifferent as to whether the term is read as encompassing the moral-legal universe of the Dworkinian judge or whether a somewhat narrower (if hardly positivistic) account seems more persuasive.
2   The best account I have seen of how legal reasoning actually feels is that in Kennedy, 'Freedom and Constraint in Adjudication'. All the ways in which I disagree with it as an account of adjudication, as opposed to legal reasoning will occupy us later.
3   Douzinas, Warrington, & McVeigh, *Postmodern Jurisprudence* 109ff.
4   Kennedy, 'Freedom and Constraint in Adjudication', 528.
5   In that sense, Dworkin's metaphor for judicial narrative and the structure of law, that of a chain novel, seems in some sense prescient. Perhaps it is more significant than he knows that the sole exemplar of the genre was a pornographic novel, *Naked Came the Stranger*, written as a parlour game. There are some very real insights here in terms of the legal system and the role it plays in our societies and our lives! See Dworkin, RM, 'How Law is Like Literature' in Dworkin, RM, *A Matter of Principle*, Cambridge, Harv Univ Press, 1985, 146, 158-162. Cf Fish, S, 'Working on the Chain Gang: Interpretation in Law and Literature' in Fish, S, *Doing What Comes Naturally: Change, Rhetoric, and the Practice of Theory in Literary and Legal Studies*, Oxford, Clarendon Press, 1989, 87.
6   Physically, it must be said, it is a 'handing down', the judge behind a raised dais (an altar, perhaps) passing judgment upon those below. The physical structure of the court remains an inherent part of the metaphysics of judgment.
7   A part of my point is that judicial speech, specifically judicial speech at the moment of judgment, is never simply speech. As Robert Cover insisted 'We begin, then, not with what the judges say, but with what they do. The judges deal pain and death. That is not all they do. Perhaps that is not what they usually do. But they **do** deal pain and death.' Cover, 'Violence and the Word', 213. If judicial speech inevitably becomes a dealing in pain and death it is, as Cover insists, because authority, government and violence are inextricably linked.
8   Haldar, 'The Evidencer's Eye', 171-172.
9   Douzinas & Warrington, '"*A Well-Founded Fear of Justice*"', 130.
10 In this context, I think, it is significant that many rape survivors, irrespective of the outcome of the trial process, understand themselves to have been raped twice.
11 Cover, 'Violence and the Word', 213.
12 See Kennedy, 'Freedom and Constraint', esp 519-520.
13 My emphasis upon **legal reasoning** is meant to be just that, an emphasis upon legal reasoning. Kennedy appears to intend his critical phenomenology to tell us something about adjudication... not simply legal reasoning.

14   As academic lawyers we enjoy the luxury of detachment... a luxury which is open to no judge. One of the difficulties with Kennedy's account (just as with the very different account given by Ronald Dworkin) is that it offers an ideal with no place in the real world, an ideal of rational detachment devoid of power, of passion, and of violence. No real judge has the luxury of purely rational reasoning detached from the obligation to render judgment. The bottom line is *always* grounded in power, not in reason, and there is always a bottom line, a reason for judgment, a matter before the court.

15   The image I have of judge's chambers suggests that this is a very pleasant little reverie indeed. A lovely old polished desk, bookshelves crowded with legal volumes, leather chairs... Pleasant isn't it, but altogether too removed from the real world for comfort. Even his self-characterisation emphasises his unwillingness to confront his own position (a position which he projects onto his imagined judge) and the extent to which it implicates him in the very structures he suggests his 'life project' as a radical judge is dedicated to dismantling and the effect this has upon the ways in which he decides. Even more disturbing is the sense I have of the degree to which his self-conscious perceptions of freedom and constraint blind him to the ways in which acts of judgment operate in the world, and in the violence which they bring to bear upon others.

16   I do not mean to imply that I regard a scenario such as that Kennedy offers as far-fetched or fanciful. It is, however, wholly removed from the contractual disputes, the compensation claims and the various tort actions that are more likely to figure in the real world.

17   It is symptomatic of the weaknesses in Kennedy's account that his interior 'dialogue' is 'dialogue' in exactly the same way as what happens behind John Rawls' veil of ignorance is a 'contract'. Kennedy may imagine all the right things but...

18   I feel that here I ought to flag my concern simply because in this area I am not actually certain what point Kennedy is making. Is he suggesting that, ultimately, it is part of the social meaning of adjudication that we reduce the parties to a legal dispute to stereotypes? If not, why, in an account purporting to be a phenomenology of adjudication, are all that remains of the parties before the court social stereotypes, images so formal and scripted that they are reminiscent of Kabuki theatre?

19   See Kennedy, 'Freedom and Constraint', 518.

20   As Kennedy insists: 'Every case is part of my life-project of being a liberal activist judge. What I do in this case will affect my ability to do things in other cases, enhancing or diminishing my legal and political credibility as well as my technical reputation with the various constituencies that count.' 'Freedom and Constraint', 528. If one were cynical one might suggest that the hypothetical outcome has the same importance in Kennedy's vision as notches on a gun belt. They mark the trophies...., but that is all.

21   'Since I see legal argument as a branch of ethical argument, I would like to know **for my own purposes** how my position looks translated into this particular ethical medium.' Kennedy, 'Freedom and Constraint', 528. If one is acting from what one conceives to be ethical or moral considerations one does not want to know how one's position looks translated into ethical language, the ethical considerations are, on some level, part of how and why one got there. If they are not understood as somehow compelled, they are not understood as ethical. This does not mean universal and need

not be take as an expression of anything akin to Kant's categorical imperative. Rather, a part of the language game we call 'ethical conduct' involves compulsion in just this sense. One does not translate. The ethical language is there from the beginning if it is truly to count as ethical. If it is not there from the beginning...then (and I do not deny this can be done and often is) ethical language is turned to rhetorical purposes, becomes a strategy of argument rather than a form of life.

22   And here I want to suggest that the decision must both be seen as according to law, and as morally proper. Not only must it reflect *droit*, it must be *juste* and *propre*. Our word 'right', standing as it does both for the correctness of the decision and for its moral standing, attempts to square the circle, insist that the one decision can be according to law and just and proper.

23   The necessity for the giving of reasons, for the willingness to attempt to persuade others of the rightness of the decision serves as the ultimate constraint upon the oft posited threat of judicial capriciousness. She who must persuade can only do so within the structure of the existing conversation, using forms and structures that have been previously legitimated.

24   For judgment to be complete rhetoric and aspiration must play their assigned roles.

25   Hobbes, T, *Leviathan*, edited with an introduction by CB MacPherson, London, Penguin, 1968.

26   Whether it ever was, or whether in fact the point of Austinian and Benthamite positivism was to emphasise the divide between law and justice and, thereby, provide a gap in which radical reform of law to bring it closer to justice might take place, is an open question.

27   We have only to remember the Third Reich, Vichy France and Stalinist Russia to recognise that rules and procedural formality are no bulwark against evil. It should come as no surprise in any case. Bureaucratic evil ultimately relies upon rules and rule-following, is utterly banal.

28   Douzinas & Warrington suggest that 'our communities have long lost any aspirations to a common idiom... [and that] therefore... justice may turn out to be impossible, just a shibboleth.' Douzinas & Warrington, '"A Well-Founded Fear of Justice"', 131. The parallel to Alasdair MacIntyre's pre-lapsarian yearning for a vanished *polis* is remarkable. See MacIntyre, A, *After Virtue*, 2nd ed, London, Duckworth, 1985 and cf Cornell, D, M Rosenfeld & DG Carlson, *Deconstruction and the Possibility of Justice*, New York, Routledge, 1992, 211, 225-226.

29   If, in what I am writing, I make the distinction between the three elements in every judicial act more distinct than they could ever be in reality, it is important to understand their functional discreteness before we consider the ways in which they interact. The discreteness of which I speak is functional, not simply or even necessarily temporal.

30   Cover, 'Violence and the Word', 235. The same is true of the civil law. The violence of which Cover speaks is as apt to describe civil proceedings as criminal proceedings. Indeed, he himself suggests this at 1607, n 16.

31   Given weighty cultural traditions privileging **speech** over writing, this is fitting.

32   Jacques Derrida tells us that '*in the founding of law or in its institution, the same problem of justice will have been posed and violently resolved, that is to say buried,*

dissimulated, repressed'. Derrida, 'Force of Law: "The Mystical Foundation of Authority"', 23.

33 Fish, S, 'Force' in Fish, S, *Doing What Comes Naturally: Change, Rhetoric, and the Practice of Theory in Literary and Legal Studies*, Oxford, Clarendon Press, 1989, 503, 504-505.

34 And we might (or more likely might not) want to think about the fact than both the act of the judge in handing down judgment and the institutional roles of all those others who act upon the decisions of judges are exculpated by a plea most recently discredited at Nuremberg and nonetheless relied upon again and again by those who seek to disclaim responsibility for the unspeakable.

35 Her insistence that she would go 'thus far and no further' is akin to that of Pat O'Shane in 1993. See O'Shane, P, 'Launch of the Australian Feminist Law Journal – 29 August 1993' (1994) 2 *Aust. Feminist LJ* 3, 4-6.

36 Cover, 'Violence and the Word', 228. It seems to me both remarkable and significant that at least in Australia it is women who are insisting upon limits. Given the paucity of women on the bench, their willingness to take the stands they do represents courage of the highest order.

37 Cover, 'Violence and the Word', 228, n 48.

38 Serat, A, & TR Kearns 'A Journey Through Forgetting: Toward a Juris-prudence of Violence' in Serat, A & TR Kearns, *The Fate of Law*, Ann Arbor, Univ. of Mich Press (1991) 209, 246-247 n 123. 'If, as Dworkin insists, officials exercise judgment but have no choice, it follows that they are neither free to soften law's violence nor are they responsible for it. Such a system when it does not manage (or bother) to conceal the fact that it deals in violence and pain, will tend to subdue those facts by claiming them as the natural or necessary results of legal standards, standards which themselves are sufficiently capacious to contain judicial discretion and minimize interpretive violence at the periphery as well as the center of adjudication.'

4   The Subversive Moment

Introduction

This chapter is about the 'subversive moment' in law, the moment (if there is to be one) at which judgment becomes unique, becomes creative, in which boundaries are broken although they are inevitably reinstated when judgment has been handed down. The potential for subversion is fundamental to judgment as process.[1] If subversion was not possible, judgment *would* be nothing more than calculation. The subversive moment is the only moment at which judgment truly 'belongs to' the judge. At last, the particularity of the case before the court is acknowledged and the uniqueness, even individuality, of the judge comes to the fore.[2] If it is not truly a moment of judicial freedom, because within law words such as freedom and constraint have become ambiguous, judgment in the fullest possible sense forces her way into the light within that moment. Creativity and responsibility are united. The judge cannot escape either. She alone is responsible for her decision.

Robert Cover characterised the subject position of a judge confronting the subversive moment as *the moral/formal dilemma*. If such a judge rejected the demands of conscience, three options were open. He (or she) might elevate the formal stakes of obedience to law to the highest possible level. He (or she) might retreat to a mechanical formalism, treating principles such as fidelity to law and adherence to precedent as absolutes. Finally he (or she) might rely upon 'separation of powers', and remit the possibility for change elsewhere.[3] If, however, as sometimes happens, she (or he) accepts the call of conscience, she must decide how she is to justify her decision, explain it to herself[4] and to the law. Once she has made this choice if her decision can never be wholly free, it will always be a decision that is wholly hers.

In short, for a decision to be just and responsible, it must, in its proper moment if there is one, be both regulated and without regulation: it must conserve the law and also destroy it or suspend it enough to have to reinvent it in each case, rejustify it, at least reinvent it in the reaffirmation and the new and free confirmation of its principle... For in the founding of law or in its

51

institution, the same problem of justice will have been posed and violently resolved, that is to say buried, dissimulated, repressed.[5]

Those who fear judicial creativity, who understand boundary breaking as a violation of the judicial role, seek to diminish the threat of judicial creativity through a repertoire of fixed responses. They may, for example, assert that what appears to be judicial creativity is something else altogether, for example a voyage of discovery which, despite its radical appearance, merely makes explicit what had always been implicit within the law as it was.[6] They may insist that what appeared to be a manifestation of judicial creativity was something else, something far more benign, for example, the exercise of inevitable and necessary judicial discretion, faced with a 'gap' in the legal texts. More often than not even the judge will believe herself compelled to represent (re-*present*?) the subversive moment as something else, as inevitable, as flowing seamlessly and necessarily from 'the facts' and from 'the law' as it is.[7] I say this despite the ethical pull of Martha Minow's insistence that:

> the judge should not disguise how he or she actually reached the decision and should explain the decision not only through post hoc justifications but also with reference to the intuitions and reasons for selecting one principled justification over other possible ones.[8]

There comes a point when every judge must decide in what terms she is to couch her judgment. She must decide what attention she will pay to developing 'the kind of reasons that would persuade [a disappointed] party or explain the result in terms that party would concede as fair'.[9] She must decide whether these reasons will *also* persuade other judges, other courts. If she is profoundly committed to her decision, she will wish it to stand, to be found persuasive by others who do not know the parties or the case as she does, others who may not share her commitments. She must decide what attention she will pay to her own moral intuitions and reasons, even to the road she travelled to arrive at her decision, if she is capable of explaining it.[10]

Judicial Subversion – Violence, Text and Choice

There are, it seems to me, a number of distinct elements in judicial subversion. There is the moment, perhaps unacknowledged, when the judge finally accepts that she cannot reconcile her understandings of the law-as-it-is with the kind of outcome for which she is prepared to accept responsibility, given the facts before her. At this moment choice becomes inescapable, whether she wills it or no.[11] If she assents to the law-as-it-is against the dictates of conscience she is telling us far more about her response to the judicial role than about her response, or lack of response, to the case before her. The priority she is giving to the judicial role, to the illusion of judicial deference, to the need to protect the role, has made it necessary for her to exclude absolutely the possibility of subversion, of boundary breaking.[12]

Robert Cover described the judicial conscience as an 'artful dodger and rightfully so'.[13] If the judge has acknowledged to herself that she cannot accept the responsibility for reinventing the law, for judicial subversion, and yet remains unwilling to reject altogether the demands of conscience, perhaps even of sympathy, and thus reaffirm the law-as-it-is, she is likely to re-*present* herself as a calculating machine. In re-*presenting* herself as a calculating machine, in denying that boundary breaking can ever legitimately be part of the process of judgment and in affirming the authority of the text of law she has made a choice. On one level, she has chosen to resile from judgment. Yet even at this moment her work is not done. One final choice remains. She can, if only she will, put forward a plea for legislative intervention, even while she remits the present decision to 'the law'. She can, on the other hand, relinquish the moment of judgment, allow herself to become one with the law she speaks. The role and weight given the text, the tangled web which will ultimately be presented (if it is presented at all) as seamless, as without flaw or blemish, may displace entirely the subjectivity of the judge. If, as individual, her subjectivity remains undiminished, as judge, it has become devoid of substance or reality. One might say she has succeeded in the greatest struggle of all. She has eradicated class, ethnicity, gender, and ultimately even self. In becoming devoid of individuality, she has become one of the boys at last.

If, on the other hand, she accepts the subversive moment within her grasp and refuses to weave her understandings of the law as it is more closely still by adding yet another layer, she has engaged in a profound and remarkable act of boundary breaking. At this instant, long before judgment is handed down, the moment of subversion ruptures the process of judgment, sunders the tangled web even while its weaving continues. At this moment the judge is both conserving the law, because, as an institutional actor she has played her role, delivered judgment as expeditiously as may be possible, and has begun the process of giving us a new law. Hers is a fresh judgment, a beginning, a reinstatement of the (trace of the founding or originary) violence which cannot be isolated from judgment itself.[14] Even when the 'balance of terror is just as [we] would want it'[15] the judge must accept and understand the violence implicit in her role. She cannot escape, whether or not she herself might wish to do so. This violence, at once conserving and originary, is not something which can be walled off, domesticated, fenced about with love or with denial or with the refusal to acknowledge that it must be a part of every judicial act. It is not something that is found only in a criminal proceeding, although most assuredly and most clearly we do not talk our prisoners into jail.[16] It is everywhere law is. And we know, even if we might wish to deny it, that

> every juridical contract, every *Rechtsvertrag* ("legal contract,"...) is founded on violence. There is no contract which does not have violence as both an origin and an outcome.[17]

And in this is Derrida telling us that there could be *no such thing* as contract without the possibility of enforcement, of in short, violence? I believe he is. He is not *simply* acknowledging what social contract theorists from Hobbes onward have been at pains to insist. We all know that in any postulated 'state of nature' the problem is that enforcement is wanting and that, *for that reason*, no agreement is ultimately binding. All of that is true enough and utterly banal. He is saying something very much more profound, that the idea of contract is at its core a legal idea, that the idea necessarily holds within itself the possibility of that agreement being enforced. A contract is not simply a promise transplanted into a legal setting. It is an agreement between individuals which is entered on the understanding by all concerned that, if necessary, it will be enforced by the power of the state, will bring those who are party to it 'before the law'.[18]

And perhaps the ultimate illusion of the idea of the social contract lies in the way it strives to pull itself up by its own (figurative) bootstraps, to imaging a founding moment devoid of force, utterly without violence.

Violent foundings there are in abundance, whether through conquest, or revolution or civil war. There one might truly speak of the imposition of law. A social contract is necessarily something else: an originary contract which, at the moment of consent is (by definition) incapable of enforcement – without violence. It is an agreement whose most profound purpose is to make itself possible. Yes, the English Civil War can be read/must be read as a sub-text to the Hobbesian contract, and in that there was violence enough and more, but that violence was not the 'force of law'. Other violent foundings foreshadow the Rousseauean contract. Rousseau speaks of the 'contract' that preceded it, in which inequality and debauchery multiplied. He speaks as well of the explicit understanding that those who fail to accept the necessity of being brought before the law will be 'forced to be free'. Perhaps most terrifying of all, he speaks of the impossible need for a 'lawgiver' to ensure that men remain before the law. Derrida reminds us that the

founding or revolutionary moment of law is, in law, an instance of non-law. But it is also the whole history of law. **This moment always takes place and never takes place in a presence.** It is the moment in which the foundation of law remains suspended in the void or over the abyss, suspended by a pure performative act that would not have to answer to or before anyone. The supposed subject of this pure performative would no longer be before the law, or rather he would be before a law not yet determined, before the law as before a law not yet existing, a law yet to come, **encore devenat et devant venir**. The being "before the law" that Kafka talks about resembles this situation, both ordinary and terrible, of the man who cannot manage to see or above all to touch, to catch up to the law: because it is transcendent in the very measure that it is he who is to found it, as yet to come, in violence... The law is transcendent and theological, and so always to come, always promised, because it is immanent, finite and so already past. Every "subject" is caught up in this aporetic structure in advance.[19]

Against this background, it is altogether unsurprising that one of the traditional 'tests' for whether or not a particular agreement constituted a legal contract was whether it manifested an 'intent to enter legal relations'. The intent to enter legal relations was an intent that, should the agreement not be performed according to its letter, the parties would allow themselves to be brought 'before the law'. One reason for insisting that agreements between husband and wife, even those which bore *all* of the other indicia of contract, were not legally enforceable was the belief that the 'intention to enter legal relations' must necessarily be absent. Husband and wife could not remain husband and wife and yet deal with one another in ways that might, in the end, bring them before the law.[20] And what I want, and need, to say in this context, more than in any other, is that they were both entirely right in their refusal to do so, and wholly, brutally, and devastatingly wrong. Right, it seems to me because contract carries within its meaning the trace of a limited relationship. Whatever commitment may exist is to the bargain which has been struck and not to the other. Right as well because to be held to be liable for breach of contract is not *at all* the same as to be *answerable* for what one has or has not done, having promised. Contract is most urgently needed, it seems to me, when people have never been or no longer understand themselves to be answerable. Wrong, brutally, horribly, immorally wrong because the fact that those people had, in that circumstance, come before the law bore witness that whatever relationship existed between them was already limited, closer by far to bargain than to commitment. Wrong as well, because the denial of legal redress could never ensure that commitment would not fade. Once commitment has gone there are worse replacements by far than bargains that both parties know will be enforced by law. Wrong, ultimately, because promising and commitment demand that we acknowledge the position of the other, that her position be taken into account, felt to matter in ways which themselves serve as reasons for acting in particular ways. Where promises are not kept, and are, perhaps in desperation, recast as bargains with all the indicia of contract, this is no longer the case.

As well, another kind of violence insinuates itself into every contract, a violence that arises out of the asymmetry of its parties.[21] Contract, bargain, negotiation – in order that we may agree we will always find it necessary to settle for something other than we might have wished. This is true even (or most particularly) when we gain that which we believe to be of value to us. That we live among others, that we must always content ourselves with other than we would wish reminds us of lack, of incompleteness, of the violence of loss. The claim implicit in the link Derrida has drawn between contract and violence goes beyond any of the claims of social contract theory. 'Contract' (and 'contractual relations') are qualitatively different from other performatives, performatives which do not from their inception contain the necessity of force. And perhaps this is why contract has seemed to modernity the perfect metaphor for the coming of law. It epitomises the entrenchment of an overarching state to regulate transactions, to ensure that the possibility of force is everywhere present behind the relations of civil society. We can, it seems, no longer conceive of a relationship between individuals which does not, in the end, require the force of law to ensure that it will endure.[22] This may be why, as Patricia Williams has noted:

> the persuasive power of the forum itself [has] subvert[ed] the polis, as well as the law, to the extent that there is today precious little "public" left, just the tyranny of what we call the private. In this nation there is, it is true, relatively little force in the public domain compared to other nations, relatively little intrusive governmental interference. But we risk instead the life-crushing disenfranchisement of an entirely owned world. Permission must be sought to walk upon the face of the earth. Freedom becomes contractual and therefore obligated; freedom is framed by obligation; and obligation is paired not with duty but with debt.[23]

Our cultural bondage to law, to the *force* of law, goes a long way towards explaining our concern with judicial decision making. If the subversive moment is always a possibility, if with every 'fresh' decision the judge must choose, it may appear that to be before the law is simply to be before an individual. At every moment, she must either re-*present* herself as a calculating machine or engage in an act of boundary breaking. If this is true, it follows that the rule of law is illusory. *On one level,* the rule of law *is* illusory. Law is always poised at the moment of change, caught at the moment of transition. On another, far more profound, level the rule of law *could not continue* unless the subversive moment was always possible, always present. It is only the possibility of boundary breaking, of judgment afresh, of an outbreak of creativity, which ensures that judgment can ever remain both free and responsible, remain, in short, judgment. If the subversive moment were *not* possible, law would be something very different, something we would not wish to see within our polity. As Martha Minow and Elizabeth Spelman remind us, if decisions could always be based upon clearly articulated precedents or unambiguous principles it

> would make [the] presence [of judges] more or less superfluous – computers in robes... [I]nsofar as the judge is simply a "craftsman", or someone who simply "grovel[s] before the letter of the law", she has to "abandon the role of a judge and assume the role of a bureaucrat".[24]

When we try to come to terms with the subversive moment we must remember to understand it within its context. On the one hand, we find its inevitable and proper connection with violence. On the other, we see the way in which the entire machinery of enforcement insulates the judge from the violence in which she deals every day. Both of these, the connection and the insulation, are equally essential.

> One of the marks of having great destructive power over others is that while one's decisions have enormous impact on others, one does not have actually to enforce those decisions. Legislators who declare it illegal to surround the Pentagon do not have to be there to haul away demonstrators; corporate executives who create policies about workplace behavior are not the on-site managers who enforce such behavior. Generals may become presidents after fighting wars, but the president who declares a war is not among those who will actually fight it... [We tend to associate] elevated positions of authority [with] distance from the concrete, messy, and ugly consequences of orders issued from that place of authority... But maintaining an image of dignity and prestige for the judge imposes conditions which in turn curb his or her self knowledge, and encourage self-deception... If it is beneath the dignity of my station for me actually to carry out what I have decided ought to happen, then I very nearly assure that I shall not understand what my decision means in the lives of those most directly affected by it...25

Yes, and no. We have insulated the exercise of judgment from its execution for many reasons. If the judge were required both to hand down judgment and to act upon the judgment handed down we would have vested far too much power in one office, in one individual. More importantly, most normal and decent individuals would be unable in such circumstances to render judgment year after year. If, at the same time, they realised that they would be required to do all that might be necessary to ensure that the word was made flesh, the burden would be too great, too personal. To cause pain to others, to cause them loss, whether of material possessions, or of liberty, or of certain forms of connection, or, in some jurisdictions, even of life itself, is never easy. To do so consciously and deliberately, and in full knowledge of one's own role in the giving of judgment is very difficult indeed. For the kind of women and men we dare hope might become judges, we would want it difficult, perhaps even difficult to the point of impossibility. Those who could contemplate judgment under those circumstances, who would not blanch before the necessity to carry out judgment, to do whatever might be required, we would not, I think, wish to see as judges.

It is not to preserve their dignity and prestige that we have shielded our judges from the consequences of their decisions. Rather it is to preserve their ability to carry out what, for decent people, must at best be brutally difficult and at worst soul destroying, work. In a world in which we 'do not talk our prisoners into jail' we dare not ask, either of those who judge or those who carry out the judgment, that the process be, from beginning to end, seamless, unbroken. To carry out the orders handed down daily by our courts is difficult under the best of circumstances. At times what is required may be brutalising... never more so than when the order brings the liberty (or even the life) of a fellow human being to an end. More often than not, necessary though it is, the need to carry out such orders day after day diminishes, rather than enhances, the sensitivity of those whose lot it is. The risk of this kind of reduced sensitivity seems to me to be greater by far than the possibility that some judges, psychically isolated from the decisions they make, will decide without a full and proper appreciation of the consequences. What does, undeniably, shield judges from truly apprehending the weight, the burden of their decisions and the consequences that attend them is something very different. It is our persistent cultural myth that it is the law which is responsible, that the judge ought to be, if never merely a functionary or bureaucrat, the agent of the law. To be a judge is to be an agent who serves the law and whose role it is to declare what the law requires, nothing more, nothing less. Once choice and will are assimilated to capriciousness so that responsibility for the content of a decision is isolated from responsibility for its form, the decision maker is also isolated from personal responsibility for the decisions which must be made.

The Web of Law: Of Seamless Webs[26] and Other Weavings

The relationship between judge and text, between law and legal text, between text and meaning creates the web of law. The web of law is much more than the seamless web of which Dworkin speaks. That seamless web we might term 'Hercules' Web'.[27] The web of law binds together judge, text, law and meaning. Because each of these is unique, because no two moments are alike, because judgment, once given, cannot be recalled, culturally we have a need, even a compulsion, to make the process seem much more straightforward than it could ever be. One of the reasons, perhaps the most compelling reason, our theories of law feel as inadequate as they do, lies in their incompleteness. For the most part, they are constructed (abstracted might be a more appropriate word) from the written texts which have been left to us by judges. That these texts are themselves incomplete goes without saying, although the reasons they are necessarily incomplete bear reiterating.

Judgment as Rhetoric: The Narratives of Persuasion

Just as not everything in the stories told by ordinary people is 'legally relevant', not everything which has contributed to the narrative developed within the courtroom finds its way into the written judgment, into the texts of law. I insisted earlier that the supreme function of the written judgment is to persuade that both its form and its substance are directed (even dedicated) to persuasion. As far as the written judgment is concerned, judgment *is* rhetoric.[28] If my fascination with the role of narrative structure within the web of law seems curiously 'nonlegal', I would ask you to bear with me. The rhetoric of judgment is far more significant than it seems, and never more so than where the judge is master of her craft.

In recent work Robin West noted that in a series of Supreme Court cases involving the application of the death penalty[29] even more striking than the increasingly narrow ambit of the protections for those charged with violent crime was

> the contrasting rhetoric of the majority and dissenting opinions, and in particular, this phenomenon: in spite of the irrelevance, legally, of the facts of the underlying crime, the majority decisions upholding these death penalties all begin in the narrative voice with a recounting of the story of the crime. The liberal dissenters, just as uniformly, eschew the narrative voice entirely, and give no account of, narrative or otherwise, and generally make no reference to, the underlying crime.[30]

She continues, after quoting lengthy excerpts from the majority narratives describing the crimes:

> These murders, as retold in these decisions, are deeply and existentially disturbing. They are, in every sense of the phrase, postmodern murders: they strip the natural world of its hierarchy of values – life, love, nurture, work,

care, play, sorrow, grief – and they do so for no reason, not even to satisfy the misguided pseudo-Nietzschean desire of a Loeb or a Leopold to effectuate precisely that deconstruction. They are meaningless murders.[31]

She goes on to consider precisely why those judges felt it necessary to include these detailed narratives in their judgments. The narratives were (on one level) irrelevant to the legal issues raised on appeal. Indeed, so far as the appeal was concerned the narratives were formally meaningless. But, as she recognises:

the narratives in these cases have the effect, whether or not intended, of pushing the reader to assign personal responsibility for the murder and its consequences, including the arrest, trial, and its outcome – imposition of the death penalty – squarely and irrevocably on the defendant. The purpose of including these narratives is not simply to convey information... Rather, these narratives create a palpable need to reassert responsibility and human agency for a momentous act and momentous deprivation, so that we can again feel in control of destiny... The narrative in the conservative opinions ultimately validates the assignation of responsibility for the death of the defendant, and by so doing reestablishes, momentarily, order and meaning in a violently deconstructed world. Curtailment of rights emerges as a small but necessary price to pay.

Of the liberal dissenters on the other hand, Robin West highlights the fact that they wholly abandon the narrative voice for formal legal argument. It is crucial, as she insists that they argue not about responsibility but about rights. The dissenting judgments tell us nothing of the defendants, nothing of how they came to be before the law. While their rights are central to the legal story told by the dissentients, they have been effaced, depersonalised. Their judgments tell a story of diminished rights and of *habeus corpus* and the Bill of Rights under threat. Theirs is a story, not of what actually happened and how those particular defendants came to be *before the law*, but of rights.

Rights protect the individual against the community's need for coherence, for order, for meaning, for assignation of role and responsibility, for assertion and reassertion of the natural order. Rights ensure us peace to create chaos, disorder, randomness, change, from which we might fashion a new order. Rights must exit [sic], should exist, even in these cases, precisely because not in spite of the fact that they frustrate our need to reestablish, through the assignation of responsibility, order and meaning onto a disrupted world. The lack of narrative in the dissenting opinions in the death cases sends an unequivocal message: responsibility for the crime is irrelevant. It is irrelevant, of course, doctrinally. Responsibility is also irrelevant, however, to the ideal inherent in the regime of rights itself.[32]

Robin West insists that both the majority judgments and the dissenting judgments are profoundly flawed. If, as she says

by dismantling and trivializing rights, [the majority judges] have refused to honor that which renders life of value... [the dissentient's failure to provide any narrative of responsibility has led to] a peculiar and disorienting disjunction between the legal issue on which the cases turn – the jury's duty and entitlement to hear and consider all aspects of the defendant's life history that might, in the jury's mind, mitigate the crime and hence the harshness of the sentence, and the defendant's correlative right to a jury so informed – and what is learned about the defendant's circumstances or the social world, from either the majority or the dissent, which is absolutely nothing.[33]

West suggests that the dissentient's failure to humanise the defendants, to offer a counter-narrative which might mitigate our horror at their crimes and allow us to care a little about them and, therefore, about their rights:

conveys the message that a world of rights is one in which fortune, death, accident, fate, privilege, and power are randomly distributed; in which no one causes anything; in which we are shielded by rights from our responsibilities and ties to each other, to our past, to the future, and to the consequences of our action.[34]

In all of this she is, of course, correct. The structure of the judgments has had precisely the effect noted. The detailed narratives in the majority texts have demonised the defendants. They have encouraged us (all of us, including future courts who may want to see things differently) to believe that any diminution in their rights is insignificant given the horrific and inexplicable nature of their crimes. As rhetoric, the majority narratives are almost perfect. As for the dissentients, perhaps West is right. Perhaps they owe it to us to tell the story of these defendants in ways that might also suggest communal complicity in their violence. We need to understand the absurdity of a culture that celebrates violence, in the mass media, in the military, in its cultural images of masculinity, and sentences to death those who re-enact that violence. Perhaps they simply cannot find any 'liberal', 'rights based' rhetoric which might be psychologically adequate to humanise these particular defendants, given the liberal reluctance to connect word and deed, image and reality. Perhaps they remain more bound than they know by all the mythologies that tie us to the rule of law, and, in particular, to the legal insistence upon the irrelevance of precisely the narrative that West insists is called for. After all, from the perspective of legality, it was the dissentient position that represented the status quo, which had, at least initially, precedent on its side. As rhetoric, the majority narratives were perfectly constructed. They were intended to persuade us that, as West herself noted, these 'postmodern murders' were not the work of people who might have been like ourselves. They were the work of creatures so beyond our ordinary comprehension that talk of rights would be, at best, inappropriate. They encourage us to see these legal changes as right, as proper, as normal, sane and comforting, in short, as a bulwark against an insane world. The dissentients should have been able to rely upon the law and upon our cultural bondage to rights talk. That they could not was, perhaps, to be expected at this point in history. Rights talk has been gradually diminished, sometimes seems nothing more than a form of special pleading for one interest group or another.

Although the greatest judges have always known how and when to employ rhetoric, and here I think of all the rhetorical devices that reduced the plaintiff in *Palsgraf* to a cipher to prepare us for her eventual defeat,[35] too often we do not stop and attend to the uses of rhetoric and its role in persuasion. When at last we do attend as much to the way of a judgment as to its outcome, we often discount the rhetorical structure as somehow 'not properly legal', not part of the judgment in the legal sense. Robin West did precisely that when she dismissed the majority use of the narrative form. In her dismissal, I believe that she was wrong. Despite the apparent doctrinal irrelevance of narrative, it formed the stable thematic core of the majority judgments. Narrative provided the 'moral weight' which was essential to balance the rhetoric of rights and displace its putative legitimacy.

Form as Substance, Medium as Message
Affirming Legalism

Of the role of rhetoric in judgment there is much more I could say. In recent Australian law, the *Mabo*[36] decision provides compelling evidence of the power of rhetoric and the purposes to which it can be turned. While it is difficult to imagine that any contemporary Australian would be unaware of *Mabo* and of its legal (and psychological) significance, it is less well known outside of Australia. The plaintiffs were a group of Torres Strait Islanders, the Meriam people, who were the traditional owners of land on the three islands known collectively as the Murray Islands. The plaintiffs argued in the alternative that they were entitled to the Islands, as owners, as occupiers, or, in the 'worst case' scenario, as persons entitled to use and enjoy the land. In a landmark six/one decision, the High Court of Australia held that the doctrine of *terra nullius* did not defeat the claim of the Meriam people to native title. It held further that the doctrine of *terra nullius* did not apply in Australia and that native title survived the acquisition by the Crown of sovereignty and radical title. While to readers in New Zealand, in the United States and in Canada, Australia's recognition of native title may appear unremarkable, in Australian terms the decision was revolutionary. It overturned a number of propositions long deemed to be settled law. Because of its revolutionary nature, a study of the rhetorical devices that are employed is fascinating. In some ways, it can be said that there are 'two *Mabos*'. The legal decision is interesting and important in its own way, but as law it is incomplete and partial. The second *Mabo*, the *Mabo* of rhetoric, tells us a great deal about how these particular judges understood the relationship between law and justice, between law and power, and between law and politics. Because of their transparency, and because judgments of this kind are relatively rare in Australian law, given the absence of a Bill of Rights, they are worth exploring in full.

The rhetorical structure of the judgments provides singular evidence of what it can mean to speak as a judge and even more remarkable evidence of different ways in which these judges understood their relationship to the law. For Chief Justice Brennan, the critical question was whether the common law was to be held accountable for the dispossession of the indigenous inhabitants of Australia or whether that responsibility was to be borne by successive political authorities. He offers us a narrative of a very particular kind. He begins with a thorough and detailed history of the Meriam people, their social and communal life, and their early contacts with Europeans. This narrative, elegiac both in tone and in style, offers an edenic vision, a portrait of primal innocence undisturbed by colonisation and by the ebb and flow of politics.[37] Having painted a detailed picture of what might be termed 'historic fact',[38] His Honour turned to the law. The movement from 'history' to 'law', from 'fact' to 'legal fiction', lays the foundation. History and law must be reconciled *if the law is to be exonerated*. For Brennan, the question is how this can be done, given that:

> According to the cases, the common **law** itself **took** from indigenous inhabitants any right to occupy their traditional land, **exposed** them to deprivation of the religious cultural and economic sustenance which the land provides, **vested** the land effectively in the control of the Imperial authorities without any right to compensation and **made** the indigenous inhabitants **intruders** in their own homes and **mendicants** for a place to live. **Judged by any civilized standard**, such a law is unjust...[39] [Emphasis mine.]

His Honour goes on to emphasise that the High Court is:

> not free to adopt rules that accord with contemporary notions of justice and human rights if their adoption would fracture the skeleton of principle which gives the body of our law its shape and internal consistency.[40]

Law is organic, 'the prisoner of its history', but while the Court is reluctant to depart from long held views concerning the common law, and even more reluctant to depart from its own prior decisions:

> no case can command unquestioning adherence if the rule it expresses seriously offends the values of justice and human rights (especially equality before the law) which are aspirations of the contemporary Australian legal system.[41]

The stage is set. On the one hand, we have the weight of tradition, the organic presence of the law as it has developed throughout history. On the other hand, we have contemporary ideals of justice and human rights, the aspiration of the law to 'work itself pure'.[42] Only after the rhetorical backdrop is fully established, does Brennan begin actually examining the arguments sustaining *terra nullius*. If we consider the structure of his judgment *as rhetoric*, his examination of the legal arguments is unimportant. What is important is whether an avenue can be found to exonerate the common law without fatally undermining the doctrines governing land tenure in Australia. He continues:

The **facts** as we know them today do not fit the "absence of law" or "barbarian" theory underpinning the colonial reception of the common law of England. That being so, there is no warrant for applying in these times rules of the English common law which were the product of that theory. It would be a curious doctrine to propound today that, when the **benefit of the common law** was first extended to **Her Majesty's indigenous subjects in the Antipodes**, **its first fruits** were **to strip them of their right** to occupy their ancestral lands.[43] [Emphasis mine.]

It is important to recognise just how far outside the bounds of legal doctrine (as conventionally understood) and the 'normal' role of an appellate tribunal Brennan has moved. He is prepared to consign to the 'dustbin of history' common law rules that have stood for centuries. He is also, and far more significantly, prepared to do so, not on the basis that the 'law' was mistaken, but upon the basis that 'the **facts** as we know them **today**' do not warrant the application of those rules. In this way, he exonerates the common law from complicity in the dispossession. His route is circuitous indeed. He argues that because the 'facts' were inadequately understood in 1788 'the wrong law' was applied to the Australian colonies. In this way, Brennan reassigns responsibility for the dispossession of the indigenous peoples of Australia. According to Brennan:

Aboriginal rights and interests were not stripped away by operation of the common law on first settlement by British colonists, but by the exercise of a sovereign authority over land exercised recurrently by Governments. To treat the dispossession of the Australian Aborigines as the working out of the Crown's acquisition of ownership of all land on first settlement is contrary to history. Aborigines were dispossessed of their land parcel by parcel, to make way for expanding colonial settlement...[I]t is appropriate to identify the events which resulted in the dispossession of the indigenous inhabitants of Australia, **in order to dispel the misconception that it is the common law rather than the action of governments which made many of the indigenous people of this country trespassers on their own land.**[44] [Emphasis mine.]

Now all of this is, to say the very least, bizarre, *if we attempt to read it as law*. As rhetoric it is exceptionally effective. We have a sympathetic, even edenic narrative, a beautifully structured condemnation of the status quo, a projection of contemporary understandings upon the canvas of 1788, and finally, a condemnation of successive colonial governments together with a valorisation of the common law. For a lawyer, for a judge, it is a remarkably effective piece of sleight of hand.

Theory and Practice, Form and Substance

The joint judgment of Deane and Gaudron, while very different in structure, in style, and in manner, is also extremely effective as rhetoric (although again somewhat 'difficult' as law). Whereas Brennan began in an enchanted garden, Deane and Gaudron offer us a dry if didactic and thoroughly meticulous lesson in legal history, in international law, and in the intellectual structure of common law doctrines regarding property.[45] Having addressed the law and legal doctrine at length, and having emphasised that, in their view, common law native title survived settlement, Deane and Gaudron note that:

> Notwithstanding that the rights of use or occupancy under a common law native title recognized by the law of a settled British Colony were binding upon the Crown, the native inhabitants of such a Colony in the eighteenth century were in an essentially helpless position of their title was wrongfully denied or extinguished or their possession was wrongfully terminated by the Crown or those on its behalf. **In theory**, the native inhabitants were entitled to invoke the protection of the common law in a local court (when established) or, in some circumstances, in the courts at Westminster. **In practice**, there is an element of the absurd about the suggestion that it would have even occurred to the native inhabitants of a new British Colony that they should bring proceedings in a British court against the British Crown to vindicate their rights under a common law of which they would be likely to know nothing.[46] [Emphasis mine.]

While this is clearly rhetoric, and very skilful rhetoric indeed, it is very different in form and structure and reveals a very different persuasive agenda. Where Brennan endeavoured to vindicate the common law, Deane and Gaudron invoke the dichotomy between theory and practice. While, in theory, the rights of the native inhabitants were respected; as a matter of legal practice, the rights, which had been fictively granted by law, were unknown and inaccessible to those who enjoyed their theoretical protection. In addition, perhaps it is worth noting that even when the native inhabitants attempted to invoke the protection of the law, they were, nonetheless, silenced. In canvassing the inability of refugees to persuade courts of their plight, Costas Douzinas and Ronnie Warrington emphasise that:

> In the idiom of cognition, fear is either reasonable and can be understood by the judge or is unreasonable and therefore non-existent. In the first instance it is the excess of knowledge and reason on the part of the judge that disqualifies the fear, in the second it is the excess of fear that disqualifies itself. But this translation of fear into knowledge and of the *style* into reasons and causes assumes that the judge can occupy the place of the refugee and share his pain. Fear, pain and death however are radically singular; they resist and at the limit destroy language and its ability to construct shared worlds.
>
> Lyotard has called this violent double bind an *ethical tort* (*differend*); it is an extreme form of injustice in which the injury suffered by the victim is accompanied by a deprivation of the means to prove it.
>
> This is the case if the victim is deprived of life, or of all liberties, or of the freedom to make his or her ideas or opinions public, or simply of the right to testify to the damage, or even more simply if the testifying phrase is itself deprived of authority... Should the victim seek to bypass this impossibility and testify anyway to the wrong done to her, she comes up against the following argumentation, either the damages you complain about never took place, and your testimony is false; or else they took place, and since your [sic] are able to testify to them, it is not an ethical tort that has been done to you.
>
> When an ethical tort has been committed the conflict between the parties cannot be decided equitably because no rule of judgment exists that could be applied to both arguments. The genre and the rules used to judge such cases will not be those of the genre judged and the outcome will be necessarily unjust. The violence of injustice begins when the judge and the judged do not share a language or idiom. It continues when all traces of particularity and otherness are reduced to a register of sameness and cognition mastered by the judge. Indeed all legal interpretation and judgment presuppose that the Other, the victim of the language's injustice, is capable of language in general... But our communities have long lost any aspirations to a common idiom. We should not forget, therefore, that justice may turn out to be impossible, just a shibboleth.[47]

And what kind of silencing, what kind of 'ethical tort' is experienced by those for whom no distinction exists between subjection and subjugation and being, in form at least, a subject *before the law*?

One might suggest that whereas Brennan's account is quintessentially 'modernist' in style, in tone, and in structure, even to its vindication of the common law and its excoriation of politics, theirs is postmodern, consumed by the gulf between form and substance, theory and practice. Deane and Gaudron have reduced the law to a pedantic footnote, an *apologia* for a brutal colonial reality. The rhetorical climax of their judgment, and its sole departure from the dry formalism that elsewhere characterises it comes in a brief and beautifully constructed passage of mounting intensity. Initially, we are told, settlement proceeded peacefully and without dispute. Only with time and increasing expansion by the Europeans did violence and conflict emerge. Mention is made of an early 'flash point', one that occurred in 1804 in the 'fertile areas surrounding the lower reaches of the Hawkesbury River'. Abruptly, the dispassionate tone of the judgment vanishes. It is replaced by a series of emotional crescendos.

> An early **flash point** with one clan of Aborigines illustrates the first stages of the **conflagration of oppression and conflict** which was, over the following century, to spread across the continent to **dispossess, degrade and devastate** the Aboriginal peoples and leave a **national legacy** of **unutterable shame**.[48] [Emphasis mine.]

At a stroke, the dispassionate tone of the judgment vanishes. In a brief and beautifully constructed passage of mounting intensity, the concrete social meaning of **practice** is sheeted home. Up to this point, Their Honours have been concerned with the legal **theory**, with the niceties of law and of legal argument and the establishment of legal rights. Abruptly, they turn their attention to the brutal world of eighteenth and nineteenth century political practice. The rhetorical movement within the passage is remarkable. Flashpoint, conflagration, oppression and conflict, dispossess, degrade and devastate – these are words intended to reach, not the mind but the heart, to evoke not reasoned acknowledgment but empathy, evocative of a national holocaust which had gone for too long unremarked. Immediately afterwards, the quiet tone of the narrative resumes. We are told of negotiations and assurances by Lord Hobart, of the acknowledged **failure of Colonial practice** to comply with the 'wise and humane' instructions of predecessors. In rapid succession, eighteenth and nineteenth century literature concerning the Aboriginals is drawn upon to substantial effect. Cook's portrayal of a people living in an idyllic 'state of nature' providing them with all the necessaries of life is contrasted with Warton's 1893 editorial comments on that passage. Warton emphasises the 'treachery' and 'savage ideas' of the Aborigines, but acknowledges as well that they have been treated by the 'coarser order of colonists as wild beasts to be extirpated'.[49] In a brief and telling return to the law, Deane and Gaudron note the paucity of references to Aboriginal people in the Constitution. They remind us that Aboriginal people were excluded from the Commonwealth legislative power and were not to be counted in population figures. Nineteenth century acknowledgments of both Aboriginal proprietary rights and their dispossession are cited, suggesting that these occasioned at least some disquiet. In rapid succession, Their Honours mention the attempt of the 1836 Letters Patent in South Australia to protect Aboriginal rights to their traditional lands, and the failure of the Batman Treaty in 1835. These early documents emphasise that by the eighteen thirties at the latest, government authorities clearly recognised that the indigenous peoples had well defined proprietary rights in the soil from which they had been and were being dispossessed. As they note:

> Inevitably, one is compelled to acknowledge the role played, in the dispossession and oppression of the Aborigines, by the two propositions that the territory of New South Wales was, in 1788, terra nullius in the sense of unoccupied or uninhabited for legal purposes and that the full and beneficial ownership of all the lands of the Colony vested in the Crown, unaffected by any claims of the Aboriginal inhabitants. Those **propositions** provided a legal basis for and justification of the dispossession. They constituted the **legal context** of the acts done to enforce it and, while accepted, **rendered unlawful** acts done by the Aboriginal inhabitants to protect traditional occupation or use. [Emphasis mine.]

Their Honours emphasise the role played in **dispossession and oppression** by the doctrine of *terra nullius* and by the thesis that the Crown had full beneficial ownership of the lands of the colony. As they state:

> the official endorsement, **by administrative practice and in judgments of the courts**, of these two propositions provided the environment in which the Aboriginal people of the continent came to be treated as a different and lower form of life whose very existence could be ignored for the purpose of determining the legal right to occupy and use their traditional homelands.[50] [Emphasis mine.]

If Brennan invoked a 'factual error' to underpin his endeavour to rescue the common law, arguing, in essence, that had the 'facts' been properly under-stood, the law would have recognised common law native title from the outset, Deane and Gaudron fatally undermine the attempted rescue, emphasising that the facts were known but, being inconvenient, were ignored.

Evidentiary Presumptions or How to do it with Facts

Of the remaining judgments, much less can be said. If, legally, Toohey's judgment is the most 'radical' of the majority judgments, both as narrative and as rhetoric it fails, and, perhaps as a consequence, seems curiously unpersuasive. For Toohey, '[t]he real question is whether the rights of the Meriam people to the Islands survived annexation'.[51] He asserts that:

> Previous interests in land may be said to survive *unless* it can be shown that the effect of annexation is to destroy them. That is, the onus rests with those claiming that traditional title does not exist.[52]

This finesse having redrawn the field of argument, Toohey **concludes** that traditional title is not extinguished by annexation, but continues until lawfully terminated. The battle is to be fought on **evidentiary** grounds. Proof of existence is the 'threshold' question. The characteristics of the interests alleged and of the society alleging them are irrelevant.[53]

> [A]n inquiry into the kind of society from which rights and duties emanate is irrelevant to the existence of title, because it is inconceivable that indigenous inhabitants in occupation of land did **not** have a system by which land was utilized in a way determined by that society.[54]

It is, of course, quite impossible to quarrel with what Toohey is saying. It is sensible, reasonable, and perversely logical if hardly 'legal'. As argument, however, it is either a failure or nonexistent, a collection of assertions devoid of justification. The question becomes what constitutes evidence that a particular people occupied a particular stretch of land. For Toohey, one suspects, this is meant to be a simplification, a removal from the halls of rhetoric and feudal doctrine and a new beginning in the fields of fact. We are dealing with a question of fact, not of law. The matter, in short, is strictly an evidentiary matter. Yet, as Haldar has noted:

> Evidence doesn't simply construct frames of reference. It is by its own nature a frame; it is what divides/connects the internal world of the courtroom (*texte*)

to the external world of reality (*hors texte*). Evidence is adjectival law, a supplementary text, law's own parergon. If it is within the evidential frame that the law reflects upon the outside, then Evidence is no longer a marginal topic for lawyers to focus upon. The laws of evidence become the aperture: the aporia, Law's gaping wound.[55]

With the details stripped away, the Toohey's optimistic propositions may be put in this form. He begins from a **presumption** that traditional interests in land survive annexation **unless** it can be shown that they have been expropriated or extinguished. The **onus** is therefore on those who would challenge native title to establish that the lands were expropriated or title was extinguished and when this occurred. Quite obviously, as a purely pragmatic matter, this makes life a great deal easier for a potential claimant. Equally obviously, it reverses the normal rule that he or she who asserts the affirmative of a proposition must prove it. How does Toohey legitimate his sleight of hand? It is really quite simple. First, occupation is a matter of **fact**, not law.[56] Second, to make out a claim of native title it is the fact of **occupation** that must be established, not anything more difficult or exotic. Those challenging native title must point to specific legal acts constituting expropriation or extinguishment in order to rebut continued (rightful) occupation together with the presumption of native title that it generates. Yet, as Haldar notes, all these facts marshalled just outside of memory, just outside of certain knowledge, are destined to become the aporia. In the end, I believe, Toohey's judgment remains unpersuasive precisely because, like the laws of evidence upon which he relies, in the best pragmatic tradition it will not let us pass through it into belief.

Formalism and Hair Splitting

If Toohey's overt radicalism remains, in the end, unpersuasive, irrespective of what one might think of the merits or even the justice of his argument, Dawson's embrace of positivism is equally so. Unlike Brennan, Deane, and Gaudron who distinguished carefully between sovereignty and its consequences on the one hand, and the acquisition of property and the proprietary rights of the Crown, on the other, Dawson displayed little interest in such legal niceties. These academic technicalities are swept aside by the simple fact that upon 'annexation the lands annexed became the property of the Crown and any rights in the land that the plaintiffs have must be held under the Crown'.[57] The question of whether, following a change in sovereignty, pre-existing rights continue to exist is, therefore, a question of **fact**, not law. As with Toohey, in the end the matter is an evidentiary matter. Whether or not the rights subsist following annexation depends wholly upon whether the Crown has, in some way, acknowledged those rights or acquiesced in their continued existence. In essence, this is a lineal descendant of the standard positivist/formalist argument. Where the law is silent in respect of what ought to happen if a given event occurs, the happening least favourable to the plaintiff's interests ought to be implied. According to Dawson, even if the Crown recognised native interests and permitted them to continue in some form:

> [t]he vesting of the radical title in the Crown upon the assumption of sovereign authority is, however, incompatible with the continued existence in precisely the same form of any pre-existing rights. Necessarily the pre-existing rights were held of a former sovereign or in the absence of any sovereign at all. After the Crown has assumed sovereignty and acquired the radical title to the land, any pre-existing "title" must be held, if it is held at all, under the Crown. This new title is therefore not merely the continuation of a title previously held, notwithstanding that it may be identifiable by reference to the previous title. If the new title is to be held under the Crown, the Crown must obviously accept it. Such acceptance may be by way of acquiescence in the continued occupancy of land by the aboriginal inhabitants and, if the native interests are accepted in this manner by the Crown, the nature of those interests can then only be determined by reference to the nature of the former occupancy by the aboriginal inhabitants. The appearance (although not the fact as a matter of law) is, then, that these native interests continue undisturbed. In this sense it may be true to say that positive recognition of native interests by the Crown is unnecessary for their continued existence and that what appear to be different views upon the subject are, on analysis, fundamentally the same.[58]

The specific indicia of recognition which Deane, Gaudron and Toohey offered as evidence of at least tacit recognition of native rights of occupancy are either wholly inconclusive or establish the contrary. According to Dawson, 'land was dealt with upon the basis that, where not retained or reserved for public purposes, it was available for settlement without regard to any claim on the part of the aboriginal inhabitants'.[59] In an exceedingly curious passage Dawson moves to the heart of his view:

There may not be a great deal to be proud of in this history of events. But a dispassionate appraisal of what occurred is essential to the determination of the legal consequences, not withstanding the degree of condemnation which is nowadays apt to accompany any account. The policy which lay behind the legal regime was determined politically and, however insensitive the politics may now seem to have been, a change in view does not of itself mean a change in the law. It requires the implementation of a new policy to do that and that is a matter for government rather than the courts. In the meantime, it would be wrong to attempt to revise history or to fail to recognize its legal impact, however unpalatable it may seem. To do so would be to impugn the foundations of the very legal system under which this case must be decided.[60]

Much in this passage warrants discussion and consideration. Dawson J has offered no arguments to support his thesis that radical title in the Crown necessitates full beneficial title in the Crown. He has made two bald assertions. First, he insists that the distinction between conquered, ceded, and settled lands is irrelevant on the facts because its only work was to determine what (or whose) law applied. Since, when the Murray Islands were annexed, the law of Queensland was stated to apply, the distinction had no work to do. It follows that talk of *terra nullius* is a red herring. This move, which is rhetorically very useful, eliminates the unpleasant and patently false pretence that the land was uninhabited at annexation. Whether or not the land was inhabited is irrelevant. Under the feudal system of land ownership, all land is held of the Crown. If all land is held of the Crown, the Crown must acquire both radical and beneficial title upon annexation. It follows that native title must be recognised by the Crown if it is to exist because, under the feudal account of land tenure, it must, necessarily, be held of the Crown. While he acknowledges the existence of authorities suggesting that a 'mere change in sovereignty is not to be presumed as meant to disturb rights of private owners',[61] he emphasises this does not mean that the rights continue despite annexation. Rather, no presumptions attend a change in sovereignty. Whether the new sovereign recognises pre-existing rights is a matter of fact, not law. Legal argument cannot establish native title when what is needed is concrete factual evidence of some act amounting to recognition.

For Dawson we must ask what evidence might suffice. If Toohey demanded 'evidence' of occupation, Dawson insists that unequivocal (textual?) evidence of recognition of pre-existing rights is an essential precondition. Without this, no recognition is possible. The evidence sought must be textual, first because it must, if it is to stand as evidence, be contemporaneous with its contextual frame, and second because:

> a glance at any textbook on evidence illustrates that written evidence is in fact more meaningful. Documents, birth certificates, computer records, written confessions considered to be "best" evidence – but **best because they are unquestionable and not subject to cross-examination**. It is not until the laws of proof are called upon to question the veracity of an event or situation that oral evidence becomes preferable... both the witness and the document are subject to the laws of vision: both are "seen-to-be-believed" and both find expression in visual imagery.[62] [Emphasis mine.]

Because there are no witnesses, cannot be any witnesses, and all non-textual evidence of recognition of pre-existing rights can, at the most, be considered hearsay, that which cannot be seen, cannot be believed. Not only must it be seen to be believed, it must have been seen and believed **at the time**. The only reliable evidence we have is that provided by the contemporaneous written record of governmental dealings in land. Those dealings uniformly show that land was available for settlement irrespective of any claim the native inhabitants might have had.[63] The evidential frame, thus drawn, reveals no outside for the law to reflect upon, no external world of reality (*hors texte*).[64]

Rhetoric and Reality: Framing Mabo

So there we have it. The rhetoric of *Mabo* lends itself to four distinct readings, two theoretical and two evidentiary. If the elegiac narrative of Brennan seeks to bring us face to face with the Other, to make us, in that face to face contact 'fully, immediately and irrevocably responsible for the Other',[65] Deane and Gaudron fatally undermine that strategy by depriving it of its moorings and casting it adrift upon the shoals of factual evidence. No one, they suggest, ever believed that Australia was, in fact, *terra nullius*, it was enough the law declared it thus. What was done was done in full knowledge, done, in short, *before and through the law*. The movement away from the question of hearsay, of unknown title, authorship, identity, a movement away from apocrypha, to the accusation of false title, false authorship, false identity, false representation – a movement to pseudographia.[66]

is already complete. If our two theoretical readings remain in tension, offering radically different visions of law, of politics, and the legal reality of settlement, our evidentiary readings cannot even agree upon what evidence is called for. If, for Toohey, all that is needed is evidence of occupation, its source is little more than 'a means of tracing an identity, an approximation based upon memory (memoria/amnesia)',[67] always, already about to become a false writing. Yet, Dawson fares no better. In the end, his standard could never be met, because it is less a standard than a refusal to acknowledge that any standard might ever be appropriate. We are left with an *ethical tort* and where 'an ethical tort has been committed the conflict between the parties cannot be decided equitably because no rule of judgment exists that could be applied to both arguments'.[68] No shared idiom exists. Reading *Mabo*, we are left with an attempted exculpation that reminds us that justice is a shibboleth, 'a gap, an unspeakable place, a password, and a pass-not word'.[69]

Notes

1   It is only the possibility of subversion, of boundary breaking, which ensures that judgment is just that, judgment. I want to emphasise that, as I understand it, the subversive moment is within the ideal of adjudication. It does not threaten the judicial ideal. It makes it possible.

2   Here I foreshadow, although I do not address in any detail, the complications which arise in appellate jurisdictions where the 'subversive moment' is itself subverted by the need to negotiate, to weave something which can, at least for the time, be given force as a 'judgment of the court'.

3   In my insistence that the judge is always responsible for her decision in the fullest possible sense what I have to say about judging and responsibility has much in common with the insistence of Martha Minow and Elizabeth Spelman that 'the judge should acknowledge what it feels like to have power over the lives of others in the act of judgment, and, if the judge does not experience such power, the judge should reflect on why, despite the actual effects of the decisions he or she will make, he or she experiences not having much power'. See Minow M & E Spelman, 'Passion for Justice' in JT Noonan Jr and KI Winston, *The Responsible Judge: Readings in Judicial Ethics*, Westport, Praeger, 1993, 257, 258. Every decision affords choice, could have been other than it is. Decisions are made by judges, not by texts. Texts are always short of fully determinate and outcomes can always be other than they are. The responsibility for the decision lies, not with the law, but with the judge. It is not indeterminacy that leads to moral horror, it is a positivistic willingness to remit

responsibility to the law and blindly and mechanistically inscribe the text upon the bodies of those who come before the law. See Cover, *Justice Accused*, 229. Cf Weisberg, *Poethics*, 93-103. I understand what drives Weisberg to his terror of indeterminacy and openness, but do not share it. It is sobering to recognise that whereas critical scholars such as Weisberg retreat to a kind of desperate positivism, feminist scholars such as Minow, Spelman and West place their faith in empathy and in passion. I can neither cling to textuality as to a rock amid rapids nor place my faith in empathy and passion. Our judges need their noses rubbed in the world. If any judge can avoid confronting the power she exercises and the impact that power has upon the lives of those before the law, the battle is already more than half lost.

4   She must explain her decision to herself as well as to others. No judge consciously sets out to move beyond the boundaries of the judicial role. It is significant that Pat O'Shane, confronting educated women with no prior convictions who had entered pleas of guilty to malicious damage in respect of a billboard depicting a woman clad only in her underwear being sawn in half acknowledged not having known how she was going to deal with the situation. In a speech given at the launch of the *Australian Feminist Law Journal* she commented that her initial reaction was one of anger and an inability to deal with her own anger. She went on:

> I really did feel all alone – often in my job one does feel all alone. Then I thought, "Bugger it! Bollen didn't think twice". I took my courage in hand and stormed down those stairs and into the Court Room, and said "Sergeant do you have those antecedents?"... Indeed I calmed my anger sufficiently to go through it very formally, and to dismiss the charges before me under the provisions of s556A. I declined to make an order as to costs and compensation. Then I folded my arms and I sat back. And then I said: "The crime in this situation is the erection of those billboards depicting violence towards women."

O'Shane, P, 'Launch of the Australian Feminist Law Journal', 5.

5   Derrida, 'Force of Law: The "Mystical Foundation of Authority"', 23.

6   And to the extent that they speak of the judge/reader 'imposing meaning' upon the (judicial) text making of it the best that it can be, the violence inherent in the judicial act is at once acknowledged and displaced, unmoored, cast adrift from its location in the social and installed in a shadow world of readers and texts.

7   In saying this I am reminding myself and my readers that the principal function of the written judgment is to persuade. Within our conventions of legality a judgment is most persuasive when it appears to be a necessary and inevitable part of the legal canon, wholly, if startlingly, ordinary and expected. While the law is far from being a 'seamless web' the judge must attempt to present it as if it were.

8   Minow & Spelman, 'Passion for Justice', 258.

9   Minow & Spelman, 'Passion for Justice', 258.

10   I am not necessarily convinced that we always know or can give voice to the way in which we reach our decisions. We are not, despite our best efforts, always so transparent to ourselves. I think it unlikely that our judges are either more or less transparent to themselves than the rest of us.

11   It is important to be mindful that whenever the case presents as a conflict between law and conscience there is always a choice. She may affirm the-law-as-it-is; she may accept the moment of subversion. Whatever decision she makes, it is necessarily a

decision, a moment of fresh judgment. She is not simply 'following a rule'. That possibility vanished at the moment she acknowledged the possibility of conflict between law and conscience, the possibility of subversion. That she may re-*present* herself as a calculating machine is, of course, a very different matter.

12   Cover's description of the process of dissonance reduction seems particularly apt. He noted that a judge who found herself driven to a decision that she could not reconcile with conscience, 'selected, as norms, those articulations of the process and its limits that invoked the highest possible justifications for formalism, that described the process in the most mechanistic terms; and that emphasized the place of others in the decisional process'. Cover, *Justice Accused*, 237.

13   Cover, *Justice Accused*, 201.

14   And here, in one moment, I have said (without seeking to and certainly without wishing to) why the thought of '*an act of power which is loving*' is unbearable. To the extent that power and love are reconciled, to the extent that, as Robin West would have it, the judge endeavours, through her empathetic response to those *before the law* (and I read that phrase with all the foreboding its linkage with Kafka demands) to domesticate power, to domesticate judgment, we also domesticate violence, bring it within the grasp of the ordinary and the bureaucratic. Hanna Arendt spoke of the sheer banality of bureaucratic evil. I think here of a violence which has been domesticated, normalised, as with all the acts of genocide which now confront us – in the Balkans, in Africa, in the 'killing fields' everywhere... These are places where violence has been normalised. Once violence has been normalised, once we no longer shudder before its mark, we are already lost.

15   Cover, 'Violence and the Word', 223.

16   Cover, 'Violence and the Word', 223.

17   Derrida, 'Force of Law: The "Mystical Foundation of Authority"', 47. And never is this truer than of those contractual shadows, those imagined foundational moments which people 'social contract theory'. This violence, the violence of the founding moment, is, perhaps, most clearly present in Hobbes, who at least understood the need for law, for authority (and saw both as absolutes) much more clearly than did Locke. It is also present in Rousseau who understood the imperative in different terms, not it terms of an absolutist state but in terms of an absolutist understanding of our relationship to law and to conscience, as that point at which we must be 'forced to be free'.

18   On the distinction between 'promise' and 'contract' Stanley Cavell has noted that promising, unlike contract, is a specifically moral idea and that it is fundamental to its meaning that, should a promise be broken whether or not that act can be justified is *not* a question which can be finally determined by an umpire, 'that no one can settle a moral conflict in the way umpires settle conflicts'. Cavell, S, *The Claim of Reason*, Oxford, OUP, 1979, 296. Cavell goes on to note that when we speak of contract, on the other hand, its offices and defences and moves are

elaborately specified, the practice is definitive, and a given conflict can be adjudicated (umpired). This, however, involves a whole way of looking at society, one in which all human relationships are pictured as contractual **rather than** personal, within which one's commitments, liabilities, responsibilities are from the outset limited, and not total, or at any rate always in the course of being determined. We still relate to one another as persons, but only insofar as we stand in certain socially defined roles with respect to one another. The picture is made clearer if we include the suggestion that the central idea underlying the English Law of Contract is that of a **bargain**. [Emphasis mine.]

Cavell, *The Claim of Reason*, 299. And one might specifically add that, because the potential for being brought before the law is a part of every contract, both parties understand, or ought to understand, at the outset that if the matter is brought before the law the 'contract' of each of the parties will be replaced by the 'law's contract'.

19 Derrida, 'Force of Law: The "Mystical Foundation of Authority"', 36.

20 And perhaps it is true as well that the courts want to avoid the contamination inevitable if the boundary between family relationships and civil society were ruptured, if contract were acknowledged to play the same role within families as within civil society. I cannot help thinking in this context that it is significant that early social contract theorists explicitly sought to account for family relationships in contractual terms... not only marriage but also the relationship between parents and children, or to be more explicit, that between father and child. It is worth musing upon why and how a fictive account of a legal relationship between juridical equals came to be superimposed upon relationships which were, in the real world, hierarchical, and whose hierarchical context was explicitly seen as acceptable by those who sought to recast them in the guise of contract.

21 There is a sense in which the parties to every contract *are fundamentally asymmetrical*, in which each has that which the other lacks. If this were not the case, there would be no contract. As the bargain is struck, we are confronted by the gulf between that which we sought and that which we have gained. After the contract has been performed, after we have gained what we thought we wanted, loss remains. No contract, whether juridical, whether social, whether sexual, has completeness rather than violence in its outcome. The lack always remains, and while it remains we will struggle to fill it.

22 The great debates over law are simultaneously moral debates, and moral debates of a very particular kind. When liberalisation is blamed for broken families, when laws proscribing homosexual relationships are defended with increasing desperation, the vehemence with which they are defended stands as an admission that the force of law is essential to maintain them. It is not law as ideal, even less law as moral teacher, a role for which it is extraordinarily poorly suited, but law as force that is sought. It is the possibility of force, of violence, of being brought before the law.

23 Williams, P, *The Alchemy of Race and Rights: Diary of a Law Professor*, Cambridge, Harv Univ Press, 1991, 43. And behind debt, and duty, lies contract, waiting in the wings.

24 Minow & Spelman, 'Passion for Justice', 259-260.

25 Minow & Spelman, 'Passion for Justice', 363.

26 Dworkin, *Taking Rights Seriously*, 116. 'The law may not be a seamless web; but the plaintiff is entitled to ask Hercules to treat it as if it were.' Does each succeeding judge weave the 'web' of law more tightly until movement becomes impossible and no gap remains? So it would seem. See Dworkin, RM, 'Law as Interpretation' 60 *Texas LR* 527, 532 (1982). All we have of these judges are their words on paper, the seamless webs they weave and leave for others to follow.

27   The allusion to 'Charlotte's Web' is deliberate and fitting. The stories we tell children
      are not that different from the stories we tell about law and about legal reasoning.
28   I do not use rhetoric in any pejorative sense, despite the currency of such usage among
      those desperate to shore up the boundaries of, for example, philosophy.
29   In speaking of Benjamin, Derrida alludes to the place of the death penalty in law and
      suggests:
>   If the origin of law is a violent positioning, the latter manifests itself in the purest
>   fashion when violence is absolute, that is to say when it touches on the right to
>   life and to death... If the legal system fully manifests itself in the possibility of the
>   death penalty, to abolish the penalty is not to touch upon one dispositif among
>   others, it is to disavow the very principle of law... The death penalty bears
>   witness, it must bear witness, to the fact that law is a violence contrary to nature.

      Derrida, 'Force of Law: The "Mystical Foundation of Authority"', 42.
30   West, RL, *Narrative, Authority, and Law*, Ann Arbor, Univ of Mich Press, 1993, 429.
31   West, *Narrative, Authority, and Law*, 431.
32   West, *Narrative, Authority, and Law*, 433-434.
33   West, *Narrative, Authority, and Law*, 435.
34   West, *Narrative, Authority, and Law*, 436.
35   See Weisberg, *Poethics*, 16-34. In a discussion of the narrative aspects of judicial
      opinions ('The Judicial Opinion as Creative Narration') Weisberg notes at 16 that:
>   the way in which the adjudicator explains the case **determines** the rightness or
>   wrongness of the opinion. Rhetoric, in other words, does not assist an argument to
>   march to a conclusion; rhetoric **is** the argument, and the perceived rightness or
>   wrongness of the conclusion may be as much based on the style and form of the
>   argument as on the extrinsic application to it of the observer's notion of what the
>   law of the case "should have been". [Emphasis mine.]

      Later in the section he discusses two of the opinions of the great American judge,
      Cardozo, those in *Hynes v New York Central Railroad* and *Palsgraf v Long Island
      Railroad*.
36   *Mabo and Ors v Queensland (No 2)* (1991-1992) 175 CLR 1.
37   To borrow the term Barbara Herrenstein Smith used to highlight MacIntyre's
      yearnings for a world of perfect innocence and morality that never existed, Brennan's
      vision is pre-lapsarian, 'before the fall'. As the prayerbook says 'In Adam's fall we
      sinned all '.
38   A slightly darker and more sardonic vision might characterise it as 'faction'.
39   *Mabo*, 29. Brennan's post-lapsarian vision is one with which we are, unfortunately, all
      too familiar. The capacity to confuse genocide with liberation and progress remains a
      familiar part of our ethical landscape.
40   *Mabo*, 29. We are, indeed, confronted by the 'body' of the law, 'bloody bones' as
      Drucilla Cornell suggests. See Cornell, D, 'The Violence of the Masquerade: Law
      Dressed up as Justice' 11 *Cardozo LR* 1047, 1051 (1990).
41   *Mabo*, 30.
42   Cf. Dworkin, *Law's Empire*, 400.
>   Sentimental lawyers cherish an old trope: they say that law works itself pure. The
>   figure imagines two forms or stages of the same system of law, the nobler form
>   latent in the less noble, the impure, present law gradually transforming itself into

43 *Mabo*, 39. What do the facts have to do with it anyway! The problem was not that
    people actually believed that the *lands* were empty, the problem was that many of the
    settlers did not regard the natives as fully human. In 1788, after all, married women
    lacked legal personality. Why should the indigenous people have fared appreciably
    better, particularly given that they were not particularly efficient at the practice of the
    only kind of warfare the British settlers understood as such?

its own purer ambition, haltingly, to be sure, with slides as well as gains, never
worked finally pure, but better in each generation than the last.

44 *Mabo*, 68-69.
45 As befits a thoroughly postmodern pair, they are post-lapsarian from the outset!
46 *Mabo*, 93. This is a more telling rejection of normativity than Pierre Schlag might have
    hoped for! See Schlag, P, 'Normative and Nowhere to Go' 43 *Stanford LR* 167 (1990).
47 Douzinas & Warrington, 'A Well-Founded Fear of Justice', 130-131.
48 *Mabo*, 104.
49 *Mabo*, 105-106. Oddly enough, those 'savage ideas' included the quaint notion that
    they had a right to their traditional lands and were entitled to drive off intruders.
50 *Mabo*, 108-9.
51 *Mabo*, 180.
52 *Mabo*, 192-3. The problem arises with regard to the nature of the bundle of rights
    given the name 'native title'. Are these rights personal in nature, as they sometimes
    appear to be, or are they proprietary in nature? Toohey's judgment suggests that the
    rights in question are interests in land that do not amount to a proprietary right.
    Dawson draws quite the reverse presumption from the same evidence. Oh well...
53 *Mabo*, 187.
54 *Mabo*, 187.
55 Haldar, 'The Evidencer's Eye', 189. Haldar defines parergon as follows in n 41:
    '"Parergon" refers to Derrida's notion of the frame, which in turn is a critique of
    Kant's parergon (in the Critique of Judgement).'
56 An obvious proposition after all, no one could dispute it.
57 *Mabo*, 122-23.
58 *Mabo*, 129.
59 *Mabo*, 144.
60 *Mabo*, 145.
61 *Amodu Tijani v Secretary, Southern Nigeria* [1921] 2 AC 399, 407, cited in *Mabo*,
    126. Dawson J also notes the expression of similar views in *Adeyinka Oyekan v
    Musendiku Adele* [1957] 1 WLR 876.
62 Haldar, 'The Evidencer's Eye', 186.
63 As Haldar notes:
    The subject of photography... may also serve to remind us of the way in which the
    laws of evidence frame the discourse of law: what matters... is inside both a
    physical and a legal frame, constructed to form the narrative of visual evidence.
    Whatever it is which is outside the frame is excluded, it cannot be inside what
    Michel Foucault calls the "order of things"... What the law frames, it controls and
    configures – but what must also be understood is that the question of form (con-
    formation) cannot be separated from the question of the frame... In terms of legal
    discourse... what is being said is that no concept determines the judgment....

However, even if we are to admit that representation is not an innocent activity, the problem still remains that whatever is internal to the frame is still approximate to, or a fraction of what probably happened, of other truths.
Haldar, 'The Evidencer's Eye', 182.

64   Haldar, 'The Evidencer's Eye', 189.
65   Douzinas & Warrington, 'A Well-Founded Fear of Justice', 119.
66   Haldar, 'The Evidencer's Eye', 188.
67   Haldar, 'The Evidencer's Eye', 188.
68   Douzinas & Warrington, 'A Well-Founded Fear of Justice', 130.
69   Douzinas, Warrington & McVeigh, *Postmodern Jurisprudence*, 183.   And if this pessimistic reading is inevitable, any imagined reconciliation can be no more than bricolage.

5   Free Will and the Judge as Subject

Introduction

Judge, subject, woman, all these are terms that evoke clouds of meaning, a surfeit of allusions that I would rather not address, but cannot avoid. Concern with subjectivity, with what it means to be a subject and with the possibility of free will has long preoccupied those working within the Western philosophical tradition. This preoccupation sits uneasily alongside other, characteristically legal concerns. Among these are the fear that 'law-making judges' will subvert democracy by usurping the role of the legislature,[1] and the oft-repeated danger posed by overtly 'political' judges. Other, incompatible, concerns also surface, predominantly among them increasing emphasis upon the unrepresentative character of the judiciary, and its bondage to the traditional elite[2] within democracies such as Australia, the United States and Canada. When it is argued that the judiciary is unrepresentative, and its unrepresentative nature is foregrounded, the demand for greater inclusion and representation implies to many that judicial decision making would be somehow different if the judiciary were more representative. Just wherein this 'difference' might lie is never spelled out. How the belief that it would be preferable for the judiciary to become more representative could ever be reconciled with pervasive concerns about the influence of 'law-making' judges remains firmly below the threshold of consciousness.[3] Both these positions are part of the contemporary intellectual and political mindscape, particularly in Australia.[4] Despite the regularity with which such images surface, the content of the debate reminds us that questions of interpretation, of voice, and of what it means to be a subject have been repressed. Such questions have been forced beneath the surface of discourse and are seldom, if ever, openly acknowledged. To acknowledge them would be to permit, even to insist upon, questions about what judges actually do and how they do it. As it is, we remain unwilling to talk about the ways in which readers and texts constitute one another through interpretation. In that way, we disregard all those details of presence, voice and imagery, which go to make up the subjectivity of the judge both as narrator and as narratee.

Of Knowledge and Subjectivity

The central epistemological problem bequeathed to modernity by the Enlightenment was the 'other minds' problem, together with the questions it foreshadowed about our capacity to know and understand others. Today it and the legacy that it left us have been overshadowed by questions about the relationship between readers and texts. We struggle to come to terms with the relationship between practices and the construction and interpretation of meanings, and that between the stories told by narrators and those which are understood by narratees. Nowhere are these interpretive difficulties greater and more perilous than when we attempt to understand what it means or ought to mean to speak as a judge.

At the most fundamental level, the epistemological problems left to us by the Enlightenment have not been resolved. Instead, they have been pushed back beneath the surface of thought. Often it seems that all of our lingering doubts about knowledge and subjectivity have become embroiled in interpretation and in our unwilling fascination with the construction of meanings. Drawn to the impossibility of certain meaning, the inevitability of interpretation, much as a moth is drawn to a flame, it is little wonder that many who are involved with law and with legality find talk of indeterminacy, and of the possibility of a different voice terrifying. Stanley Cavell has suggested that (at least as we normally understand it) philosophical scepticism is a specifically masculine intellectual position, that it resonates with masculine insecurity regarding paternity. Both scepticism, and its alter ego, positivism, are symptomatic of a crisis within epistemology, an attempt to render knowledge fixed, stable, possessable, an image of knowledge as property. When, as was always inevitable, knowledge escaped the confines set out for it, we abandoned our faith in the possibility of knowing, and insisted that without certainty all that remained was the abyss. As Cavell notes:

> The violence in masculine knowing, explicitly associated with jealousy, seems to interpret the ambition of knowledge as that of exclusive possession, call it private property... This linking of the desire of knowledge for possession, for, let us say, intimacy, links this epistemological problematic as a whole with

that of the problematic of property, of ownership, of the owning or ratifying of one's identity. As though the likes of Locke and Marx, in relating the individual to the world through the concept of laboring, and relating the distortion of that relation to the alienation or appropriation of labor, were preparing a conceptual field that epistemology has yet to follow out. "Appropriating" seems to have the same stress put on it in relating the individual to the world through the ownership of property as "belief" has in relating the individual to the world through the acquisition and power of knowledge... It remains to be seen how the institution of law takes its bearing here, particularly in relation to the demand for consent to a social contract. I assume that if there is a skepticism with respect to belonging and to belongings, the fact of law will not settle it, any more than the existence of science will settle skepticism with respect to the external world. On the contrary what we call law and what we call science have become modified as part of the historical trauma that sets the scene for skepticism...[5]

Traumas such as these come together in adjudication in a critical way. On a simple level, the fundamental presuppositions of our legal system depend upon our conviction that words and phrases alike, not only have an intelligible meaning but also one which is somehow shared and accessible and fixed. We dare not begin to imagine a legal system in which phrases such as 'beyond reasonable doubt' are simply up for grabs. The trial enables us to secure those meanings and realise them. Only in this way can we persuade others that the outcomes that flow from our decisions can be justified, both to ourselves and to others. Only if meanings are stable, fully replicable, does justification seem possible.

The sceptical tradition that emerged during the Enlightenment has called our capacity to attain this stability into question at a fundamental level. We are left with a sense of loss and failure, 'a doubt [not] about whether we can know but by a disappointment over knowledge itself'.[6] Nowhere are that fear and that disappointment more problematical than within the context of judicial interpretation and indeed within the practice of adjudication more generally. While religion has generally not concerned itself with the death of god, legal theory seems paralysed by the suggestion that the text has gone the way of god. Faith, after all, needs nothing more. Reason demands proof, and proof is precisely what reason is unable to provide.

Our political and legal traditions encourage us to demand that our knowledge here be seamless and more complete than elsewhere. This ought, to, I think, specifically be figured against the possibility of the 'other' as judge. If difference signifies human separation, no matter how much we know about the other, we will never know enough to satisfy the demand for proof which we have constructed. The attempts to confine judicial interpretation to rule application, to hold on to the idea that meaning (and therefore knowledge) have a stable core, represent a response to Cartesian scepticism and the other minds problem. Our demand for certainty fuels our desire to ensure that our own legal system epitomises the rule of law.[7] We believe, even if we can no longer justify our belief, that for this to be true our legal texts must bear their meaning on their face, so that in the ordinary way of things that meaning cannot be mistaken. Our fear that the knowledge which we have can never be enough to suffice for the tasks which we have set it is, in the end, a fear that no knowledge could suffice, and that ultimately we must recognise our own fallibility and our own responsibility.

Earlier I spoke of the way in which our courts and the ritual dramas played out within them were epistemically akin to the rituals woven through Western religious traditions. Ordinary men (and women?) both want and need to believe that the decisions made daily within our courts represent justice under the rule of law. We expect a very particular kind of decision making from our judges. Ordinary, fallible, human knowledge can never be sufficient. What is needed is a kind of transcendence, an ability to isolate the self from context, from partiality, from the affections and fallibilities that make up the daily lives of ordinary people.[8] We expect our judges to become the kind of subjects which, in our saner moments, we know to be beyond possibility, beyond comprehension, beyond understanding. In short, we want them to possess knowledge that is complete in itself. We want them to possess knowledge that is so certain that it is beyond the possibility of scepticism.[9]

For this project to be intelligible, we must understand both the subject and what it is to know in very special ways. First, I believe, we must understand knowledge as something which can be grasped, possessed, seized. That which is known must be and must remain uncontaminated, lie beyond congress or commingling. The subject acts upon the object of knowledge. Neither the subject nor the object is altered by the encounter, but, nonetheless, the subject knows and therefore possesses. My need to, and insistence upon, using a visual analogue for the getting of knowledge undoubted derives some of its compulsion from the 'visuality' of Cartesian scepticism. The decay of vision into the perception of 'sense data' signalled a 'crisis of faith' in vision as a mechanism for obtaining (fixed and certain) information about the world. While I might trace this scepticism about vision further, invoking Plato's myth of the cave, that would be to invoke a very different problematic. Our contemporary enslavement by visual imagery, and our despair over its inability to provide the certainty we seek seems to me to have quite specifically enlightenment origins.[10] The idea of knowledge as property, as something that can finally be reduced to possession, tamed, put on display for all to see is central to this despair.[11]

In law, the longing for self-interpreting texts, texts that bear their interpretation on their face, continues to linger. Here the violence never far beneath the surface of ruling economies of knowledge is joined by another violence, the violence Robert Cover immortalised in his understanding of the jurispathic economy of the courts.[12] Every decision, every instantiation of law's violence, hacks through the thicket of meanings. It opens a clear and final path, but a path which succumbs at once to the inevitable alterity of the interpretive act at the moment it is invoked as authority.

Paradoxically, of course, the kind of text our folktales of law demand became impossible for us at the precise moment the scholars of the Enlightenment challenged us to seek it. Let me explain. The lasting intellectual lesson of the Enlightenment is not, as some might have it, the still unfulfilled and wholly contemporary desire to somehow realise the 'liberal polity'. The lasting intellectual lesson of the Enlightenment is that of Descartes. In seeking to rival god in knowledge and in wisdom, in seeking to render knowledge of the world perfectly transparent, certain beyond even the slightest possibility of deception, he called knowledge itself into fundamental question. So doing, he fatally undermined the possibility of confidence in knowledge and in our ability to know. The kind of certainty Descartes sought is beyond possibility, beyond all reason.[13] It is **always** possible that perception could deceive us, that what we believe that we see could be a mirage, a hallucination, or a dream. Mostly, however, it does not. The fact is that we proceed upon the basis that our eyes do not deceive us, that all the ordinary artefacts of perception are no more and no less than what they appear to be. If we did not, we would not act at all.

What Descartes bequeathed to us was a standard, a metric bar for certainty against which we continue surreptitiously to measure our vaunted knowledge. If, for most of the time in most of our lives, we make do with our ordinary language and our ordinary standards for knowledge, we have always, subconsciously at least, held our judges to a different standard.[14] And here, I believe, I must at last abandon, at least for the moment, the 'political we'. The standard to which judges have been held, the standard demanded by paradigms of rule application, and more latterly right answers, the standard which, in its darker moments, imagines itself as simultaneously absolutely free and totally constrained, is, I would suggest, none other than that standard to which women have always been held – by men. Only if utterly confined, totally circumscribed by education, by role, by convention could trust become possible. Here I think of Rousseau's ultimate political work, *The Emile*, in which he at last made it clear that the figure of the citizen became possible only to the extent that woman as property and as speculum was utterly confined within the private household.[15] This presents a further complication. Once the one economy of knowledge that might provide perfect certainty in adjudication is acknowledged to be unattainable, the judicial enterprise is threatened. The confusion that seems inevitable when the body of a judge becomes the body of a woman emerges from figure to ground.

Here, it seems critical to flag the way in which the procedures and traditions of the common law foreground the visual. The trial can be understood as a public spectacle both in the importance of an open court and in the idea that justice must be **seen** to be done. The rules of evidence conventionally require that the accused **confront** her accusers. While in some jurisdictions video-taped evidence is allowed for the victims of child sexual abuse, efforts to extend this concession to other instances where testifying in an open court might prove unduly traumatic for the victim have been resisted. The law knows well the violence of the gaze. The interposition of a filmed representation, substitutes the hidden and surreptitious gaze of the voyeur for open confrontation in pursuit of the truth. The emphasis upon visuality is also central to the characteristic refusal of the laws of evidence to admit hearsay evidence. Only that which has been seen can be believed.

The trial as we know it today replaces another kind of public spectacle, trial by battle. As with trial by battle, outcomes must be clear, and public and certain. The kind of certainty sought demands a masculine economy of knowing and understanding. To shift from a 'different voice' to the exploration of a masculine economy of knowing and understanding, is more than a shift of perspective. It is this economy of knowing which seems to me to be hopelessly entangled in the web we call the common law. If I am correct in identifying a masculine economy of knowing and understanding as the dominant *leit motif* in common law method, how can I, as a woman, know the law within that economy of knowledge? How can I, who but lately have myself escaped ownership, claim not only knowledge but also my right to possess it. Wherein lies the word, if I venture outside it?

When, repeatedly, some judicial decisions[16] are excoriated as judicial law making, a (but lately vanished) golden age is invoked.[17] In that 'golden age' legal texts bore their meanings on their faces.[18] If, upon occasion, language might prove deceptive and disagreements might arise, those disagreements had a single and simple source, a want of precision in the rule itself. Some rules were open to two or three meanings – were not, in other words, fully determinate. To say that rules were not fully determinate, however, was not at all the same as to suggest that interpretation inevitably contaminated the text. If interpretation inevitably contaminated the text, so that the line between text and interpretation was always on the point of collapse, the implications for law were profound. The possibility of that contamination signalled that the boundaries of textuality are not closed but porous and open. The difference is central. The mere fact that texts were not always fully determinate signalled, not illicit congress between the object of interpretation and the interpreter, not the possibility of seduction, but simply the potential for error. Error was never a threat, could never undermine knowledge as such. Any error was, of course, regrettable, but that was all. This point is, I think, quite important. It suggests that the justice of particular outcomes is, in the end, seen as very much less significant that the continued integrity of the law itself. One of the reasons that a 'close reading' of *Mabo* has proved so revealing is because of the defence mounted of the common law by both Brennan and Dawson. Both, in radically different ways, are desperately eager to shore up the boundaries, keep the prize labelled common law beyond contamination. If the common law is always already contaminated, if they are part of what they fear, what refuge have they?

In a profound and paradoxical sense, error affirmed, and continues to affirm, the certainty of knowledge. Our ability to recognise an error has often been taken as proof that certain knowledge lies before us, is potentially within our grasp.[19] Only when we can no longer escape the insight that to interpret is **always** to **supplement** does the line between (innocent) interpretation and (illicit) supplementation collapse. Once the line between interpretation and supplementation vanished the figure of the judge becomes a lightening rod for all of our fears and concerns.

And what of the subject in all of this? Once the boundary between supplementation and interpretation was revealed to be, not a impenetrable barrier safeguarding 'the law' against judicial law making, but a mirage, the judge **qua subject** is necessarily always already contaminated. There is no perspective from which judicial decision making can be described as the act of one whose 'subject position' is irrelevant. To speak as a judge is to speak in the certainty that one's subject position is always potentially relevant and, as a consequence, always potentially open to question.[20] Because the limits of knowledge are constantly with us, because what society expects of its judges and of its courts is a kind of certainty (and of objectivity) which no judge and no court could ever attain, to speak as a judge is to struggle to embody a certainty which is unattainable. The judge must speak and must be seen to speak with the authority of law, as the embodiment of law or, more precisely, as the *body* of law.

It is at this point that I confront the idea of law as something that is (necessarily?) **unspeakable**. (By me? By any woman? Why **un**speakable?)[21] If to speak as a judge is to speak as the *body* of the law, to embody authority, to become authority in that place and at that time, who or what may speak as a judge now that the line between interpretation and supplementation has vanished? What constitutes the law and from whence does its authority derive if each decision is a supplement? Can a woman's body, a pregnant body, a menstruating body become the *body of the law*, embody[22] the authority of law? For such a body, is law speech possible, speech which has no choice (because a decision must be made) but to supplement? What becomes of law, what becomes of authority, when plurality fractures the framework[23] of the law, the framework of the court?

Yet I cannot help but wonder if here I am straying too near the edge, allowing myself to be mesmerised[24] by the master discourse. Whose fear is it that seeks to exclude disorder, open boundaries, plurality rather than unity? Why do I accept 'the master's voice'[25] even as I would refashion the master's tools?[26] Traditionally, images of law have emphasised order, rigid and impermeable boundaries, unity, skeletal principles.[27] Why not multiple possibilities, osmotic transmission, plurality, cellular division? What madness was it that led Brennan to imagine common law principles as a brittle skeleton at the point of fracture? Is the ultimate threat that we will no longer know what to do and how to do it? Was Hobbes right? Is it that without certain rules, the war of all against all still waits?[28] Or is it simply that, if men relinquish the dream of order, of rigid frameworks, unequivocal right answers, settled and impermeable boundaries **they must rediscover the capability to take what is given on faith**, learn to risk relying upon the knowledge of (an)**other**.[29]

Authority, specifically the nature of authority, is one of the problems. Kathleen Jones suggests that within political discourse

> Authority and the authoritative act... as disciplinary devices. They construct order; they enforce obedience, conformity and acceptance; they silence opposition. Authority constructs rules with which to organize behavior, to master and control it, to fix it in its (proper) place. The authoritative, as an interpretive reading of values and practices, "locate[s] the unruly meanings of a text in a single coherent intention". (Citation omitted.) Conceptualized in this sense, both authority and the authoritative establish boundaries.[30]

Earlier I suggested that no explanation of our obligation to obey the law was needed, that when an explanation was demanded, the obligation had become, in every important sense, already history. The truly authoritative is beyond question, beyond explanation. At the point at which the decisions of judges are called into question, as increasingly today, the authority of the judicial office is also called into question. We are forced to question whether any avenues remain through which we can understand the meaning and source of authority, specifically judicial authority, if rules are no longer sacrosanct. If the rules no longer confer certainty, if the boundary between the rule and the authority it constitutes is itself permeable, the distinction between (legitimate) authority and (illegitimate) force collapses. Not only does interpretation inevitably become supplementation, the judge herself, as she oscillates between narrator and narratee, is altered by her participation. To be beyond alteration, beyond seduction, is to be beyond being a part of ordinary discourse. The office no longer confers its authority upon those who fill it.[31] If neither subject nor text is absolute, fixed and impermeable, unalterable, from whence does authority derive? How does it attach and how is it recognised – what remains of authority under such conditions? What criteria could ever be sufficient to establish legitimacy beyond **un**reasonable doubt? Hart's secondary rules have long since gone the way of his primary rules, in unwilling obedience (obeisance) to the law of infinite regress. If god and the author are both dead what could ever constitute authority? Who or what is it that brings men and women before the law and authorises violence?[32]

Before the Abyss

If neither author nor text are fixed and stable, if our understandings of law and of the violence it entails cannot be legitimated by reference to the democratic process, to shared principles of political morality, to the canons of economic discourse, to a 'glass menagerie'[33] of eternal verities, to be brought **before the law** is to be brought before the abyss, or so it might seem. In fact, it is business as usual. The parade of prisoners before the bar (or, in the case of OJ Simpson, across cablevision networks),[34] the queues of plaintiffs seeking access, if not to justice, at least to authoritative decision and finality, has diminished not at all. What, one might well ask, is going on? Put another way, if as seems to be the case, we accept that knower and knowledge are always already contaminated, that there are no fixed poles to which we may repair, how is it that the law has continued more or less unchanged, neither more nor less in question than before? Judges continue a-judging, lawyers continue a-lawyering, in Australia, as in the United States, politicians continue a-mending,[35] as if nothing had happened. Is it, perhaps, as Stanley Fish has suggested that:

> judging or doing judging is one thing and giving accounts or theories of judging is another, and that as practices they are independent, even though the successful performance of the first will often involve engaging in the second.[36]

Is it, in short, that nothing has changed except, perhaps, the stories judges tell us? Is the passage from Enlightenment verities to 'standpoint jurisprudence' nothing more than a shift in discursive paradigms, an alternative approach to legitimation? If so, the transition from 'skeletal principles' to an open acknowledgment of law as the context within which dispossession and violence were legitimated signifies nothing of importance.[37] Perhaps. Even so, the distance between skeletal principles and an open acknowledgment of law as a critical player in the process of creating an 'environment in which the Aboriginal people... came to be treated as a different and lower form of life whose very existence could be ignored...'[38] seems more than the harbinger of an alteration in fashions of legitimation. As an open acknowledgment of the interpellation of law and politics it speaks of a revolution in one judge's understanding of what it is to be a judge. It acknowledges that 'to speak as a judge' is always, potentially at least, to speak as one who, because of who she is and where she is placed, is deeply and profoundly complicit in the existing order. 'To speak as a judge is to speak in a way which cannot be bracketed.'[39]

Of course, I do not deny that law has a formal existence, that it can be seen as it wishes to see itself, as separate and apart, distinct from politics. **Of course,** judges reach decisions on grounds and for reasons that are, in important respects, wholly distinct from those which operate within political fora. **Of course,** all the things that have always set adjudication apart and marked the judicial branch as the 'least dangerous branch' remain the case. One can race through them, nodding at the appropriateness of each. Judges cannot choose the issues with which they must deal. They determine particular cases, not generalised political programmes. Law is the 'prisoner of its history' and thus, inevitably, profoundly conservative. Even the highest court must rely upon others to carry out its decisions, and is thus bound by invisible chains to what is.[40] One might even add that judges who are willing to speak truth to power are rare.[41] All of this is true, and yet all of it is somehow not quite acknowledged by those who wish to see the judge and her role as separate and unique. They insist that this very separateness and uniqueness resides in fidelity to role and to rule, in the idea of a role whose metes and bounds insulate the judge from contamination by text, by political discourse, by context. It is **this** image of the judge which is threatened by the idea of a text which overflows, which is always about to escape its margins and become something else.

Images of choice, of consent, of a **social** contract make their way, at last, to the surface of textuality. A contract is never simply a promise. It depends always and utterly upon the possibility of being enforced.[42] In a world in which author, text and interpreter escape their boundaries, until intentionality becomes chimerical, what room remains for that most cherished of all icons of Western culture, the idea of free will? Is free will, perhaps, an idea that can have meaning only within an economy of fixed and determinate boundaries, in a vision in which subject and object remain resolutely apart, unambiguous? Is it an idea from which we dare depart? The iconography of free will is woven through our cultural conventions. It pervades our understandings of responsibility, of ethical conduct, of all the potentialities which make it marginally possible for us, at least in some times and in some places, to live as a community.[43] Any threat to our understandings of what it means to experience ourselves as beings for whom choice is possible, and thus as beings for whom responsibility is possible confronts us with the horror of a world without either. Unless we understand ourselves as free, as capable of rational choice, we cannot say to any among us that what has been done is blameworthy, that responsibility cannot be evaded.[44] If we figure a world of permeable boundaries as a world in which choice is chimerical,[45] in which our responsibility is never limited, never able to be confined within fixed boundaries, what remains of ethics, what morality becomes possible? We have not yet even begun the work of imagining the lineaments of ethics and morality in an economy of permeable boundaries. In such an economy, its central metaphor being, not the disembodied rational mind of the Enlightenment tradition,[46] a mind capable of casting off the moorings of its own corporeality, but the placental membrane, what are the lineaments of individuality, of responsibility, and upon what bodies dare we inscribe them? What elaboratives make themselves available within an economy of permeable boundaries? What might it be like to act morally in a world in which cares and commitments always extended beyond the limits set for them, in which the ultimate terror is that:

> another may be owed acknowledgment simply on the ground of his humanity, acknowledgment as a human being, for which nothing will do but my revealing myself to him as a human being, unrestrictedly, as his or her sheer other, his or her fellow, his or her *semable*.[47]

I want to speculate a little more about what this kind of acknowledgment might entail, about what it might mean to be unable to set bounds to the acknowledgment one offered.[48] What right have I to impose my acknowledgment upon the other, insist that she accept the burden of my acknowledgment, nothing hidden, nothing held back? Disorderly bodies and total acknowledgment, an openness that becomes a kind of imposition, a demand that the other also holds nothing back, abandons all defences. In an economy of gendered bodies and permeable boundaries, is this what it might mean to reveal oneself – unrestrictedly – **simply as a human being**? What kind of humanity is there in such a revelation, what space for the will, for choice, for, dare I say it, freedom? Holding back nothing foregrounds the body, the gendered body, the body whose boundaries are never entirely certain. In an economy whose central metaphor is the placenta, that through which all nourishment passes and all waste is eliminated, which holds nothing back but yet ensures that bodies remain separate, how can limits be set and choices made. How are we to figure the body of a 'human being', what are its lineaments, its flesh? If I must oscillate between the disembodied rational mind of Descartes (as ever staking its existence upon the goodness of god) and an economy of gendered bodies and permeable boundaries how may I speak as a judge? To speak as a judge is to speak the law, to inscribe the law upon the bodies of those who are brought before it. What bodies are those which are brought before the law? Do those who come before the law come simply as human beings or do they come as gendered bodies? If, as I suspect, before the law there are no 'human beings' but only bodies coded by race, by ethnicity, by gender, by sexual preference, no determinate categories but only gendered bodies and permeable boundaries, who or what do I become if I speak as a judge? Confronted by the necessity of finality, of determinate decisions, of clôture, how do I, having no choice, decide?

> If gender, race, class, and sexual preference are not to be used as mere "markers to describe the race [etc.] of the respondent" nor as disciplinary devices to police the borders of identity – either by keeping some "outside" or by insisting on the faithful being "inside" – then we must abandon the search for sovereignty through any of them, or even all of them in combination, and work toward solidarity – solidarity based on what Stephen White calls the responsibility to act combined with the responsibility to otherness. We cannot succeed politically to unseat those who have monopolized power and authority, and thus continue to insist on their definitions of these terms, if we play according to the rules of their game; this is, if we continue to insist on territorial sovereignty for our identities. We may not agree on all the issues, but those who watch our vituperation from the wings are, in Ntozake Shange's words, "the same old Men ".[49]

As an unseeing witness to this unwilling oscillation between 'human beings' and 'gendered bodies', the figure of 'blind justice' attains spectral significance. On one level, blind justice seems an anomalous figure within the essentially visual spectacle of the trial. If the central theme of the trial (at least the criminal trial) is visual confrontation, the right of the accused to confront those who accuse her, the demand that the victim visually identify those who have wronged her, is it not the ultimate irony that our cultural traditions figure justice as **blind**? As symbol, the figure of **blind justice** is truly striking. If she were not blind, what might she see? Yes, I know, of course, we all know, that her blindfold signifies utter fairness, total impartiality in the pursuit of the truth. That it is a blindfold is striking. Blindfolded justice with sword and scales... our dominant cultural symbol for the trial. She is not blind, but she deprives herself of sight in order to see more clearly. It is worth asking where else the iconic blindfold figures in our culture. Most often, I believe, as an image of utter powerlessness – the blindfolded prisoner being put to death, the captive or kidnap victim being conveyed to a secret destination. The figure is ambiguous, on the one hand shielding the prisoner from the necessity to visually confront the immanence of death, on the other, shielding the executioner from the gaze of the one to be killed – one might say, shielding the executioner from responsibility. Blind justice, she for whom the only permissible and possible evidence is hearsay evidence!

If justice must be blindfolded to function within the fundamentally visual process which is the trial, is it perhaps that she must be blind to the disorderly bodies that are brought before her? They are bodies whose corporeality has been systematically rejected by the law and by a legal process that emphasises reasonableness above all. Is it that for judge and prisoner alike, for all of those who come to law, the disorderly body with its permeable boundaries and its (threatened) contamination must be tamed, rendered obedient, lawful. If so, this can happen only if we repress all ambiguity and reinstate the oppositions from which we have but lately escaped.

Notes

1   Here, of course, free will becomes, not a precondition to subjectivity and personhood, but the threat of subversion.

2   An elite, it must be said, based upon class, upon race and/or ethnicity and gender. The stereotypical member of the judiciary is a male White-Anglo-Saxon-Protestant.

3   When such images do surface, they surface in a way which emphasises the threat. The plea for a more representative judiciary is conflated with the very different idea that judges (like parliamentarians) ought to **represent** particular interests. At times this becomes bizarre, as when it is insisted that increasing the representation of women, for example, will ensure that the interests of women are treated fairly, that increasing the representation of various ethnic minorities will ensure that adequate attention is given to their interests. At a conference entitled 'Courts in a Representative Democracy', a significant part of the discussion following a presentation by former magistrate, now

Family Court judge Sally Brown, centred around the threat that broadening the base from which the judiciary was drawn would somehow increase 'forum shopping'.

4   One might, in fact, suggest that these concerns represent the flip sides of a single coin. It is because we know that judges 'make law' that the unrepresentative character of the judiciary is of significant concern. On the other hand, the demands for greater inclusiveness, and in particular for enhanced representation for group which are presently under-represented heighten fears regarding judicial creativity.

5   Cavell, S, *Disowning Knowledge in Six Plays of Shakespeare*, New York, Cambridge Univ Press, 1987, 10-11. Subsequently (13) Cavell alludes to a connection between the denial (or loss) of the mother's body and the denial of the world.

6   Cavell, *The Claim of Reason*, 440.

7   The alternative, the chilling acknowledgment that ordinary men and, today, women, having become judges, inevitably 'contaminate' the law they speak, that the history of the 'common law' instead of epitomising, as Dworkin would have it, the law 'working itself pure' might better be represented as process of ongoing confusion and contamination, as the interaction of disorderly boundaries, suggests we might want to reconsider the entire idea of the 'rule of law', at least if any alternative presented itself!

8   In that respect, if in no other, Dworkin's positioning of Hercules is entirely apt. His position on Olympus at once ensures a kind of transcendence and isolates him completely from ordinary human feelings and forms of life.

9   We would like to believe that our judges have wisdom and knowledge like that of god. While, in our saner moments, we know that is impossible, we would like it to be true.

10   Generally see Jay, M, *Downcast Eyes: The Denigration of Vision in Twentieth-Century French Thought*, Berkeley, Univ. of Calif. Press, 1994. Other connections also seem relevant, most particularly the connection between objectification and violence, particularly the (metaphorical) violence of the pornographic gaze, that gaze which figures woman (solely) as the object of male desire. The Rousseauean transformation of the beloved into a mirror in which her lover may see himself reflected larger than life also seems relevant here. See Berns, SS, *Add Woman and Stir*, 1990, unpublished doctoral thesis on file at the University of Tasmania, 230-256.

11   A background theme here is the idea of the getting of knowledge as somehow erotic, sexualised, of coming to know as equivalent to sexual conquest. The elision between erotic love and the getting of wisdom has been with us at least since the Platonic exaltation of homoerotic love in the *Symposium*. It is well to note that this remains a masculine economy of knowledge, knowledge as property, specifically sexual property. What, for a woman, the getting of knowledge might be or become must remain, at least for the moment, an open question. Within law, it is well to note, the theme of knowledge as property is most completely embodied in 'intellectual property' regimes, so-called. It is symbolically significant that, in *Moore v Regents of the University of California* 249 Calif Rptr 494 (Cal App 2 Dist 1988), the 'intellectual property' of surgeons and researchers in the cell line cultivated from cells removed from his cancerous spleen prevailed over the physicality of his spleen and over any image of his body as his property.

12   Cover, R, 'Nomos and Narrative' in Minow, M, M Ryan & A Sarat (eds) *Narrative, Violence, and the Law*, Ann Arbor, Univ of Michigan Press, 1992, 95, 138-139.

13   It belongs in short to god.

14   We want, I think, an impossible court, an authoritative instantiation of the 'War Crimes Tribunal' summoned by Bertrand Russell and Jean Paul Sartre to 'judge' American conduct in the Vietnam war. Cover, R, 'The Folktales of Justice: Tales of Jurisdiction' 14 *Capital Univ. LR* 179, 200-202 (1985).

15   Rousseau, J-J, *The Emile*, trans by B Foxley, Melbourne, Everyman's Library, 1911. Everything in Sophie's education was directed to a single goal, that of fitting her to serve as a mirror for Emile's particularity. Many of the resonances in my figuring of woman as property and as speculum are explored in Berns, SS, *Add Woman and Stir*. See also Gatens, M, *Feminism and Philosophy: Perspectives on Difference and Equality*, Cambridge, Polity Press, 1991, 9-26. This image may also be figured as the image of figure and ground and the oscillation between them in common optical illusions.

16   Always those with which the speaker or writer profoundly disagrees...

17   Golden ages are, of course, always but lately vanished.

18   That golden age seems to me to be akin to another... one in which men were men, women were women, all families were happy and the 'angel of the house' was the ruling metaphor for woman as possession!

19   Mistakes are always 'easy' to address. Our ordinary criteria are sufficient, once we have accepted the error of our ways.

20   Only those who understand themselves to be devoid of 'subject position' can escape this insight and the terror which accompanies it.

21   'Only if ethics were something unspeakable by us, could law be unnatural, and therefore unchallengeable.' Leff, 1229.

22   I use 'embody' here quite deliberately and literally, represent **in the flesh** the body of the law. Moses is said, upon Sinai, to have glimpsed the hind parts of god, and that glimpse gave weight and form to the text in which Moses' fears were inscribed. We demand of our judges that they **embody** the law, to be precise that they embody the law as it exists as our cultural icon.

23   Those familiar with the jurisprudence of the Australian High Court may wish to read these fractures as a 'supplement' to Brennan's 'skeletal principles'. See *Mabo*, 29.

24   The image that comes to mind is the stage hypnotist of vaudeville, with tails and hat and cape and pocket watch, and his inevitably female subject.

25   It is important to double back to the icon of 'His Master's Voice' – the visual image of the dog, head cocked, listening to the sounds (which we now deem scratchy and almost beyond recognition) of 'His Master's Voice'.

26   Yes, I know, the master's tools..., but like it or not we remain within the master's house. Violent revolution seems unworthy as a feminist goal, and we ought, perhaps, think long and hard about the institutions which ought to replace those we have and how we are to get there from here, and how many bodies we are willing to sacrifice on the way. One of the minor, and nasty, things about wholesale rejection of the master's tools, is the likelihood of substantial and violent unpleasantness on the way from here to 'destination unknown'.

27   This memorable phrase is that of Brennan J in *Mabo*. He insisted at 29 that the High Court is 'not free to adopt rules that accord with contemporary notions of justice and human rights **if their adoption would fracture the skeleton of principle which gives the body of our law its shape and internal consistency**'. [Emphasis mine.]   The

organic metaphor is striking – *skeleton* of principle, *body* of the law... As Drucilla insists – bloody bones. And perhaps these metaphors – giving us in their own way '**images** of the fragmented body' akin to those 'identified by Lacan as the classic signs of what the discourse of psychoanalysis calls aggressivity: the torn flesh and the ruptured separated organs, the shattered frame and the severed limbs insist in the speech, the fantasy and the dreams of the subject as the marks of an unrelieved violence as an inherent condition of its very subjectivity' are ways of seeing law. Barker, F, *The Tremulous Private Body: Essays on Subjection*, London, Methuen, 1984, 89. The body of law is always in danger of shattering. Is the law, akin to Marvell's 'coy mistress', always in danger of dismemberment, always vulnerable. Is it Brennan's dark secret that the law's brittle skeleton has been hostage to the dispossession of the Aboriginal people, our detritus. Brennan's judgment can, in fact, be read as a text for the skeleton left behind when the bodies of the dispossessed were transformed by the carceral order from socially visible objects to ones which can no longer be seen... and, in particular, the removal to mission settlements to transform 'disorderly bodies' to obedient (and disembodied) servants?

28 Rawls believes it does. In his view, all of today's disputes are wars of religion waiting to re-emerge – the Hobbesian backdrop of the English civil war all over again. On a sombre, and deeply pessimistic note, Bosnia, Palestine, Rwanda do make me wonder. Is it perhaps the fear that there will be no more like cases, that law itself will become an impossibility, a wilderness of single instances with no connecting thread.

29 It is precisely this that is impossible within a masculine economy of knowing.

30 Jones, KB, *Compassionate Authority: Democracy and the Representation of Women*, London, Routledge, 1993, 191.

31 I am hinting at the possibility that an individual judge attains authority *qua* judge only when/because the office frames the body of the judge – in an echo of parergonality – or is it that the body of the judge/the body of the law frames the office of the judge.

32 'And what rough beast, its hour come round at last, slouches towards Bethleham to be born?' Yeats, WB, 'The Second Coming', Colmer, J & D, *Mainly Modern*, Adelaide, Rigby, 1969, 185. Well might we ask what it is that comes... today more than ever.

33 Conventional understandings of the law are like a glass menagerie, brittle, fragile, captivating but wholly removed from the world of power and authority that the courtroom performance frames. If so, *The Glass Menagerie* of Tennessee Williams has more in common with the 'skeletal principles' of Brennan J's common law than might appear! Both are essential to sustain the worlds of those whose mindscapes they rule, both are illusory, indeterminate, removed from reality, ready to shatter into a million pieces.

34 If the symbolism of the trial has its origin (as I believe) in the public and wholly and immediately visible spectacle of the trial by battle, the move to the voyeurism implicit in the trial as 'cablevision spectacular' is of immense importance. If the trial as **public spectacle**, emphasised the immediacy of sight, the necessity of immediacy and confrontation, in the flesh as it were, the voyeurism of the media trial emphasises perspectivity, multiple angles, possibilities, openness rather than finality, ultimately raising further and fascinating questions. Even within the courtroom, trial as spectacle blends indistinguishably into trial as media spectacular, encouraging surreptitious glances away from the trial itself to any one of a dozen **re**-presentations of the action,

each from a minutely different angle. If, as Roland Barthes suggested, the photographic image 'is a message without a code' the simultaneous visual images of the trial as media circus might well be described as perspective devoid of standpoint! Barthes, R, *Image-Music-Text,* trans. Stephen Heath, New York, 1977, 17. Well might we ask what it might be to speak as a judge if a trial by jury becomes a media circus.

35 Here as elsewhere, it is perhaps well to acknowledge the slippage between the grandiose implications of 'amending the law' and our lingering doubts as to what politicians actually do when they go 'a-mending'.

36 Fish, S, 'Dennis Martinez and the Uses of Theory' in Fish, S, *Doing What Comes Naturally: Change, Rhetoric, and the Practice of Theory in Literary and Legal Studies,* Oxford, Clarendon Press, 1989, 372, 378.

37 This is, perhaps, an opportune moment to add a further layer of ambiguity. The shift in voice from 'skeletal principles' (which must at all costs be protected against fracturing) to 'standpoint jurisprudence' is also a shift from a decisively masculine and unequivocally liberal voice, to the equivocal and sexually ambiguous voice of a joint judgment, specifically a joint judgment one of whose authors is the only woman on the Australian High Court. It is worth noting that it is rumoured that to which I have circumspectly referred as the joint judgment of Deane and Gaudron JJ, is in fact the work of Mary Gaudron, albeit veiled in plural ambiguity.

38 *Mabo,* 108 per Deane & Gaudron JJ.

39 Berns, SS, *Concise Jurisprudence,* Sydney, Federation Press, 1993, Berns, SS & P Baron, 'Bloody Bones – A Legal Ghost Story: To Speak as a Judge' (1994) 2 *Australian Feminist Law Journal* 125, 127.

40 One might even make the deeply pessimistic observation that even those decisions which seem most revolutionary and aspirational, those which most clearly strive to realise a vision which is not simply business as usual are in a very real sense decisions whose time has come – decisions which are inescapable. In the United States, *Brown v Board of Education* was such a decision. In Australia, *Mabo & Ors v Queensland* struck much the same sort of chord and became an emblem of national healing.

41 Robert Cover tells some marvellous tales of judges and courage in Cover, 'The Folktales of Justice', 187–190.

42 In this, perhaps, we see the truth of Rousseau's famous insistence that **social contract** is finally secured because what is consented to above all else is that men shall be forced to be free. See Rousseau, J-J, *The Social Contract and Discourses* translated with an introduction by G.D.H. Cole, London, J.M Dent & Sons, 1913.

43 I do not intend to suggest even the possibility of a 'presocial' state, a 'state of nature'. The 'boy's own adventure' scenario of states of nature and states of war I leave to others. Nonetheless, community is always fragile; the threat of disorder and dissolution always at hand. Our movement beyond the family, the clan, the tribe, remains perilous. Even within them, the peace is often uneasy and purchased by force.

44 In this context I think of all those pleas in mitigation so well known by the criminal law, of those whose minds are so disordered that the distinction between right and wrong has lost all meaning, of others so enraged by a wife's infidelity, the withholding of a child, that control vanishes, of all those other attempts to excuse because, at bottom, it is claimed that rational choice was beyond the capacity of the individual.

45   In figuring the possibility of choice as chimerical, a doubling back to the figure of the chimera as a monstrous is explicitly left open as a reading. Not simply illusory, then, but monstrous, a febrile imaging with lion's head and serpent's tail, too many choices, too many possibilities – responsible for too much for it to be bearable.

46   Here I think of Rene Descartes in his study, retreating from this table, this chair, from bodily sensation, from the evidence provided by sight, to an inability to distinguish between reality and dreams, between the febrile luxuriance of insanity and the evidence of his own rational mind. *Cogito ergo sum.* I think therefore I am, but I can be certain only because of my faith in a god who is both infinite and good, who would not condemn me to a madhouse in which I – the disembodied rational mind of the Enlightenment – could not believe the evidence of my own senses.

47   Cavell, *The Claim of Reason*, 434-435.

48   Perhaps it is well here to note that a conventional term for one who owes this kind of unrestricted revelation is – mother. Another figuring may be found in the following lines of poetry.
'And all the while, for every grief,
Each suffering, I craved relief
With individual desire;
Craved all in vain! And felt fierce fire
About a thousand people crawl;
Perished with each, – then mourned for all!'
Millay, E St Vincent, 'Renascence' in *Collected Poems of Edna St Vincent Millay*, New York, Harper & Row, 1956, 3.

49   Jones, *Compassionate Authority*, 228-229.

6   From Polyvocality to Narrative Coherence

Introduction

Every legal case begins in polyvocality. It begins, that is, as stories, each story offering one possible reality, one window on events. My need to account for polyvocality with explicitly visual analogues, snapshots of reality, windows on events, highlights a hidden ambiguity. Inevitably, each story begins in a particular time and a particular place, begins as one way of looking at events, framing them. I believe that it is of critical importance to insist that events are 'framed'.[1] Our perceptions always frame events. Every event becomes such through a process of interpretation, through selection. Those that bring us 'before the law' are no exception. An event is not a natural phenomenon but a cultural performance, a way of organising what has become, for some of us, a reality. The stories we tell about these performances become, over time, more real than the performances themselves, and these performances in turn are always more real than the details of which they are comprised. In this chapter, I want to interrogate the process by which the ordinary stories of (more or less)[2] ordinary people become 'legal stories'. I also want to explore the way in which those legal stories are transformed into a single authoritative account whose narrative coherence locates it within the 'seamless web' of law.

Ordinary Stories

We will begin with that most utterly banal of legal stories, a dispute between neighbours, perhaps over whether or not a boundary fence is accurately positioned or concerning overhanging branches or encroaching roots. The sheer ordinariness of such a story, and its frequent intractability, seems an ideal vehicle for a preliminary sketch of the way in which ordinary stories become legal stories. It is ideal in another way as well, as an illustration of how the texts of law frame ordinary stories, dictate the terms of their transformation. In the ordinary way of things, such disputes are seldom about the precise positioning of boundary fences, about overhanding limbs, about all the inevitable aggravations of urban life. In the ordinary way of things, whether in cities or in suburbia, defective surveys, fences reconstructed upon the relics of fences past, trees and shrubs which refuse to confine their growth to the area where they have been planted, are part of the fabric of life. Most of the time, for most of us, as long as the fence remains standing it will do well enough. The overhanding limbs may or may not be pruned back to clear the path or rescue a view, and life goes on pretty much as usual.

How is it, then, that for some, these minor aggravations of urban life become something altogether different? In many cases, I suspect, while the 'legal' story is one of mistaken boundaries or of encroaching limbs, the human story is about something very different. Perhaps it is about a breakdown of neighbourliness. Perhaps its origin lies in the transfer of property from one who had been a neighbour to someone new who did not understand the rituals of neighbourliness and the way they had been woven around conversations over a back fence. Perhaps the misunderstandings go deeper still, with different customs straining at the bounds of neighbourliness. Other stories are possible as well. Often a dispute originates in relationship fractured over long years with small bitternesses, all of which have come together until overhanging branches or a fence but slightly askew becomes the symbol for everything which has gone wrong between neighbours.[3] When this happens, the dichotomy between the legal story, that story which will be fashioned out of the misplaced fence, the encroaching limbs, and the human story, the story of vanished neighbourliness and increasing rancour, is stark.

Even the human story, the narrative told by one ordinary person to another, is not self-announcing. The images and feelings that make up the narrative have been selected out of a kaleidoscope of happenings. They are made up of words spoken and unrecalled, imagined slights, perhaps the inch or more the fence is misaligned magnified into thousands of dollars, the possibility of an extension foregone. Memory is selective. Stories are not accidental. More often than not, stories are told because the telling of them meets some need or hunger in the narrator. It is worth insisting that stories are told in the consciousness of having an audience. This is emphasised rather than that; these images brought into sharp relief, those relegated to the shadows, because each narration is a performance, one which we hope will be understood in a particular way by a particular other. It matters, then, whether the story is told to a friend or a child; a rival or a partner, a lawyer or a judge.

I have begun in this way because I wanted to emphasise that although our legal stories have their origins in other, far more ordinary, stories, the two are not the same and must not be conflated. And even when we are simply dealing with what I have called ordinary stories, the same story can be, and often is, told to a hundred people. Inevitably it will be, simultaneously, the same and different, both in the telling and in the hearing. None of what I am talking about has anything to do with error, with misunderstandings and the like. These shifts in meanings, in tone, in emphasis do not involve misunderstandings. They do not even inhibit our ability to recognise misunderstandings, to insist to the other **that** was not what I meant. They are wholly different. When we tell stories, we are conscious of the context within which they are told, so nuances of emphasis, tone, of manner become part of the story itself. This should not be surprising. Were it otherwise, were we indifferent to setting, to purpose, to all of the ways in which our stories reach out to their intended audiences, we would simply not be telling stories. We would be doing something else, engaging in a performance which was essentially solitary, one in which speech served, not as a way of engaging with others, but as... as what? If speech were not a way of engaging with others, were not a performance by which narrative bound the narrator to the narratee, what could it be?[4] And if, at times, the intended connection fails, the story falls **on deaf ears**, that should be no more surprising than that, at other times, we come to see our own stories, our own performances, in a new light.[5]

We begin with an ordinary story, but a story that comes to be told, not to friends or to neighbours, but to a lawyer. And the fact that it is being told to a lawyer, told either because having been summoned,[6] the narrator accepts the inevitability of being brought before the law, or because she seeks redress, seeks to bring some other before the law, becomes a part of the story. It could not be otherwise. Something else becomes part of the story as well. It is the understanding that this story will be retold, not by its author, but by one who is **authorised** to recast it, couch it in legal language, render it in the grammar of law. In this context, it is appropriate, I think, that to render is also to cover over with a thin film of concrete or mortar, to present a seamless surface to the world. To render an ordinary story in the grammar of law is simultaneously to cover it over with lawness and to rip it apart, shred the flesh of its meaning. The author may give evidence, may tell, both in examination in chief and under cross examination, her story, but it will not be **her** story, it will be the **authorised** version,[7] her story seen through the **eyes of the law**.

Her story will be no longer her own, but a legal story, a legal story told through the arguments of her counsel and told in a semblance of her own voice, but not in her own words. To be brought 'before the law' is also to give evidence (even if, in the end, one gives evidence by declining to do so). It is to tell one's story, newly minted and given legal form, and to answer questions with 'one's eyes on the prize'. By the time a story reaches the court what is important is not what really happened, over time, between those who used simply to be neighbours, not the events that led to a lawyer's office, not even the sense of being aggrieved, of wanting to compel another to see for themselves how it 'really' was. What is important is the 'legal story', the narrative, couched in legal language through which, it is hoped, a judge (and perhaps a jury) may be persuaded. The legal story, it goes without saying, may or may not be true to the human story. Some stories are familiar, easily assimilated by law; others are not. Some narrators, too, are readily believed, the law always already familiar with the cadence of their voices. Others, their voices, even when rendered into legal language, strange and unlawlike, lack credibility. The law has its own rules for stories, and for storytellers. We flout them at our peril should we come before the law.

It matters, therefore, not only what the stories are, and the ease with which they slip into legal language, but also who tells them. It matters who the counsel are, and the parties, who the judge is, and how she hears the stories which are told. All these are strands in the web being woven, strands which, together, will determine its shape and form. These strands, the warp and weft of the law, are the raw material from which judgment will be fashioned and further narratives created.

In characterising the process of generating the 'courtroom drama' as a process of translation, I am traversing familiar ground, conventional ground even. Legal scholars from a range of perspectives have long been aware that the process of transforming ordinary events into a persuasive legal narrative is a process of translation. Every beginning law student is uncomfortably aware, from quite another standpoint, that part of the process of learning the law, of learning to think like a lawyer, involves mastering a language which is at once familiar and foreign. If the words of which the law is comprised are, for the most part, always already familiar, until the language of the law has been mastered their meaning remains tantalisingly out of reach. Legal language is itself the product of narratives and the nature of those narratives and those who were allowed to bring them before the law has had a profound influence upon law itself. It is important that this is understood. Too often law takes on (or is surreptitiously given) a spectral quality, as if it were devoid of antecedents, as if its shape and form emerged without human agency. It is for this reason, I believe, that it often seems (or is made) more mysterious than in reality it is. Too often it seems cloaked in an authority which is a simulacrum of the authority with which religious texts are conventionally cloaked, becomes, in essence, revealed wisdom.

Within the common law tradition, this spectral quality is most obvious in the narratives of contract and tort. Beneath the carefully constructed seamlessness of the legal record, the silhouettes of the human participants can sometimes be glimpsed. Either their identity and their narrative were critical to the structure of a particular judgment, or the art of transforming the parties into ciphers had not yet become critical to the structure of legality. What we can learn from these shadowy dramas is that legal narratives have a past. Because they have a past, because that past was not inevitable, not a product of 'right answers' but of the ordinary activities of daily life, we need to ask whose stories have become legal stories. We need to know what kind of stories the law understands and who is entitled to tell them. Even after the human stories, and those who told them, have long been consigned to dust, those stories, recast through the eyes of jurists, remain law, remain potent, remain able to shift and shape events. They are powerful stories and their power is not captured by any single image. They are the stories which tell us what a contract is, and what the law demands of those who would bind themselves in this way. They are the stories that shaped the law of wrongs out of the events that disrupted communal life and once threatened a return to older ways.[8] Because, at every turning, these stories might have been other than they were, because they shaped the law in unexpected ways, we know both that in the future stories will have the power to shape the law in ways that may surprise us and that no outcome is ever certain.

The heart of the law lies in the movement from polyvocality to narrative coherence. If law begins with ordinary people and ordinary stories, each story must be honed, stripped of inessential elements and tested in the fire of argument. Nothing may be said which cannot be verified. No room remains for poetry, for images and ideas that shift and shimmer in the mind's eye. The law is concerned with facts, and not just any facts, but facts that are, in particular contexts, legally relevant. Just what facts are legally relevant depends, of course, upon a reaching back into history, for law can no more escape its history than it can avoid the necessity for making a decision. Precedent is all about history, stories which were found persuasive once upon a time, in one setting, stories which have been spun into the fine strong thread of which seamless webs are made.

Legal Stories and Seamless Webs

One such story, one which was persuasive not that long ago, is that recounted by the Irish Court of Appeal in *Hegarty v Shine* in 1878.[9] The story is simple enough, albeit redolent of the sexual and social mores of the late Victorian era. The plaintiff, who, we are told, had contracted a 'loathsome disease' whilst cohabiting with the defendant, brought a civil action against him. As originally framed, the action alleged breach of promise of marriage and an 'assault' as a consequence of which the plaintiff claimed to have become infected with venereal disease. The writ of trespass averred that the 'defendant assaulted and beat the plaintiff, whereby she became infected'. We are told by the Court of Appeal that no evidence was led at the trial in respect of the first cause of action. As to the second, we are told that the trial judge directed the jury:

> as a matter of law, that an assault implied an act of violence, committed upon a person against his or her will, and that, as a general rule, when the person consented to the act, there was no assault; but that if the consent was obtained by the fraud of the party committing the act, the fraud vitiated the consent, and the act became in view of the law an assault, and that therefore if the defendant, knowing that he had venereal disease, fraudulently concealed from her his condition, in order to induce, and did thereby induce, her to have connection with him; and if but for that fraud she would not have consented to have had such connection; and if he had with her the connection so procured and thereby communicated to her such venereal disease, he had committed an

assault, and one for which they might on the evidence award substantial damages.[10]

By the Irish Court of Appeal, we are told both that it is 'unnecessary' for the purposes of the appeal to 'enter into the details of the evidence'. We are also told that the learned trial judge had arrived at 'so absurd a charge to the jury not of his own volition', but rather, because he believed he was constrained by authority to adopt this position.[11] While the words of the Court of Appeal are profoundly revealing, its silences are even more so. Because, so we are told, it is 'unnecessary' to canvass the facts, the reported case becomes a curious mixture of Victorian prurience and unexplained silences. We are told precious little of the plaintiff, save that her 'circumstances are so pitiable that they must necessarily excite compassion in the breast of every man'.[12] We do not know why the complaint of breach of promise was dropped. Because the 'facts' are irrelevant to the appeal as constituted, we also do not know whether in the count as stated the sexual act itself and the violence palpable upon the face of the writ were the same. The second count was also stated in somewhat different terms, that 'the defendant assaulted and beat the plaintiff and infected her with venereal disease'. This alternative formulation introduces a further level of ambiguity. On either reading, the nexus between violence and sexuality is unmistakable. This too is wholly and fittingly Victorian. It may be that the relationship between plaintiff and defendant was a violent relationship. On the other hand, counsel may have appropriated language redolent of physical violence in an attempt to locate the wrong alleged squarely within existing legal categories. If this were the case, of course, counsel would have been carrying on a tradition well established by the time of the first Year Book cases in the fourteenth century. Whatever richness or inflection might have emerged from the interaction of these images is lost in the judicial insistence that it is 'unnecessary' to canvass the facts. The facts, the stories, fractured narratives glancing off one another which might have shimmered beneath the surface of brute facticity are thereby silenced. Within the bounds of the appellate jurisdiction, all that remains are legal stories. Nothing in any of the judgments provides us with a picture of either the plaintiff or the defendant – although utilising late twentieth century hindsight it is easy enough to picture them as stock characters in a Victorian melodrama. Still less do we learn of any relationship between them. This is I believe, of almost unbearable importance. In chapter 4, we began to learn of the relationship between law and narrative. Of the understandings gained in that chapter, perhaps the most important was that the way in which the judge understood the relationship between the judge and the law was of critical importance. Whether the judge valorised the common law, or whether the common law was profoundly implicated in the events that transpired, the relationship between judge and law was central. Here we begin to explore a very different relationship between the judge and the law. The statement that the appellate judge found it 'unnecessary' to canvass the facts speaks of a world view in which fact and law are potential contaminants. It is not simply that it is unnecessary to canvass the facts. It is that these facts will bring down the law. The law dare not canvass facts that must enmesh it in matters best left unacknowledged.

In the end, Ball C upholds the order for a new trial made by the Queen's Bench Division and avers that 'an action of this character cannot be maintained'. Were it to be sustained the court would be complicit in the provision of a remedy for the consequence of an immoral act, thus compromising the integrity of the court itself. Immorality and illegality fuse, a fusion which seems unremarkable until we consider the fervency with which they were, at much the same time, held to be immutably separate and apart where what was at stake was 'freedom of contract'.[13] Sex and law, law and sex. For law, at this time, in this place, sex becomes unruled and unruly, destructive of the essence of legality.

While the basis for his rejection lies deep within the Victorian character, his judgment suggests that for such a remedy to be granted a 'contractual obligation' between the parties was essential. Only contract, it seems, can generate a duty to disclose which a court may properly enforce. Such an obligation could not arise where the relationship itself was immoral. The immorality of the relationship meant that the duty asserted was one in aid of indulgence in the immoral act alleged. This is, in itself, curious. We are prone to view the collapse of the border between contract and tort as a late twentieth century phenomenon. Yet, well before this it is suggested that for the plaintiff to be afforded a remedy in tort it is essential to establish a prior 'contractual' relationship between the parties, one capable of generating an enforceable duty of disclosure. Exactly what sort of 'contract' might be required is not specified, perhaps understandably. The law, it is clear, is incapable of recognising the existence of interpersonal duties that are not a product of a contract or trust known to law.

A couple of unstated presumptions drift ambiguously in the background of this sorry little tale. First, although Ball C does not put it in quite this way, in the absence of a pre-existing contractual relationship, the defendant would not have any enforceable duty to inform the plaintiff that he suffered from such a disease. Only contract is capable of generating a duty to disclose information such as that withheld. The defendant might have disclosed his condition if he were a 'nice guy', but any obligation involved would be 'moral' rather than 'legal'. While the plaintiff's condition is acknowledged to be 'pitiable indeed', her condition forms part of a classically Victorian morality play which is, by unhappy mischance, being played out in a court of law. As Ball is at some pains to emphasise, it is, nonetheless, 'no fit subject for the attention of a Court of Justice'. The fear of contagion and pollution and the atmosphere of 'moral panic' are remarkable.

Whatever the relationship between the plaintiff and the defendant might have been before the action commenced we learn nothing of it from the reported judgment. Answers to the other questions alluded to above are also lacking. Only when we look elsewhere[14] do we discover that the relationship between the plaintiff and the defendant is that of master and servant. The plaintiff, entrapped by her own immorality in the authorised version is simply a young female servant infected with a venereal disease by her master. We learn nothing of this in the decision of the Irish Court of Appeal. That august body found it 'unnecessary' to canvass the facts. To gain access to the 'facts' it is necessary to repair to the judgment of the Queens Bench Division.

The court is beset by moral panic. Deasy LJA notes that if recovery were allowed the appellate courts would be overrun by similar cases.[15] In any case:

> In the present case the woman has led an immoral life – a life, one of the frequent consequences of which is the contraction of a loathsome disease. For two days a most able judge and a jury have been engaged in investigating the details and occasions of this course of immorality, in order to discover whether the probable consequence of that course of immorality did actually originate from it. I am of opinion that such an investigation is **no fit subject for the attention of a Court of Justice, and that no such investigation ought to receive judicial sanction.**[16] [Emphasis mine.]

If we find this account perversely mannered, both the language and the holding tell us far more about the judges and how they saw themselves and the common law than about the parties and the events which brought them before the law. The case is extraordinary. Upon the frame of reference of the tort of battery, the court superimposes a contractual requirement. Only if a valid contract exists between the plaintiff and the defendant can she argue that he was obliged to disclose his condition.[17] Mercifully, the court was spared any need to grapple with the complications inevitable had the plaintiff and the defendant been married (rather than simply cohabiting). The plaintiff would not have been able to bring the action had she been married. This was the case both because, being a *femme covert*, a married woman would have been required to sue through her 'next friend' and because the law did not permit suits between husband and wife. Because the (unhappy) couple in *Hegarty v Shine*[18] were unmarried, the plaintiff had standing to bring her action but could not recover, her misfortune being a consequence of her immoral life!

The missing contract, the missing ground of obligation in *Hegarty* was, of course, marriage, but marriage imposed a permanent bar on recovery! It is also worth noting that at common law the conventional legal position is that one cannot consent to serious bodily harm.[19] Its application on the facts of *Hegarty v Shine* would, of course, be fraught with difficulty. If it had been applied, it would be clear that, *had the plaintiff been aware that the defendant suffered from a venereal disease* she could not have given a 'legally valid' consent to sexual intercourse. We are left with the bizarre position that the appeal court will not entertain a remedy for an injury arising out of circumstances which, had she been aware of them, could have rendered any consent she might have given invalid. Within the court's masculine economy of knowing and understanding, none of this matters, indeed, it passes from view.

Spousal Immunity and the Journey from Tort to Crime

When *The Queen v Clarence*[20] confronted the English courts some ten years later, matters were complicated both because the victim was married and because the matter came before the courts as a criminal rather than a civil matter.[21] Deprived of the ability to castigate the prosecutrix by the fact that she was, to all appearances, a respectable married woman, Wills J exhibited a salacious fascination with the 'subtle metaphysical questions'[22] involved. His Honour rejected outright the possibility that a husband might be found to have *assaulted* his wife by having sexual intercourse with her whilst suffering from gonorrhoea. In his judgment, the language of assault became entangled with the language of rape. The oscillation between the discourse of 'assault' and the discourse of 'rape' suggests that an attempt to blur the distinction between sex and violence failed utterly. Subsequently he emphasised that there was no distinction between:

> consent obtained by suppression of the fact that the act of intercourse may produce a foul disease, and consent obtained by the suppression of the fact that it will certainly make the woman a concubine, and while destroying her status as a virgin withhold from her the title and rights of a wife.[23]

While he conceded that the plaintiff would have been entitled to deny her husband sexual access whilst he suffered from venereal disease, that was immaterial. The legislation dealing with rape, defilement and abduction made no mention of the present circumstances. That what His Honour could only understand as 'sex' was the structural equivalent of an 'assault', that is, an act of physical violence causing bodily harm was inconceivable. His insistence that it ought to have been canvassed by the legislature under the 'appropriate' categories of rape, defilement and abduction, is another way of saying that an act such as that alleged was incapable of being criminal. At that time, rape, defilement and abduction were, at that time, structurally property offences.[24] The wrong lay not in the injury to the victim's interests, but in a devaluing of the worth of the proprietary interests of her father or husband. Here the victim was married, her body having become by virtue of marriage, the property of her husband. Because a husband has property in his wife's body, he is entitled to use it as he sees fit. The language is remarkable in a number of respects. According to Wills J,

> if we are invited to apply the analogy of the cases in which a man has procured intercourse by personating a husband, or by representing that he was performing a surgical operation, we have to ask ourselves whether the procurement of intercourse by suppressing the fact that the man is diseased is more nearly allied to the procurement of intercourse by misrepresentation as to who the man is or as to what is being done, or to misrepresentation of a

thousand kinds in respect of which it has never yet occurred to any one to suggest that the intercourse so procured was an assault or a rape.

His Honour goes on to make a range of further rhetorical comparisons concluding with the implicit suggestion that His Honour's experience well fitted him to pontificate upon the views of women in respect of the matters considered. Deprived of the safe harbour of 'a course of immorality', Wills J resorts to speculation about the almost infinite variety of circumstances in which consent as to intercourse might be called into question. Having become convinced of the impossibility of distinguishing consent obtained through bigamy from consent obtained by withholding information about disease,25 he concludes that the statutory prohibition against assault had never been intended to apply in such circumstances. Given that such diseases had been known for almost four centuries, it seemed to him improbable that, at this late date, the criminal law might be invoked to deal with such a transgressor.26 Even the enhanced rights of women seemed to him a 'strangely insufficient reason' for a new fangled reading of the criminal law! Such a reading would open the door to new forms of extortion. His Honour exclaimed with (feigned) horror that –

> the unmarried woman [common prostitute?] who solicits and tempts a perhaps reluctant man to intercourse which he would avoid like death itself if he knew the truth... must surely... come under the same criminal liability as the man.27

His Honour's difficulty seems to have arisen primarily from his reluctance to accept that a prosecution involving sexual intercourse as an element in an assault inflicting actual bodily harm did not, necessarily, amount to an a prosecution for rape. It is, undoubtedly, somewhat difficult for a woman to rape a man (although through the years the law has been able to treat her as a party to that offence). If the scenario is as His Honour would have it, and our hapless and reluctant man has succumbed to the blandishments of a wily woman, he might well have an action in assault should he choose to pursue it. Perhaps he was unable to conceive of an assault in which the 'victim' (who would not have consented to intercourse had he been aware of the danger of contagion) was not the passive recipient of an unwanted physical contact. The dialectic of desire and deceit, one beloved of the Victorian sensibility, renders such a possibility wholly untenable.

Ultimately the problem became clear. Such an action merely illustrated the futility of any attempt to use the criminal law as an instrument of moral instruction. Yet, this reading wholly elides the context within which the court made its decision. The *Contagious Diseases Acts* and the discourse of the 'common prostitute' were already a reality. During the period between 1864 and 1886 the State routinely invoked the criminal law as 'an instrument of moral instruction' and took a proactive role in regulating immorality.[28]

For Stephen J, master of the criminal law that he was, the matter was comparatively simple. Given that the injury was a consequence of the suppression of the truth, it was an abuse of language to describe it as an assault. As His Honour insisted:

> In this case there was no intention, and therefore no attempt to infect, and it seems anomalous to make a consequence which, though highly probable, was neither intended nor necessary, relate back on its occurrence in such a way as to turn an act not punishable in itself into a crime.[29]

His Honour's search for an appropriate *mens rea* is bizarre. In most instances of common assault, the 'intention to cause grievous bodily harm' is inferred from the character of the assault and from the fact that grievous bodily harm eventuated as a consequence of that assault. Here, perhaps because of the sexual matrix, the defendant's intention to claim his 'marital privilege' apparently overrides his (one assumes certain) knowledge that, as a consequence, grievous bodily harm will in fact be caused. Moreover, and perhaps even more to the point, Stephen J disputed the applicability of the maxim that fraud vitiates consent in matters such as that before the court. According to Stephen J:

> It is commonly applied to cases of contract, because in all cases of contract the evidence of a consent not procured by force or fraud is essential, but even in these cases care in the application of the maxim is required, because in some instances suppression of the truth operates as fraud, whereas in others at least a suggestion of falsehood is required. The act of intercourse between a man and a woman cannot in any case be regarded as the performance of a contract. In the case of married people that act is part of a great relation based upon the greatest of all contracts, but standing on a footing peculiar to itself.[30] In all other cases the immorality of the act is inconsistent with any contract relating to it. Thus in no case can considerations relating to contract apply to it. The effect of fraud is to render it voidable at the option of the party defrauded.

This clearly cannot apply to sexual intercourse. It is either criminal if the woman does not consent, or if her consent is obtained by certain kinds of fraud, or it is, as this was, a breach of matrimonial duty, or it is not criminal at all... The injury done was done by a suppression of the truth.[31] It appears to be an abuse of language to describe such an act as an assault.[32]

In *Clarence*, as in *Hegarty v Shine*, the discursive regime of contract intrudes upon the text in a way that obliterates the parties and the act alleged. Contracts, legal, sexual and, perhaps, ultimately social, become entangled with the question of consent in ways which seduce the mind into bizarre channels. The passage cited immediately above provides the clearest example. When Stephen J insists upon reading consent exclusively through the lens of contract, his reading makes it inconceivable that sexual relations could be the subject matter of a valid contract. If the parties are married contract is irrelevant because sexual intercourse is always already implicit in the marital relation.[33] If the parties are not married, the purported contract is void for illegality and against public policy for that reason. The nature of the act leaves nothing for an allegation of fraud to operate upon, given that 'the effect of fraud is to render it voidable at the option of the party defrauded'. In the context, **it** can only be the act of sexual congress itself. If the parties are married contract collapses into doctrinal treatment of husband and one as one person, the husband being that person. If single, contract flows seamlessly into *contra bones mores* and so good night. No space remains in which an allegation of fraud could be made out.

Stephen J's rhetoric heightens the tension between the language of (criminal) assault and the language of rape, subtly encouraging the reader to acknowledge the absurdity of treating sexual intercourse as the **subject matter** of a voidable contract. We do not stop to inquire what else **it** might be in the matter before the court. The slippage between a refusal to treat sexual intercourse as the performance of a valid contract and a passage which makes sense only if the sexual act itself is the 'it' voidable at the option of the defrauded party vanishes. If, as the construction of this passage demands, **it** refers to the sexual act itself, it **is** absurd to treat the **act** as voidable. There is simply no such thing as a voidable act. Within the paradigm of contract, it is the contract[34] which either is or is not voidable, not the act or acts constituting performance. An act is not, in the ordinary way of the world, something which can be 'avoided' in the legal sense. In the real world of course, most of us find avoiding sexual intercourse easy enough most of the time, but we avoid it before it has taken place, not after! After is just a little late, and it is this very lateness, of course, upon which Stephen relies to persuade us. If, despite the context in which this passage is located, **it** refers instead to all the normal contractual formalities of 'offer', 'acceptance', 'intent to enter legal relations' and 'consideration', one wonders why on earth the paraphernalia of contract is relevant. Strictly speaking, the matter before the court would appear to lie securely within the discursive boundaries of either tort or crime. Within the paradigm of 'assault'[35] consent operates, not as part of an investigation into whether or not a binding agreement has been concluded, but as a fact that (radically) alters the character of the act itself.

Ordinarily, at least within the paradigm governing the intentional torts, consent signifies not agreement but permission. The difference is important. To consent to a touching, or to a blow (as within the sport of boxing), or to a lawful tackle (as within the sport of football) or to an operation (as within the medical context), or even to sexual intercourse (as within the law governing sexual assault) is to negate the potential wrongfulness of the act in question **in advance**. It is for this reason that an understanding of the nature of the act consented to is critical. While it might seem as if the consent that negates the tortious character of an act is functionally equivalent to the consent without which a binding contract cannot come into existence, these 'consents' are, I think, phenomeno-logically very different.

In tort law consent, whether tacit or explicit, functions as a mechanism to **exclude** legal redress for what would, **absent that justification**, be a wrongful act. Within contract, on the other hand, consent is an essential precondition if an alleged contract is to be legally enforceable. Because **consent is a precondition** for legal enforcement, where agreement is obtained by fraud it follows that the contract may be avoided by the injured party. The injured party is put to her election. She must decide whether, even given the defendant's fraud, she prefers the bargain as it is written, or whether she wishes the entire transaction to be set aside. That these are the alternatives are important. She cannot effectively rewrite the contract as it stands by eliminating the fraudulent element only. In avoiding the contract, the injured party is eliminating the possibility that the contract may be enforced against him or her. As noted earlier, it is important to note precisely what is avoided in this context. The **contract in its entirety as a legal entity** is avoided, not the specific acts which would otherwise have constituted the 'performance'. Those acts, whether performance has been concluded or whether some among them remain to be done, become legally relevant only in the context of determining whether *restitutio in integrum* is available. If the *status quo ante* can substantially be restored *restitutio* will be appropriate. If not, either damages or, perhaps, an account of profits, will be the remedies available.

Throughout his narrative, Stephen J subtly deforms relatively uncomplicated doctrinal issues. He insists that the allegation be of rape or nothing at all. This insistence prepares the way for his assertion that the maxim that fraud vitiates consent can not apply in circumstances such as those before the court. He is not prepared to entertain the possibility that the presence or absence of disease might alter the nature of the act.[36] Once the matter before the court is, in essence, 'rape or nothing', other possibilities vanish. The tort doctrine of spousal immunity is the root of the problem. Like *terra nullius*, spousal immunity, once abrogated, threatens to 'fracture' the skeleton of the law.

Dissenting Paradigms: The Negative of the Fiduciary

Hawkins J, in dissent addressed precisely this possibility stating that:

Rape consists in a man having sexual intercourse with a woman without her consent, and the marital privilege being equivalent to consent given once for all at the time of marriage, it follows that the *mere act of sexual communion is lawful*; but there is a wide difference between a simple act of communion which *is lawful*, and an act of communion *combined with infectious contagion* endangering health and causing harm, which *is unlawful*... If a person having a privilege of which he may avail himself or not at his will or pleasure, cannot exercise it without at the same time doing something not included in this privilege and which is unlawful and dangerous to another, he must either forego his privilege or take the consequences of his unlawful conduct.[37]

Hawkins J was, notably, also prepared to entertain the possibility that, in some circumstances at least, an assault would also occur where the parties were unmarried.[38] Where Stephen J, in particular, seems to have been bewitched by the metaphor of contract, and by the role of fraud within the contractual paradigm,[39] Hawkins J eschewed altogether the language of contract. For Hawkins J, at least within the marital context, sexual access was a privilege. The subtle distinction between the discourse of 'privilege', a discourse that emphasises that the 'privilege' can never be absolute, and the language of contract and contractual rights is critically important. It signals a different legal paradigm altogether, and one equally well grounded in authority. In this paradigm, even under a legal regime that refused to recognise marital rape as rape, a wife was entitled to withhold consent to sexual congress if it would endanger her health. Within the paradigm invoked by Hawkins J, the husband's marital privilege meant that he stood in a fiduciary relationship to his wife. Where discretion can be exercised unilaterally and the exercise of that discretion unilaterally affects the interests of another, those interests must be taken into account. [40]

On one level, such cases seem little more than curiosities today, relics of a bygone era, although it is well to note that *Hegarty* remains good law. On another level, the competing discourses, the rhetoric of contagion and moral pollution on the one hand and of privileges and consequential responsibilities on the other, provide a compelling illustration of the way in which legal storytelling works. It obliterates individuality, obliterates context, indeed, obliterates the stories of the parties, replacing them with the stock characters and legal precedents.

Hegarty v Shine and *R v Clarence* are fascinating cases, not because of the law they establish, but because of the way in which they detach the law from the events which brought the parties before it. Their insistent depersonalisation highlights what we risk when we come before the law. The stock characters of a Victorian melodrama replace the parties. In the end, we are confronted by a Victorian morality play, one in which the voices of the victims remain forever lost.

From Victorian Silences to...

Norberg v Wynrib[41] is a contemporary Canadian case raising many of the same issues. It is notable both for the comparative verisimilitude with which the parties are sketched, and for a willingness on the part of some members of the court to elide the boundaries between the discourses of contract, tort and equity which parallels that in *Clarence*. Of the plaintiff, we are initially told (by La Forest J) that when the saga began she was a 'modestly educated young woman in her late teens'.[42] Because of a failure to adequately diagnose an abscessed tooth, she became addicted to painkillers. Her addiction was supported in part by her sister who was also an addict. Her addiction ultimately led her to consult Dr Wynrib, described as an elderly medical practitioner. He initially provided her with drugs in response to various pretexts. After he realised that she was addicted he suggested 'if [she] was good to him he would be good to [her]', reinforcing his suggestion by gesturing to his private quarters above his office. Initially:

> the sexual encounters took place in the back examination room of his office. He kissed her and fondled her breasts. In time, he required her to meet him upstairs in his bedroom where he kept a bottle of Fiorinal in his dresser drawer beside the bed. She managed to stall him for a while by asking for the Fiorinal first and then leaving after she obtained it. But this device did not work long... The pattern was that he would tell her to undress and put the bottle of Fiorinal by his bed for her to see. Both parties would lie on the bed. Dr Wynrib would kiss the appellant, touch her and then get on top of her. He would go through the motions of intercourse. There was no penetration, however, because he could not sustain an erection. On at least one occasion, however, he penetrated her with his fingers... At trial, the respondent did not testify. However the appellant admitted that Dr Wynrib did not at any time use physical force. She also testified that he did things for her such as giving her money as well as coffee and cookies. She agreed that she "played" on the fact that he liked her and that she knew throughout the relationship that he was lonely.

Yet here, and it is a measure both of the passage of time and of a way of looking at events, the a majority (La Forest J, Gonthier and Cory JJ concurring) had no doubt that the appellant's consent could not be characterised as voluntary. As La Forest J explained it:

> To summarize, in my view, the defence of consent cannot succeed in the circumstances of this case. The appellant had a medical problem – an addiction to Fiorinal. Dr Wynrib had knowledge of the problem. As a doctor, he had knowledge of the proper medical treatment, and knew she was motivated by her craving for drugs. Instead of fulfilling his professional responsibility to treat the appellant, he used his power and expertise to his own advantage and to her detriment. In my opinion, the unequal power between the parties and the exploitative nature of the relationship removed the possibility of the appellant's providing meaningful consent to the sexual contact...
>
> In my opinion, the principle of *ex turpi causa non oritur actio* does not bar the appellant's recovery for damages... The respondent forced the sex-for-drugs transaction on the appellant by virtue of her weakness. He initiated the

arrangement for his own sexual gratification and then impelled her to engage in it. She was unwilling to participate but did so because of her addiction to drugs. It was only because the respondent prolonged the appellant's chemical dependency that the illicit relationship was available to him. The respondent has been found liable in this appeal because he took advantage of the appellant's addiction. To apply the doctrine of *ex turpi causa* would be to deny the appellant damages on the same basis that she succeeded in the tort action: because she acted out of her desperation for Fiorinal. Surely public policy would not countenance giving to the appellant with one hand and then taking away with the other.[43]

Here, as in *Clarence*, consent provides the fulcrum upon which judgment turns. If, in *Clarence*, the question of consent was entangled in an oscillation between contract and crime, in *Norberg* consent is vitiated by the eradication of the appellant's agency. While there can be no doubt that, on one level, the appellant 'consented' to the respondent's advances, questions of power and exploitation vitiated the consent itself. She acted as she did only because of her need for drugs. Because the respondent used his medical knowledge to gratify himself rather than for the benefit of his patient, her consent signifies nothing within the frame of reference of the relationship between the parties.

Yet, as Sopinka J notes, **in contract itself** it is not clear whether unconscionability and inequality of bargaining power function within the discourse of consent to render a particular consent invalid. **It may be (even within the paradigm of unconscionability) more profitable to analyse the relationship between the parties without reference to consent.** Sopinka J offers a different reading of unconscionability and suggests that the real question (in contract at least) is whether, in all the circumstances, the transaction was such that it could not, in justice, be allowed to stand. As he notes:

> La Forest J... reasons that "[i]f the 'justice factor' of unconscionability is used to address the issue of voluntariness in the law of contract, it seems reasonable that it should be examined to address the issue of voluntariness in the law of tort"... There is, however a fundamental difference between these two concepts. If the former, the court may refuse to recognize the validity of a transaction voluntarily entered into by reason of the unfair use of power. The factor of unconscionability would be more appropriate here if the respondent were seeking to enforce the transaction as opposed to defending himself against an allegation that he committed an intentional tort by the strong

against the weak.[44] In the latter, the court is asked to saddle a party with damages for a wrong inflicted on the plaintiff. In the latter case, there is no wrong if there was consent. In the former, the issue is not consent but whether it was fairly obtained.

Accordingly, the weight of academic and judicial opinion is that the doctrine of unconscionability operates to set aside transactions even though there may have been consent or agreement to the terms of the bargain. It is not that this doctrine vitiates consent but rather that fairness requires that the transaction be set aside notwithstanding consent.[45]

For Sopinka J, 'transposing unconscionability analysis into the context of a battery claim may lead courts astray'. His Honour correctly notes in particular the dangers of invoking community standards matters concerning consent to sexual contact. He continues:

One example of how transposing unconscionability analysis into the context of a battery claim may lead courts astray is La Forest J's statement that if the type of sexual relationship at issue is "sufficiently divergent from community standards of conduct", this may indicate exploitation. This reasoning is drawn directly from an unconscionable transaction case... in which... the key question is "whether the transaction, seen as a whole, is sufficiently divergent from community standards of commercial morality that it should be rescinded"... While community standards of commercial morality may be a relevant consideration in determining whether there has been such exploitation as to warrant setting aside a commercial contract, with respect, community standards of sexual conduct have no bearing on the question of whether or not there was consent to sexual contact in a particular case.

I therefore do not find the contractual doctrine of unconscionability of assistance in attempting to answer the factual question of whether the appellant consented to sexual contact with the respondent. Furthermore, in my view, the facts of this case are more accurately reflected by acknowledging that the appellant consented to the sexual contact and by considering the respondent's conduct in light of his professional duty towards the appellant.[46]

Like all texts, and most particularly all judicial texts, this text lends itself to a variety of readings. On one hand, and I believe that this is important, it gives some credence to the appellant's agency, acknowledging that, even in a addicted state and undergoing withdrawal symptoms, she was capable of giving or withholding consent. In this respect at least, she is not simply a victim, one whose consent is always already given and awaiting negation. From within this same reading, I find it refreshing, particularly after the Victorian imagery of cases such as *Hegarty* and *Clarence*, that 'community standards' are given short shrift, most particularly in the sexual context! I cannot but agree that community standards have no bearing on whether the appellant consented to the sexual desires of the respondent. To the extent that community standards might be thought to come into play, their role can only be ambiguous and ambivalent, the voice, in short, of the moraliser, and a voice which has, historically, been wholly unsympathetic towards women.

On the other hand, this text also lends itself to a reading that emphasises the sanctity of contract, the (potentially) fiduciary character of a physician's duties and the (inegalitarian) discourse of professional and client. At once breaking down hierarchy by affirming the appellant's agency, her capability, even in the circumstances, to choose, it reinstates hierarchy by locating the discourse within the already framed and prismatic discourse of client and professional. The discourse of the professional remains profoundly dangerous, at least within this context. It subsumes categories that might once have been addressed in various ways into a master discourse of authority. On a very different level, the discourse of professionalism strips the (newly) agentic appellant of any agency. Yes, she 'consented', but both the meaning and the value of her consent disappear into the questions of breach of professional duty and breach of fiduciary duty. Because the text focuses upon the respondent, as professional, and, potentially at least, as fiduciary, its central concern must be the ways in which his agency is mediated by role and by status. Her agency is wholly irrelevant to the question before the court. She becomes, in this way, simultaneously present and absent.

Yet if in the preceding judgments the matter before the court has oscillated between contract and tort, Sopinka J considering but rejecting the possible fiduciary aspects of the situation, for McLachlin J

> the doctrines of tort or contract [do not] capture the essential nature of the wrong done to the plaintiff... [T]o look at the events which occurred over the course of the relationship... from the perspective of tort or contract is to view that relationship through lenses which distort more than they bring into focus.[47]

While it is indeed tempting to concur in McLachlin J's sentiment, the fiduciary alternative he posits offers more than a little cause for concern. He adopts as his paradigm for the application of the fiduciary relationship to the doctor-patient relationship the unreported judgment of La Forest J in *McInerney v MacDonald*. La Forest J quotes with apparent approval the following passage from the 1956 judgment of Le Bel J:

"It is the same relationship as that which exists in equity between a parent and his child, a man and his wife, an attorney and his client, a confessor and his penitent, a guardian and his ward"... [McLachlin J continues:] I think it is readily apparent that the doctor-patient relationship shares the peculiar hallmark of the fiduciary relationship, trust, the trust of a person with inferior power that another person who has assumed superior power and responsibility will exercise that power for his or her good and only for his or her good and in his or her best interests... The essence of a fiduciary relationship... is that one party exercises power on behalf of another and pledges himself or herself to act in the best interests of the other.[48]

Yet, in the end, there are only so many 'legal stories', only so many prisms through which this (comparatively simple) story can be viewed. There is the story of the 'star-crossed' lovers of contract and tort, the (almost clinical) tale of fiduciary relationships, the story of crime (which was, after all, invoked in *R v Clarence*, only because spousal immunity rendered tort unavailable). The legal stories are, always, inferior to the human stories. If we fill out the human stories in *Norberg v Wynrib*, the 'social stories' are sad, familiar, and beyond the resolution of the court. Ms Norberg, the modestly educated young woman of the facts, was almost certainly at best semi-literate, from a working class family, and without either clear goals or understanding of how to formulate goals in life. She was, in short, one of a hundred thousand girls who leave school at the end of year ten without any understanding of who they are or who they want to be. Dr Wynrib, pathetic in his own way, was a 'hack doctor', competent on good days to dispense sympathy and Tylenol, confronted as increasing numbers of GPs are with addicted patients who are vulnerable in a whole range of ways. In the end, he chose to assuage his own needs rather than confront those of his patient. It is, I think, almost possible to feel sorry for an aging man, who, because he was a 'professional' continued to work rather than being compulsorily retired, and whose judgment, bluntly put, retired years before he did.

In a context such as this, what it means to speak as a judge is always (already) up for grabs. Locked into an adversarial frame of reference, viewing 'truth' through competing prisms of competence and knowledge, only sure that within an adversarial frame of reference, someone must win and someone must lose, no one wins! Ms Norberg has, perhaps, won one fragile victory, she has (for the moment) conquered the addiction which led to the case. The victories she has not won remain worth noting – she is still a 'modestly educated young woman', her sister is still a 'drug addict', and, for all one knows from the case, she is still without a clear path. Yes, she may marry, but given the pattern of vulnerabilities already established, that prospect is perilous at best. If it is hard to feel sorry for Dr Wynrib, it is likely that even if he is more affluent than the plaintiff, he will almost certainly be pushed into a 'retirement' for which he is not prepared. If she began her life 'at the end of the line', he has reached the 'end of the line' in another way. As for the judge, to speak as a judge means that if an outcome is never dictated by 'the law', judgment is always already inescapable. The world of right answers becomes a vanishing echo of the northern lights as one acknowledges that to speak as judge is to be, always already, on the verge of ambiguity. To speak as a judge is to speak within a social order that veers uncertainly between incompetence and evil, to confront the necessity to render decided judgment upon the undecidable.

Notes

1   A more specifically photographic image would be cropped. Both framing and cropping emphasise the partiality of our perceptions of events.

2   Of course, some of those whose stories become legal stories are not ordinary people at all. Indeed, some are neither ordinary nor people, but corporate persons of varying descriptions. Their stories, and the further perspectives with which those stories interact, add a further, and enormously suggestive dimension to the constitution of authority, for us, in our times. We do, after all, live in a world in which corporation persons have been held to be constitutionally entitled to freedom of religion. In such a world, the process by which 'corporate stories' are woven into the seamless web of law warrants careful attention. This fact should, as well, remind us that legal personality has, historically, been an enormously powerful instrument for both exclusion and inclusion, and that the legal story that is has been profoundly shaped by all those exclusions and inclusions.

3   If Robert Frost insisted that 'good fences make good neighbours' he also reminds us, and in the same breath, 'something there is that does not like a wall'. Frost, R, 'Mending Wall' in McKenzie, JA & JK, *The World's Contracted Thus: Major Poetry from Chaucer to Plath*, Melbourne, Heinneman Educational Australia, 1975, 226-227.

4   This is another way of asking about the relationship in which I stand to my own voice. Most of us have the experience of speaking to ourselves, trying out turns of phrase, levels of argument. What is at issue is not a private language, but a way of figuring oneself simultaneously as narrator and narratee.

5 Here the relationship between narration and seduction assumes a further dimension, a dimension in which we are, in some sense, capable of seducing ourselves.

6 The way in which we are brought before the law is noteworthy. Most of us, most of the time, dare not resist. See Yablon, CM, 'Forms' in Cornell, Rosenfeld & Carlson, 258.

7 Again I want to double back, insist upon the parallels between law and religion.

8 The 'invisible hand' beloved of Adam Smith and legions of economists after him might well have had its inspiration in the development of the common law. The common law evolved out of power and community, out of acts that threatened violent disruption or the dissolution of trust. Because of the time when it developed, some people might bring their stories to the law and others might not, or might only through the agency of another. The incremental development of the common law through time, through the accretion of matters and decisions acts, it seems to me, in exactly the same way Adam Smith believed the market to act. Had he but considered, he might have also doubted whether this sort of agency had the potential for good with which he credited it.

9 *Hegarty v Shine* (1878) *Cox's Criminal Cases* 145.

10 *Hegarty v Shine*, 145-146.

11 And in the telling we are also told, I think, that no *reasonable judge* could have charged a jury thus had he (yes, he) not been constrained by authority.

12 *Hegarty v Shine*, per Deasy LJA at 148. In this context, the connection with the Victorian fascination with images of dead and dying women, and in particular, with such images where the subject might be characterised as a 'fallen woman' is worth reflecting upon. The undertone of sexual excitement in the judgment is notable and is worth thinking about.

13 Here, of course, immorality becomes irrelevant!

14 See *Hegarty v Shine* (1878) 4 LR Ir 288 (QBD). Within the discourse of immorality issues of power, of status, of economic need are comprehensively obliterated and replaced with the moralistic discourse characteristic of the Victorian era with its obsession with dead and dying women.

15 In this context, the familiar allusion to 'floodgate fears' invites interpretation as a sardonic comment upon Victorian sexual mores, or rather, a judge's eye view of Victorian sexual mores.

16 *Hegarty v Shine*, 148. The language is remarkable. Apparently, discussion of such matters was unfit for judicial ears...

17 While the tort of battery is actionable per se, the act alleged to constitute the battery must be without consent or lawful authority. Here, the plaintiff alleges that had the defendant disclosed his condition she would not have consented.

18 (1878) 4 LR Ir 288 (QBD).

19 The recent English decision in *R v Brown* [1993] 2 All ER 75 provides an interesting example of this principle in action.

20 *R v Clarence* (1888) 22 QBD 23.

21 Just what sequence of events led to the defendant husband being brought before the law to be tried upon a criminal indictment specifying that he was charged with 'unlawfully and maliciously inflicting grievous bodily harm' upon his wife is impossible to ascertain from the reported judgments. It can hardly have been ordinary,

in 1888, for an aggrieved wife, whatever the cause, to invoke the aid of the criminal law against her husband. Of the narratives leading up to the trial before the recorder and subsequently to the case stated being reserved by the Court for the consideration of all the judges we know nothing. Given the state of the law at that time, criminal law was the only option available to the plaintiff, a wife being unable to bring action against her husband in tort. In Australian jurisdictions the doctrine of interspousal immunity was statutorily abolished in the recent past. See, for example, *Law Reform (Husband and Wife) Act* 1968 (Qld), *Married Women's Property Act* 1965 (Tas) s4, *Marriage (Liability in Tort) Act* 1968. In some Australian jurisdictions (NSW, WA) the immunity persisted as recently as 1993.

22   *R v Clarence*, 29-30.

23   *R v Clarence*, 30.

24   In many ways, they remain property defences. If our understandings have changed during the ensuing years, it is simply that women are now, in some circumstances, seen to have property in their own bodies.

25   I as well do not see any reason to differentiate between that particular pair of scenarios. Given the conditions of the era, both warrant compensation. His Honour's perspective, of course, may have been somewhat different.

26   One might suggest that these musings represent an unacknowledged reading of the provision through the lens of the 'mischief rule', and his masculine certitude that, whatever mischief this provision was meant to prevent, it could not possibly have been intended for such use.

27   *R v Clarence*, 32.

28   For a discussion of the Contagious Diseases Acts see McHugh, P, *Prostitution and Victorian Social Reform*, London, Croom Helm, 1980, 35-90.

29   *R v Clarence*, 45.

30   He means peculiar in that the terms of the marriage contract lay outside the will of the parties. So far as they were concerned, the contract was unenforceable and made it difficult, if not impossible, for any other contract to be concluded between the parties, it being presumed that the intent to enter legal relations would be lacking.

31   The reasoning here is slightly bizarre. Even taking the medical knowledge of the day as given, it seems unlikely that anyone could seriously contend that venereal disease was caused by suppression of the truth, although, if this **were** true, it could readily explain the 'moral panic' induced by the suggestion that the law might afford a remedy!

32   *R v Clarence*, 44.

33   There is, in short, no subject matter for a contract to operate upon.

34   In this context, the only contract which Stephen could acknowledge is the marital contract and it is **this** contract which must be avoided if fraud is to operate in the normal way. Yet, as shall be seen shortly, it is the insertion of the discourse of contract into the discourse of assault that is the root of the problem.

35   I am conscious as I write this that the language of assault used in both of these cases is itself illustrative of slippage. In *Hegarty* at least, battery would be more precise. In criminal law the slippage between assault and battery is sanctified by long usage.

36   Our ease in doing so, perhaps, lies in the necessity to figure sex against the background of AIDS, and our recognition that just such a deceitful act could be the source of a potentially fatal disease.

37   *R v Clarence*, 54-55.

38   *R v Clarence*, 54-55. Hawkins J discussed the issue against the background of the concerns of the majority that awarding a remedy in these circumstances would encourage undesirable prosecutions. In his view, it was highly unlikely that either party would invoke the criminal law where prostitution was involved, and in any case, in His Honour's view, in such arrangements, the parties consented to all risks. Where the parties were not married but prostitution was not involved, willingness to invoke the aid of the criminal like was likely to be constrained by shame.

39   The present author is unwilling to go further than suggest that this particular stance is profoundly linked to his affinity to natural law and its images.

40   One way of reading Hawkins J's discourse of 'privilege' is as an allusion to a fiduciary relationship, a foreshadowing the judgment of McLachlan J in *Norberg v Wynrib* more than a century later. See *Norberg v Wynrib; Women's Legal Education and Action Fund, Intervener* (1992) 92 DLR (4d) 449, 484ff.

41   *Norberg v Wynrib*, above.

42   *Norberg v Wynrib*, 451 per La Forest J.

43   *Norberg v Wynrib*, 468.

44   It is refreshing to find a judge who is prepared to acknowledge that perspective is critical, that it matters profoundly and centrally whose point of view is adopted.

45   *Norberg v Wynrib*, 477.

46   *Norberg v Wynrib*, 479-480.

47   *Norberg v Wynrib*, 484.

48   *Norberg v Wynrib*, 486-487.

7 Texts, Authority and the Force of Law

Introduction

This chapter will explore the connections between the way particular speech acts are clothed with authority, the written word, and the ways in which writing facilitates the transmission of force through time and space. If the figure woman seems absent in all of this, her absence is hardly strange. Throughout much of our history, the lineaments of authority and of the force of law have been drawn in ways that specifically excluded the presence of woman[1] and excluded as well the possibility of a connection between woman and authority. Underlying this meditation upon the connection between authority and the authorised text is a further question, whether, and how, texts may themselves be 'gendered'. We need to ask what the gendering of a text might mean to its force as law. It is important to be very careful here. The reason that we do not ordinarily think of legal texts as gendered, is, perhaps, that being gendered male, they have been coded 'human' in some uncomplicated way. Once texts are understood as gendered, questions of perspective and of voice become inescapable. Texts can be gendered in a range of ways that are not immediately apparent upon the face of the text. I am not talking about something as easy and obvious as pronominal reference. Rather, I am talking about a deeper and more subtle form of gender coding so that all superficial signs of gendering can be eradicated and the text will nonetheless remain unequivocally gendered.

Further questions also suggest themselves. I want to ask how, or if, the kind of authority vested in the judicial text can be reconciled with the presence of woman as author and as interpreter. A further question seems, in this context, both essential and unanswerable. If, as has been suggested, the author has gone the way of god, wherein lies the distinction between author and interpreter? In law, it often seems that the entire edifice of legality depends upon the insistence that law is a text with a fixed and certain identity. The figure of the text guards the abyss between author and interpreter, insists that the chasm between authorship and interpretation is unbridgeable. If, instead, the boundary between author and interpreter is permeable, what or who is invested with meaning and authority? Fishian reliance upon interpretive communities vests both, not in the text, not in the author, not even in the interpreter, but in the interpretive community itself. Yet I cannot help but wonder if an interpretive community is not, in law at least, as much to be feared as the other communitarian tropes that abound. I have, as woman, but lately scrambled out of invisibility and begun to claim independent agency. If, then, I accede to the idea that all meaning and, perforce, all authority, lie in the interpretive community, I have become an agent only to proclaim with my first 'agentic act' the irrelevance of my own agency.

Authority is not an easy idea in this context. The vesting of authority in particular kinds of texts, and, inevitably, in their silences[2] as much as in what is said, is of enormous importance. Moreover, the relationship between the female body and authority is profoundly difficult and ambiguous, and raises deeply troubling questions. Kathleen Jones suggests that:

> The current post-structuralist turn in feminist theory has compounded resistance to authority. The question "What makes actions rightful?" depends on judgments and, in the discourse of genealogy, judgments are disciplinary by definition. Once one accepts the thesis that every authoritative interpretation of public life opens up certain options for living only by closing down others, the temptation to suspend all judgment and to refuse to speak or to act increases. Who can speak for/as/about whom, who can use the term "woman" knowingly, authoritatively? Every interpretation becomes an imposition, every action a constraint. Doubts about certainty and truth seem to render impossible the articulation of any clear plan of political action.
>
> Doubts and guilt abound. If there can be no generally accepted principles of action, then political theorizing itself becomes suspect, political inertia threatens, and the temptation is strong to retreat into private fantasy...
>
> Once the secure foundation of the truthfulness of any interpretative claim has been called into question, to speak with authority about gender, about women and men and what sexual differences have represented, becomes both impossible and undesirable. Speaking about gender becomes impossible because skepticism immediately supplants acceptance of any generalizations about gender as even provisionally true. It becomes undesirable to speak about gender because even temporarily fixing categories such as gender, or even provisionally making statements such as "in the interests of women, we should secure reproductive rights", are seen as politically dangerous since they risk

reproducing, at the level of theory and strategy, the hegemony of binary oppositions.[3]

Undoubtedly what Kathleen Jones describes as the post-structuralist turn in feminist theorising has made many of us more alive to the patterns of exclusion and domination inherent in the positions we claim. Perhaps, as we struggle to come to terms with our own prejudices and untested assumptions, we do not make truth claims as readily as once we did. Perhaps we are (if only belatedly) becoming aware that the representative voice carries with it a profound and deep-seated responsibility. The representative voice is one that we should never assume lightly. Whether or not Jones is correct in blaming the 'post-structuralist turn in feminist theorising' for what she terms a kind of paralysis of the will,[4] it is instructive to explore how, and, indeed, where, this paralysis is felt. If post-structuralist thought has eroded the legitimacy of our attempts to claim the subject position 'woman' as legitimately our own, this is as much because of the kinds of truth claims associated with the representative voice as of 'existential angst'.[5] Cartesian scepticism is an unlikely (and largely unwelcome) champion of these doubts.

Once we elevate 'speaking for' to unwarranted heights, yes, it is illegitimate to claim any potentially universalisable subject position as our own. Every attempt to do so becomes a kind of silencing, a kind of hegemony.[6] We no longer speak representatively and for the consent of others, but as if that consent was always already given. Feminist theoreticians have no reason to be surprised by this particular difficulty; the evidence of its currency is all around us. It is a consequence, not of the current 'post-structuralist turn in feminist theorising', but of deeply ingrained traditions of speech and culture. Often quasi-universal figures such as 'woman' have been contrasted to, for example, Aboriginal women, not least by those who claimed to speak in the name of woman.[7] Yet resiling from any attempt to speak representatively, as a woman and for the consent of other women, is no answer at all. To do so is less an answer than an abandonment of the political and a retreat from engagement. We dare not withdraw from engagement, as if to be engaged is sufficient to make us complicit in oppression, but must seek an avenue for engagement in which uniqueness is fully recognised and representation is negotiated, not assumed. Speaking from within legal discourse, Helen Stacy argues:

I press for the necessity of moving towards a method within legal discourse that provides for the uniqueness of each woman's voice, while allowing for fruitful connections amongst and between women...

...Relativism therefore needs a supplement which recognises that knowledge claims are both constructed *and* situated. As juridical subjects, women need to be able to make a claim to legal protection that rests upon a certain level of constructed realism about their female sexuate identity – claims that are "essential" (for here and now) without enframing their identity as they make that claim for protection. We need, instead, to press for methods that allow for connections across diversity without thereby erasing the uniqueness of each voice.[8]

In law, as in politics, it seems that the pitfalls are endless. Each new claim reinstates another form of the oppression that it seeks to alleviate. When outsiders claim the right to speak both as representatives and as outsiders, they are claiming to speak for the disenfranchised. The simple fact of their ability to speak and to put forward truth claims sometimes suggests that they speak for a constituency to which they no longer belong. The question then becomes whether they are entitled to do so.

In other settings the representative voice seems beyond question. We are all familiar with these other settings, whether as lawyers or as citizens in a democratic society. It is to this 'unexceptional' dimension of the representative voice that I now turn. Among the issues with which we will be concerned is why, in these particular contexts, the representative voice seems less at issue. It may be that in these contexts the representative voice becomes a part of the formal structure, a trope of power.

Law as Representation: Blind Justice and her Servants

For those of us who work in and through the law, the representative voice is inevitable. As lawyers, as judges, we cannot help but speak representatively. When we speak on behalf of a client, we speak representatively, on their behalf. We do not do so in the sense of the quasi-illegitimate position suggested above, in which consent is presumed and difference eradicated in pursuit of an unargued universal, but in another rather more subtle (but, perhaps, equally disturbing) sense. As lawyers, as simultaneously representing the interests of our client and acting as officers of the court, our voice, for the duration of that service, is bound to the service of others and bound as well to the law. If we speak, we speak representatively. The alternative is silence and to be silent is to reject the law and our role within it. For judges, the double gesture, at once facing the parties and their competing claims and facing as well those by whom they will themselves be judged, offers no escape from the representative voice. For many of us, the challenge is to discover a form of speech through which it is possible to address these varied constituencies simultaneously. At all times, it remains essential to be faithful to each and to the core of one's own being so that selfhood remains intact. Stanley Fish speaks very clearly of the pitfalls of negotiating roles (most particularly those which are at variance with one's own identity) and the potential for role conflict:

> I am old enough to remember when it was not a simple matter to be both an academic and a Jew (now almost an identification), when the academic culture, especially in literary studies, was so insistently, if unselfconsciously (precisely the measure of the insistence) Protestant that one was faced with a choice between assimilating – imitating one's senior colleagues down to the patches on their elbows – and various forms of "acting out", a choice even more sharply posed today to those blacks who are simultaneously being recruited by the academy *as* blacks and required to comport themselves just like everyone else, that is, according to academic "standards" that are supposedly indifferent to race, sex, ethnic origin, etc. What sense does it make to speak in such situations of being constrained by belief, when one's beliefs, rather than cohering, pull one in different directions... An academic who is also a feminist is not two persons, but one – an academic-who-is-also-a-feminist. That is, when her feminism weighs upon her, it takes the form specific to the situation; it is feminism-as-an-academic-might-be-concerned-with-it. Being a feminist is a state no less complex than being an academic, and when they come together, they do so not as sovereign and separate obligations, but as obligations that have already been defined by their relationship to one another. Nor is that relationship itself stable: a feminist-academic may have worked out a modus vivendi that allows her to satisfy and even make capital of her "divided" loyalties, only to find in a moment of crisis that the two loyalties cannot both be satisfied and that, for the present at least, she must shut herself off from considerations to which she would otherwise be attuned.[9]

It would not be difficult or inappropriate to substitute judge for academic in this passage.[10] This fact perhaps serves as a reminder that for those of us who do not understand ourselves as 'liberal selves'[11] 'speaking as' inevitably forces us to confront our loyalties, and learn to deal with the (complex) relationships between them. It also begins to sketch the possibility of a kind of role conflict in which divided loyalties threaten one's sense of self.

The representative voice in law signals a different relationship both towards authority and with language than the questions sketched earlier. Many beginning law students have an almost instinctive sense of the pitfalls of that relationship, and describe finding their law studies profoundly alienating and destructive of self, particularly in the early years. Underlying this alienation is a series of questions about the representative voice, about power, about authority and about what it means to negotiate these relationships, both for self and for others. Those of us who write and speak about the law, cannot afford the luxury of resiling from questions of authority. That is even more true of those who write and speak about how, or if, women may come to speak authoritatively within law (while retaining as well a voice which is other). If we are to survive, and to function within law, resiling from authority is not an option. The discourse of authority is inseparable from the discourse of law itself, the two intertwined. In this context, it is worth thinking about the multiple ways in which hierarchy and authority are figured within law. The various court hierarchies are only the most obvious surrogates for authority. Less obvious are the divisions within the legal profession such as those between solicitors and barristers. More subtle still is the weighting accorded the various texts which might be proffered as 'authority' for various propositions of law, until lowliest of all, we encounter the statement of a publicist whose stature is diminished because she is still alive. That death should be a mark of authority is truly remarkable and limns the fascination of law with the fixed, the permanent, and the unchangeable. Once dead, after all, if only the text remains stable, the author cannot change her mind! The text has become truly canonical.

In a chilling image, and one which resonates with the insights of postmodernism, Robert Cover described the courts of the imperial state as jurispathic, law killing – each judgment silencing competing possibilities, competing laws. Judgment, for Cover, reduces polyphonic discourse to right answers, answers that are right because they are authoritative and final and not because of any characteristic of the answer, or the method by which it was obtained. As Cover explains it:

> It is remarkable that in myth and history the origin of and justification for a court is rarely understood to be the need for law. Rather, it is understood to be the need to suppress law, to choose between two or more laws, to impose

upon laws a hierarchy. It is the multiplicity of laws, the fecundity of the juris-generative principle, that creates the problem to which the court and the state are the solution... The state of unredeemed controversy, the problem of too much law, is thus seen to be either solved by the authority of the courts or caused by the failure or lack of authority of courts.

A little later, Cover quotes a passage from the *Federalist Papers* of Alexander Hamilton in which Hamilton emphasises the need for one supreme tribunal, one ultimate appellate court:

> To produce uniformity in these determinations, they ought to be submitted, in the last resort, to one SUPREME TRIBUNAL... If there is in each state a court of final jurisdiction, there may be as many different final determinations on the same point as there are courts. There are endless diversities in the opinions of men. We often see not only different courts but the Judges of the same court differing from each other. To avoid all the confusion which would unavoidably result from the contradictory decisions of a number of inde-pendent judicatories, all nations have found it necessary to establish one court paramount to the rest, possessing a general superintendence, and authorized to settle and declare in the last resort a uniform rule of civil justice.[12]

Speaking and writing within law holds another lesson as well, one that is of the highest importance. For those of us who speak as judges, the possibility of silence, of retreat from and denial of the call to judgment is forbidden from the outset. The post-structuralist moment of which Kathleen Jones speaks, truly heard and obeyed within law, is a moment which accepts the imperative to action. It accepts as well the knowledge that every authoritative interpretation of law (as a micro-instantiation of all of social life) both opens and forecloses options. All judgments are disciplinary by nature. Those of us who think and write within law, do not have the luxury of 'pure' or 'impure' theory, have no study to retreat within, no freedom to suspend judgment, to postpone or deny the disciplinary moment. This is, I think, enormously important. It is important for a number of reasons. Because legal judgments (and this they have in common with the judgment of god) are **disciplinary**, cannot be other than **disciplinary**, the political theorist's existential angst is the legal theorists *sine qua non*. 'The judges deal pain and death. **The judges deal pain and death. *The judges deal pain and death.*'**[13] These are bottom lines. If you, man or woman, do not like being involved in the pain and death business, get out of law. You can 'cop out', you can deny culpability,[14] but 'silence' is not an option.

Authority and the Gender of Judgment

It follows, and follows importantly and significantly, that the obligation to weigh speech, to consider, to ensure that judgment is, in the fullest possible sense, judgment, is paramount. Within law, within judgment, the truth of the post-structuralist moment is often elided, as increasingly frantic attempts are made to resile from the responsibility it makes inevitable. Despite increasing acknowledgment that the moment of judgment is the interpretive moment, despite increasingly widespread acceptance that, as Richard Posner said, 'interpretation... is as much creation as discovery',[15] the search for a post-structuralist instantiation of the 'philosopher's stone' continues. We seek a principle or set of interlocking principles that will confer both certainty and authority upon judgment.[16] Our doubts about our capacity to justify even the most rudimentary kind of judgment, to say that this is preferable to that, send some of us fleeing in terror from judgment itself. In law, unsurprisingly, these doubts (and the insights that accompany them) have more often led to a refusal to acknowledge precisely where our unwilling flirtation[17] with the borders of post-modernism has led us. The image of unwilling attraction, compulsion, even, is one that captures precisely my ambivalence, as a lawyer. I see no alternative to the insights about textuality and about meaning to which post-structuralism has led us. Equally, and even more strongly, I accept the impossibility of the kind of certainty which Descartes demanded that we seek. Nonetheless, I do not believe myself as an individual, or my culture, as a culture, to be bereft of judgment in the way some would claim and fear. Canonical texts come and go. To the extent that they remain canonical, they remain so because their truth is as much a truth for us as it was for those who first came to those texts, as authors and as interpreters.

If textuality on its own cannot provide a bulwark against uncertainty, if the author has gone the way of god, if precedents are merely texts, nothing more, nothing less, from whence comes their authority? We purport, in law, to be dealing with canonical texts, texts which, both within jurisdictions and across them, instantiate hierarchy. Authority, in law at least, is a property not only of the individual author, the individual judge, but also of a particular court. We understand the particularity of the court in a number of ways. On the simplest level, a level understood by every beginning law student, its particularity is relevant to issues of jurisdiction and hierarchy. The court is thus located spatially, becomes part of an organisation chart sketching the disciplines of judgment.

On a different level, the particularity of a court may be understood in terms of the judges who comprise it and sometimes even the character of its Chief Justice. Thus it is that we might identify the 'Warren Court' in the United States or the New Zealand Court of Appeal of which Sir Robin Cooke was the President. Lord Denning's stewardship of the Court of Appeal in England also comes to mind. I suspect that the time will come in Australia when we will look back at a particular period as that of the 'Brennan court'. Once upon a time, it also depended upon whether the report (the actual, physical text) consulted was an 'authorised report' or one of 'lesser' status.[18] Authority is simultaneously personal and institutional (and perhaps cultural as well). At the intersection of personal and institutional authority questions force themselves to the surface about what it might mean to speak at once as a judge and as a woman. If, as seems likely, much if not all of law is coded male, if law's voice remains male, what voice emerges when it is a woman who speaks the law, even more, 'embodies' it? In this context, yet another layer of difficulty emerges with the notion of 'speaking as'. The intersection of 'speaking as' with another idea which we will explore shortly, the idea of obligations of role and the way in which these obligations interact with individuality and personality is also relevant. It is only recently that questions such as these have even become askable within our culture. If (as I suspect) law continues to be coded male, how can a woman speak it with the full authority which the law demands, and yet, while maintaining that authority, maintain as well her identity as a woman?

Here as well, another layer emerges, a layer that is intimately linked to the discipline of the text. To write from within a position of institutional authority is to submit to the discipline and the judgment of others. One must accept that it is inevitable that in doing so one will be deprived, ultimately, even of the capacity to insist that **that** was not what one meant.[19] These questions become much more urgent when the speech one attempts and the writing compelled by the need to persuade is disciplinary. When this fact is inscribed upon the face of what one does, not buried beneath the surface, it cannot be escaped.

The lines of authority simultaneously run in two ways. The judge writes from a position of authority. Her writing is not simply writing, at least in the sense that a literary work or a book such as this can be **simply** writing, but a memorandum of judgment as written in and on the flesh. As an official account of the disciplinary moment, a record of that which was ordered to be done, a record of a command and of that which should and must count as sufficient obedience to that command. In this lies her power. She cannot resile from it and remain a judge. Nonetheless, she writes also as an act of submission. She is institutionally required to attempt to persuade others of the rightness of the judgment that she has given. In this way, every judge necessarily submits to the judgment of others.[20]

Yet, truth and falsity retain the meanings that they have always had. If our understandings of them have changed, if we are less willing to see ourselves as representative, as entitled to speak for others, this may be a salutary corrective to the enduring legacy of the Enlightenment. When Rousseau insisted (and, more importantly, wrote, created a text whose lineaments continue to haunt our mindscapes) that the ultimate power of the social contract was the right of the community to 'force men to be free', he spoke truly. When speaking of the community's right to compel men to submit their particular (self-interested) wills to the general will, he bequeathed to us an image of authority from which we do not yet know how to extricate ourselves. In insisting that the individual was responsible to himself alone, so that the ethical will and the individual will are fused, even while submitting absolutely to the will of the community, Rousseau left us impaled upon a contradiction. The libratory text and the disciplinary text had their genesis at the same moment. In all of the ways that matter most, for those of us who are, willingly or unwillingly, the children of the enlightenment, this was the moment. The libratory text, the text that celebrated the individual above all else, sought to fuse perfect freedom and ethical absolutism, is also the text that sought to impose absolute sameness, to eradicate even the possibility of competing allegiances. In this way, the state was secure and the general will uncontaminated. The community of the social contract could succeed only if the other was repressed and denied.[21]

The oscillation between 'force' and 'freedom' that epitomised the enlightenment, an oscillation that traced the lineaments of authority in a wholly new way, is one from which we have yet to escape. Once we are driven[22] to acknowledge that meaning is a property, not of texts but of their interrogation by agents, some may feel that the need for both meaning and stability commits us to a particularly strong conception of community. I am not suggesting that texts exist in a pure and holy realm in which they await encounters with meaning bearing agents (as if meaning were a 'property' that could somehow be possessed) but rather that meaning is interactive. Authors, readers, even the commentators are among those who confer meaning upon texts, participate in their realisation. Some of us can remember being first introduced to particular texts by a guide who 'breathed life' into those texts. This is an essential part of the meaning making process. While it is fleeting, it can be infinitely replicated. We interpret texts within the contexts of their multiple genealogies, not in isolation from them. To come to a text without this kind of context one would, I think, need to come to that text from wholly outside the intellectual (and cultural context) to which it belonged. No one with the linguistic skills required to gain meaning could be 'outside' in the absolute sense required. The search for a strong conception of community, I believe, lies underneath diverse attempts to provide a secure foundation for interpretation after 'the death of the author'. It may be found in Stanley Fish's image of an interpretive community strong enough to yield meaning and certainty as surely as it may be found in Ronald Dworkin's account of associative obligations. Albeit in different ways, both seek to vest meaning in a supra-individual entity, even if, as Dworkin insists, the community to which he refers is metaphorical rather than actual. Both, in this way, seek to locate meaning and authority in the community rather than the individual. The search for a strong conception of community that has emerged in contemporary thought owes a great deal to the work of Rousseau. Initially pursued by communitarian political philosophers such as Michael Sandel[23] it is a dominant influence underlying the work of civic republican legal theorists such as Frank Michelman and Suzannah Sherry.[24]   While the resurgence of community in the work of Ronald Dworkin is partly the legacy of his affinity for Gadamer, it has deeper roots. Within the liberal paradigm, the legitimacy of both law and government seemingly require recourse either to some form of 'strong community' or to classical contractarian discourse. This trope, this flight from (newly decentred) text to (newly recentred) community, foreshadows particularly difficult questions when the text in question is a judicial text. It is perilous in the extreme when the question we struggle to answer is what it can or should mean to speak as a judge.[25]

Meaning, Community, Authority

While Ronald Dworkin and Stanley Fish negotiate the 'death of the author' in very different ways, as suggested above, both seek to locate meaning and authority in a strong account of community. For Dworkin, the community is, in an important way, a product of the understandings of those within it. While the community with which he is most profoundly concerned, the nation state, is, on one level, wholly determined by its boundaries, the nation state of the cartographer's imagination inhabits the realm of the purely conventional. So doing, it remains transfixed by the legacy of positivism. Wholly determined by its (physical) boundaries, boundaries which are established by the dictates of (positive) rules, such community as exists within it is purely 'conventional', a matter of nationality as established by law, nothing more. The cartographer's nation state speaks solely of nationality, and delineates the spatial dimension of domicile. As defined by the rules of nationality and domicile, the citizen is a paltry thing. It is a very long way indeed from the 'lawyer's citizen' to an equal member of the *polis*, a member in good standing of a deliberative community of equals. As I understand citizenship, it is very different. Citizenship bespeaks membership, belonging, and a mutuality of rights and obligations that bind people together. History suggests that this is most easily and quickly achieved by delineating those outside the bonds of community as other. Our task is to reimagine it, find ways to understand membership and belonging which do not depend upon exclusion and denial.

Dworkin believes that, given the death of the author, the conventional state can never be other than arbitrary and tyrannical. If we are as the conventional account describes us, isolated individuals for whom community is simply the formalisms of geography and nationality, the death of the author has robbed law of authority beyond that of the gunman. The rhetorical moment in which the judge seeks to persuade her constituency[26] that her decision can be justified is barren. Justification becomes unthinkable. What meaning is left for an understanding of law as rules if each interpretive paradigm we pursue yields only infinite regress as each new source of meaning fades into nothingness. To reclaim law, to escape the purely arbitrary, Dworkin reaches backward into a (pre-liberal)[27] under-standing of community and relationships, hoping that, by reclaiming a meaningful concept of the ties of community, law's authority will be *re*placed upon a secure footing. His vehicle for this imperial[28] attempt at the legitimation of law and of its authority is the notion of 'associative obligations', a concept which he acknowledges largely replicates 'obligations of role' under a new and (hopefully) more evocative name.[29]

Stanley Fish confronts the same problem. Like Dworkin, he wishes to legitimate the interpretive process and thereby validate both his own enterprise of literary interpretation and, by extension, the interpretive acts of judges. He is also concerned to put the ghosts of positivism to rest. He has attacked on a number of occasions the positivist insistence that meaning is a property of texts and that it is possible to distinguish between a 'legitimate' interpretation and one which makes a mockery of those 'texts'. Fish begins from the (pragmatic) assumption that meaning is not individual but social. Within each community of interpreters unspoken conventions establish what counts as an interpretation of a text within that community. These conventions set bounds, ensure that interpretation is not an arbitrary exercise and that meaning remains relatively stable. They determine what counts as a reason, what amounts to a justification, establish the bounds of appropriate discourse within that community. On one level, this is unremarkable, even banal. For Fish to tell us that interpretation follows conventions and standards that are specific to particular interpretive practices is hardly news. We are familiar with 'schools of interpretation' in law as in literature and we are familiar with the implications that those schools have both for meaning and for our understandings.

For Fish, the interpretive community, as he calls it, is the arbiter of both 'truth' and 'meaning' in interpretation. Fish argues that interpretive communities, whether academic schools of thought[30] or professional communities of lawyers and judges, conduct their discourse according to particular conventions. These conventions determine which meanings are legitimate. The process is identical whether the setting is the New Criticism or a courtroom. While these conventions operate beneath the surface of the discourse, they identify the arguments that count within that discourse as rational and as meaningful.

On a very different level, however, this pragmatic view of meaning and of interpretation reinforces already pervasive doubts about our ability to challenge existing distributions of power.[31] If the interpretive community determines what counts as meaningful speech (as surely on one level it must be) real questions arise as to the space available to those who wish to subvert traditional distributions of power from within. To move beyond accepted conventions of meaning is to risk exclusion.

While superficially very different, the account of associative obligations which underpins Dworkin's account of political and legal obligations leads to many of the same questions. Eschewing Fishian pragmatics in favour of a critical examination[32] of a variety of social practices, Dworkin seeks to persuade us that practices such as these have their own interior logic and rhythm. Among friends, within armies, even within orchestras, interpersonal obligations arise between members if certain conditions are met. Paramount among these conditions, Dworkin tells us, is an assumption that the practices of the group reflect equal concern for each of the members of the group.[33] In this way, Dworkin seeks to avoid the crass bondage to the status quo that some critics suggest characterises Fishian pragmatics, while still developing an image of community that possesses sufficient *gravitas* to provide legitimation for contemporary social practices.

Here, however, a very different problem emerges. In relying upon social practices and upon the rather mysterious idea of the 'group's assumption'[34] Dworkin's account inadvertently calls both the nature of community and that of collective assumptions into question. If political obligations arise where community members **assume** that communal practices reflect a defensible conception of equality, we need to understand whose speech counts within those practices. All too often, that 'assumption' merely enables the powerful to inscribe[35] their interpretation upon the bodies (and minds) of those whom that community understands to be, for whatever reason, other. Communal assumptions are always fraught with peril. Words such as community all too often conceal difference, reject otherness, and reinstate hierarchy under the name of equality.[36] Most of our communities (most of the time at least) understand themselves as such through multiple processes of inclusion and of exclusion. Often it seems that people cannot understand themselves as a community at all except by reference to those whom they exclude; to those whom they perceive as other. Equally of course, as Dworkin's own examples make clear, the relationships within many of these same communities remain unable to transcend the role definitions to which they subscribe. While Dworkin attempts to delineate an egalitarian community through the 'group's assumption'[37] that its practices value each member equally,[38] his

example, that of an 'egalitarian' patriarchal family, reinstates multiple
levels of exclusion even while purporting to be inclusive and to value each
of its members as equals.[39] Its assumptions regarding the daughter from
whom 'equal concern' requires submission to her father's will in all things,
are assumptions which both expect her to remain voiceless and identify her
silence as speech.[40] I can only repeat what I have elaborated upon
elsewhere. Groups do not assume. Neither do they speak. Rather, those
who speak for those groups (whether with or without the consent of their
members) assume, and their assumptions are identified as the assumptions
of the group.

If Dworkinian community founders upon his failure to attend
sufficiently carefully to the dynamics of power, and, in particular, to the
dynamics of collective assumptions, that offered by Fish fares little better.
If, as Fish has suggested, 'interpretive communities are no more than sets
of institutional practices',[41] and if those practices themselves are
profoundly implicated in existing distributions of power and authority,[42]
they seem unlikely agents of change.[43] If he is right, at best, we
simultaneously act within and against existing practices and, at our most
successful, are able to nudge them this way or that. While Neurath's image
of a sailor rebuilding her boat at sea remains a potent metaphor for change
and renewal under conditions of uncertainty, such desperate and hasty
repairs are unlikely to yield more than cosmetic improvement. Unless the
lineaments of the present are faithfully replicated, the renewal seems likely
to fail at the point it is most urgently needed. While

> those practices are continually being transformed by the very work that they
> do, the transformed practice identifies itself and tells its story in relation to
> general purposes and goals that have survived and formed the basis of a
> continuity.[44]

Their transformation cannot escape its historicity. Its bondage to the past
and to the distributions of power forged in the struggles of the past
remains.

Despite the bleakness of this image, it is in this feature, I believe, that
Fish's account has its truest application to law. Like the other interpretive
communities of which Fish speaks, law cannot escape its historicity, its
bondage to precedent and, though less often acknowledged, to power.
When it moves beyond those (as upon occasion it must) it is most open to
challenge and to attack. The virulence of the attack upon the Australian

High Court by assorted state governments in the wake first of *Mabo*[45] and subsequently of *Wik*[46] is a measure of law's bondage to both. The rhetoric of betrayal deployed with increasing panic by various interest groups, mining companies and cattlemen's associations being notable among them, is increasing in virulence and in its insistence upon drawing the lines of community in particular ways. The Aboriginal people are again 'other' to the Australia which is represented by these interests and which, having proclaimed itself the injured party, is now pursuing political redress. The rhetoric used is specifically a rhetoric of equality. The successive judgments in *Mabo* and in *Wik*, have become, for Australia, contested terrain. This terrain is akin to that which, in the United States, was captured first by *Brown v The Board of Education*, and subsequently by *Roe v Wade*.[47] Change and growth are always frightening, and never more frightening than when they manifest themselves within a canonical set of texts such as those identified with the law.

The transformative moment, that moment at which we struggle to escape the tangled web of the past, in much the same way the moth struggles to escape the cocoon of its larvaehood, is always already a failure. If we emerge as moths, we emerge within the charnel house of existing structures of power and authority. Like the moth that struggles out of its chrysalis only to find itself trapped within a jar too small to allow its wings to expand fully, we struggle to fly, but are unable. The freedom essential if we are to transform the practices within which we are embedded is precisely the freedom that the general purposes and goals of the past have refused to make available.

Against this background, Rousseau's prophetic assertion that should any within the polity refuse to submit their arbitrary and individual wills to the demands of the general will they might be **forced to be free** acquires renewed force.[48] Like the moth, its impulse to liberation thwarted by crumpled and hardened wings, we can indeed be **forced to be free**. Just as we may release the moth upon the pavement and allow it to struggle step by step up the path to make its way freely within the world,[49] we may also be released, allowed (or forced) to make our way within the world-as-it-is. Dworkinian and Fishian community, it would seem, offers scant hope for anything more.

Both Dworkin and Fish struggle to locate meaning and authority in the social rather than in the textual. Meaning is not a 'given', a property of texts and of authors, but a social phenomena, one which is located within particular communities at particular historical moments. If successful, this gambit enables them to escape the oscillation and instability of the text. Their theories insist that if fixed and certain meaning resides neither within the text-as-artefact nor within the conventions of authorial intent then for the legal enterprise to sustain its legitimacy a 'mother-lode' of meaning and stability must be found. Both Dworkin and Fish have seized upon the image of community as source of meaning and stability. Both scholars acknowledge that if no such source is available, we remain trapped within the infinite regress of textuality. Within this frame of reference, each new sign of textual instability threatens to destabilise the legal enterprise and deprive it of cultural authority.

The Violence of Meaning

Within law, the debates that characterise literary theory seem far more portentous than they could be elsewhere. While the debates of literary theory may (upon occasion at least) momentarily rupture the fabric of the academy, the violence without which law as such could not exist gives these debates a wholly different dimension. As Robert Cover recognised, the violence of law sets judicial interpretation utterly apart.

> In this [judges] are different from poets, from critics, from artists. It will not do to insist on the violence of strong poetry, and strong poets. Even the violence of weak judges is utterly real – a naive but immediate reality, in need of no interpretation, no critic to reveal it. Every prisoner displays its mark. Whether or not the violence of judges is justified is not now the point – only that it exists in fact and differs from the violence that exists in literature or in the metaphoric characterizations of literary critics and philosophers. I have written elsewhere that judges of the state are jurispathic – that they kill the diverse legal traditions that compete with the State. Here, however, I am not writing of the jurispathic quality of the office, but of its homicidal potential.[50]

This homicidal potential, a potential that is present even in jurisdictions such as Australia where it remains mere potential, stands as the sign of law.[51] Our understanding of the sign of law is, I believe, incomplete unless we join with Cover in recognising that legal interpretation is simultaneously an interpretation and a performative utterance 'in an institutional setting for violent behavior'.[52] Judges and lawyers never simply interpret; they interpret in order that their words may provide the institutional mandate for acts that would otherwise be criminal under the laws of that same jurisdiction.

I think that it is important to understand legal interpretation in this way. Its justificatory dimension is simultaneously an exculpatory dimension. Property is transferred, rights are finally and authoritatively determined (subject to any appeal) through judgment. The relations determined by law are the antithesis of voluntary contractual transactions. They are takings, pure and simple, but they are takings done under colour of right.

There is another dimension as well. If the act of judgment gives the warrant and colour of authority to deeds which, absent that act, would be criminal, the act of judgment must (particularly if it moves beyond the routine and the predictable) ultimately be justified. Here, the violence is submerged beneath the surface of the text, has rhetorical force, not actual force. Today, justification is, perhaps more than ever, open to analysis and scrutiny. If, in the not so distant past, it spoke primarily to the legal community, and its success or failure was known primarily through the mechanism of legal texts, that is no longer the case. In Australia, as the High Court ventures beyond the secure harbour of a but lately departed formalism,[53] no less a personage than the former Queensland Attorney-General has, according to the *Courier Mail*, 'warned' judges that they have a duty *'to consider the effects of their decisions on the justice system and the community'*.[54] As the Attorney General is reported to have said:

> It is not evident that in applying high principles the courts have had appropriate regard to all of the practical consequences of the decisions for the community.[55]

In this recasting of the political, a crude and unsophisticated version of Dworkin's insistence that even a 'best interpretation' will be rejected by integrity if it would 'take the community by surprise' is emerging.[56] I spoke earlier in this chapter of the profoundly ambiguous trope 'community' and, in particular, of the patterns of inclusion and exclusion implicit in that too easy rendering. Here, perhaps, as we struggle to understand what speaking as a judge can mean for us, now, it is important to consider the symbolic dimension of the relationship between judge and community. In Dworkin's text, the tension between the 'understandings'[57] of the community and the 'best interpretation'[58] which the judge can offer is palpable. Nothing in this passage helps us understand the relationship between that particular judge and the best interpretation she can offer, and the understandings of a community (her community?) which finds that interpretation unthinkable. Dworkin's figure of integrity excludes the judge from the community that she judges. Were she not excluded, she would be taken aback by her own judgment, find it beyond her comprehension.[59] Nothing Dworkin tells us enables us to come close to guessing where his mythic judge Hercules[60] is situated, where his community is to be found, although that, perhaps, is the meaning of the image. If the sign of Hercules is a sign of exclusion, of being outside all community (beyond that, perhaps, formed by sitting judges, a sort of community of the bench)[61] how are we, as ordinary women and men, to judge those whose task it is to give judgment among us.[62]

The Ethics of Judgment

If Derrida and Cover insist upon the violence of law and of the giving of judgment, theirs is only one way of approaching these texts and the acts for which they seek to provide the justification. James Boyd White suggests that:

> we can see text-making-writing and talking-as a kind of action itself, and thus within the field of ethics; and, conversely, that we can see an important part of the meaning of a text as lying in the ethical action it performs.[63]

For White, the giving of judgment is an ethical action on, not one, but two distinct dimensions:

> Obviously, the judgment or result reached by the court – the resolution of the case–is a form of ethical action, subject to ethical judgment. But can we also see the opinion, the text in which the judge explains that judgment, as a form of ethical action too, in some sense independent of the result?[64]

Here, I want to relate White's remarks to arguments put earlier about the structure of judicial proceedings. When I spoke of that structure, I emphasised the movement from an institutionally mandated openness to persuasion by others to an equally institutionally mandated attempt to persuade others. Within this dynamic, the result of which White speaks, is both embedded in the act of judgment and distinct from it. White insists, quite correctly, that the result is an ethical act. Here I want to focus upon the fact that it is simultaneously an ethical act in White's sense, an act that is subject to ethical judgments, and an act of violence. That ethical judgment will fix, in the end, upon whether the violence that has been authorised can be justified or whether it is beyond the limits we believe to be acceptable. Something else is interesting as well. The ethical action of which White speaks is, like the rhetorical justification which follows it, on another level, less an act than a text. As text, it sets the bureaucratic machinery responsible for executing the orders of the court into motion. The ethical significance attaches to the outcome. The act of judgment may, in this sense, be compared to a physical act, to the pulling of a lever, perhaps (or a trigger). What can we say of the actions between text and consequence, those of bailiffs, warders, and even executioners? Are we willing to say that these are actions of no ethical significance? If we are, what, if anything, does this fact say about us as a community, indeed, what could possibly be of ethical significance if actions such as these are not?[65] What I want to interrogate here is another aspect of the idea of obligations of role, this time in a more familiar, if more disturbing form. As we saw earlier in this chapter, Dworkin wants to use the idea of associative obligations (aka 'obligations of role') to legitimate the legal and political machinery of the modern nation state. Here, we see role based obligations at work in a very particular form, in calling forth (and legitimating) the actions of the bailiffs and warders who carry out the terms of the judgment.

When we move from the act of judgment to the text that purports to legitimate that act, while it may be possible to judge the text in ethical terms,[66] I am not certain that it is appropriate. White, in keeping with the overall tenor of his theorising, speaks of the community the text establishes with those who read it. He speaks as well of questions of tone and voice, modes of address, patterns of inclusion and exclusion, drawing, inter alia, upon Lincoln's Gettysburg Address. I spoke earlier of the rhetorical function of the written judgment and I want now to return to that aspect and to discuss it a little further.

Historically, written judgments within the common law tradition evolved within the context of very particular traditions. Some of the earliest written records of judgment, those of the Year Book cases, do not even record the outcome. Typically, these early reports summarise the writs and pleadings that were used, and sometimes, where the matter involved an action on the (special) case, the particular facts upon which the plaintiff sought to rely. They are written, not by judges, but by serjeants-at-law attending the court as pupils-at-law. In these early reports only rarely does the justificatory dimension emerge that became the dominant *liet motif* of the common law tradition.[67] Not until the appearance of 'private law reports'[68] in 1537 did the practice of citation and reliance upon authorities became firmly established. In many early reports the text consisted almost exclusively of citation rather than the argumentative form which is now common.[69]

Only as the jurisdiction of the King's (Queen's) Bench matured, did the rhetorical dimension of law acquire a life of its own. The most significant aspect of this transition may be found in Coke's reports. Concerning Coke's reports, Goodman comments:

> Coke's reports were not based on what would now be regarded as accurate reporting, nor do they reveal anything other than a hazy notion of precedent. Rather he used cases for his own purpose. That purpose was defence of the common law. According to Coke, the law which the judges declare is unwritten and immemorial. Precisely because it is native to England, im-memorial custom, it embodies the wisdom of generations, as a result not of philosophical reflection or theorising, but of the accumulations and refine-ments of experience. This is Coke's concept of 'artificial reason': what speaks when the judge declares law is the distilled knowledge of many generations of men, each decision based on the experience of those before and tested by the experience of those after. In accordance with that theory, Coke always purported to 'declare' what the law was because it already existed in nature and therefore had merely to be found. He regarded the common law as the embodiment of reason and coterminous with natural law. Common law was supreme. It followed that in the event of conflict the common law was fundamental and must prevail over any statute which did not conform with common right or reason.[70]

As the importance of the rhetorical dimension of common law method increased, so too did the length and significance of the actual reported cases. What had, in former days, occupied at most the space of half a page stretched out until it covered dozens and later hundreds of pages. This growing rhetorical dimension is of immense importance. It recognises that judgment cannot simply be given, what has been ordered to be done must be justified, explained. In a very particular way, the court has become accountable, and the written judgment evolves within the context of an increasing pressure towards public legitimation. Psychically, it may be that this marks the point in common law history at which role of the courts in foreclosing 'self-help' remedies and private vengeance has been overtaken and finally superseded by its legitimation function. It is no longer enough to secure the 'King's Peace'. Instead, it has become essential to account for what has been done in a way which ensures that the law may be seen to have an identity of its own and a legitimation of its own. The autopoetic dimension of law has emerged.

If even in civil proceedings the acts that are performed are takings done under colour of right, it is no longer enough that the judge[71] is convinced that the outcome can be justified. In her turn, she must justify it to others. This act of prospective justification, which proclaims not only what has been done, but why it had to be done, provides its own ethical dimension, a dimension that reflects our understanding that all exercises of power must be justified.[72]

A central part of the ethical dimension of law is located in the rhetorical and justificatory dimension of the judicial text. For this reason, I am interested less in the community the judicial text establishes with its readers,[73] than its ability to persuade others the outcome is right.[74] It is not simply the parties whom the text must persuade, but a wider constituency, the legal community, both now and in the future. As the act of judgment becomes increasingly politicised (not by the judges but by interest groups with particular agendas), some of these texts must have the capacity to persuade the community at large. What is required is always more than an explanation of how a particular decision was reached. If the text is to be persuasive to this wider constituency, the reasons that it gives must resonate along an ethical as well as a legal continuum. Only where this is the case will it have the capacity to persuade others.

The need for this rhetorical dimension, this act of persuasion, generates its own questions. First, in this context, what are we as a community to make of the practice of some courts[75] to eschew the rhetorical dimension wherever possible? It cannot, I think, be simply that within some juris-dictions the matters before the court seldom involve questions of law. In such cases, the task of any judgment proffered would be to justify the decision in terms of the facts before the court. Here, or so it seems to me, the task of justification is more urgent, more immediate. It cannot be either that the task of justification is too immense, so that whatever decision is reached is beyond justification the moment it is handed down. Surely, in the end the same could be said of any decision, of any court. It cannot even be that the decision turns upon the exercise of discretion, perhaps a broadly drawn discretion, by the trial court. Even in cases where, for an appeal to succeed, the discretion must have been exercised in so egregious a manner, that no reasonable judge could have acted in that way, justification remains possible. Surely, the understanding, among lawyers and litigants, that some aspects of some decisions are, to all intents and purposes, unappealable, suggests to the ordinary person that those decisions are in greater, rather than lesser, need of justification. To justify a decision which, at bottom, turns upon the exercise of discretion, a particular way of interpreting the facts, the judge must justify the habits of mind and character that are both fundamental and utterly beyond justification. She must justify her own performance as a judge, her own intellect, and her own understandings.

Notes

1   Except, of course, in the guise of 'blind justice'. See Berns & Baron, 'Bloody Bones', 138. Baron notes:

> As a child, I remember being profoundly disturbed by the image of blind justice. That sense of disturbance remains today. I had never, in the past questioned why it was that I dislike the image so much. On reflection, I recalled thinking as a child that the woman was maimed, and so, powerless. She had a sword, symbol of authority, of physical power, of violence and even of death. She held aloft scales, symbols of justice, of wisdom, of intellectual power. But she could not see. She was unable to use the sword because she had no eyes. She could not assess what was on the scales, what it was she was weighing, whether she was comparing like or unlike things, because she had no eyes.

2   As we saw in the last chapter, there are cases, *Hegarty v Shine*, for example, where the silences are far more revealing than words.

3   Jones, KB, *Compassionate Authority*, 8.

4   I do not think, in fact, that she is. See Hunter, R, 'Deconstructing the Subjects of Feminism: The Essentialism Debate in Feminist Theory and Practice' (1996) 6 *Australian Feminist Law Journal* 135; Parashar, A, 'Essentialism or Pluralism: The Future of Legal Feminism' (1993) 6 *Canadian Journal of Women and the Law* 328.

5   For an attempt to negotiate these issues see Stacy, H, 'Legal Discourse and the Feminist Political Economy: Moving Beyond Sameness/Difference' (1996) 6 *Australian Feminist Law Journal* 115.

6   What I have described as a new kind of silencing is new only because it is done under the sign woman. But for this, it differs little from the forms of silencing it attempts to challenge: the male universal that denies that it is necessarily both gendered and raced.

7   See Behrendt, L, 'Black Women and the Feminist Movement: Implications for Aboriginal Women in Rights Discourse' (1993) 1 *Australian Feminist Law Journal* 7. And what, in this context, are we to make of a middle-aged white man (Leon Carmen) who could, or so he claims, only speak about the issues which concerned him through the persona of an Aboriginal woman (Wanda Koolmatrie)? On one level, what fiction

is always about, has always been about, is the capacity of the author to enter into the identities of her characters. Is it so different when the work purports to be a memoir, and the author identifies 'herself' as Aboriginal and as a woman in a bizarre (and ultimately self-interested) kind of intellectual cross-dressing? *My Own Sweet Time* the work styles itself, and in this context it is important that we think about the kind of 'speaking as' represented by this and both other recent examples of self-induced 'mistaken identity'. Did Leon Carmen even wish to speak as a woman, specifically, an indigenous woman, or did he wish something very different? His is truly, I believe, a perversion of the representative voice.

8   Stacy, 1.

9   Fish, S, 'Going Down the Anti-Formalist Road' in Fish, S, *Doing What Comes Naturally: Change, Rhetoric and the Practice of Theory in Literary and Legal Studies*, Oxford, Clarendon Press, 1, 31-32.

10   It is equally plausible to substitute 'woman' for Jew (and male for Protestant).

11   Alasdair MacIntyre says of what he terms 'the liberal self': 'The liberal self moves from sphere to sphere compartmentalising its attitudes.' MacIntyre, A, *Whose Justice? Which Rationality*? Notre Dame, Univ of Notre Dame Press, 1988, 345. Subsequently, he suggested that:

> in a society in which preferences, whether in the market or politics or in private life, are assigned the place which they have in a liberal order, power lies with those who are able to determine what the alternatives are to be between which choices will be available. The consumer, the voter, and the individual in general are accorded the right of expressing their preferences for one or more out of the alternatives which they are offered, but the range of possible alternatives is controlled by an elite, and how they are presented is also so controlled. The ruling elites within liberalism are thus bound to value highly competence in the persuasive presentation of alternatives, that is, in the cosmetic arts. So a certain kind of power is assigned a certain kind of authority.

12   Quoted by Cover, R, 'Nomos and Narrative' in Minow, Martha, Michael Ryan & Austin Sarat (eds) *Narrative, Violence, and the Law*, Ann Arbor, Univ of Michigan Press, 1992, 95, 139-140. More generally see 139-144 on the idea of the courts of the state as 'jurispathic', law killing.

13   Cover, 'Violence and the Word', 213. I suspect that Robert Cover would have understood my need for emphasis, and also my acknowledgment that how we deal with this fact about law gives law and legal institutions whatever legitimacy they have.

14   Legal positivism attempts to relocate responsibility for judgment from the individual giving judgment to a tyrannical and external 'law'. Robert Cover spoke of the judicial conscience as an 'artful dodger'. Cover, *Justice Accused*, 210.

15   Posner, R, 'Legal Reasoning From the Top Down and From the Bottom Up: The Question of Unenumerated Constitutional Rights' 59 Univ of Chicago Law Review 433, 435 (1992).

16   In Australia, in the recent past, as novel cases make their way before the courts and judgment is duly handed down, politicians clamour for judges to eschew 'judicial lawmaking'. Most recently, the Premier of Queensland has demanded a 'court' chosen by state governments, to judge the High Court. The underlying assumption is worth spelling out. So long as the court decides in a way that does not disturb the political

status quo, its decision making is legitimate. It becomes illegitimate precisely at the point at which it has measurable consequences. The quarrel is not with the legal process, but with the political outcome. On this accounting, the most important distinction between the 'legal' and the 'political' lies in the potential impact of a decision. Where the impact of a decision is limited and does not obviously affect a wider range of stakeholders than the immediate parties and others in like positions, it is properly legal. Where, on the other hand, the impact of a particular decision is not constrained in this way, it is political, and, by definition, one which the courts ought not to make. The determination is not a legal matter, indeed the legal reasoning is normally irrelevant to the perception.

17   I owe this turn of phrase to a conversation with Bob Moles of the Australian National University. While he used the phrase explicitly to refer to the work of Ronald Dworkin, for me this phrase resonates much more deeply.

18   This is, I think, one of the subtle chains binding authors to their texts, within law at least. One may wish to speculate about the impact of electronic publishing upon this particular kind of authority.

19   This seems to me very important. Ordinary authors may cast their texts upon the waters but, in some sense at least, during their lifetimes they can always insist **that** was not what they meant. In jurisprudence, the Fish-Dworkin debate, stretching on interminably in legal and literary journals, is a well known exemplar of the corrective impulse. This sort of debate, is, however, profoundly at variance with the judicial office. In a sense the language of law is a language founded upon the pretence that meaning is fixed and certain, that there is a 'thing' which can be identified as the *ratio* of any particular case, that all else is purely *obiter*. While even the most relentlessly positivist account allows for modification and correction over time, both are founded upon the tacit assumption that the text remains certain and stable. Errors within the text, and even errors in the reasoning, can be corrected, but the text itself remains stable, knowable.

20   This includes, and it should go without saying, even the members of the highest court in each jurisdiction. By their texts they are and shall be judged.

21   Charvet, J, *The Social Problem in the Philosophy of Rousseau*, London, Cambridge Univ. Press, 1974 discusses this and associated difficulties at length. See also, Berns, *Add Woman and Stir*. Charvet suggests that for Rousseau relationships were only possible to the extent that he found in those around him a reflection of himself and his understanding of that self. Thus, a community devoid of otherness might be forged.

22   In law, in particular, we have been, quite literally **driven** to acknowledge. Only as a last resort do we acknowledge that meaning is not a property of individual texts.

23   Sandel, M, *Liberalism and the Limits of Justice*, Cambridge, Cambridge University Press, 1982.

24   Michaelman, FI, 'Foreword: Traces of Self-Government' 100 *Harv LR* 4 (1986), 'Law's Republic' 97 *Yale LJ* 1493 (1988); Sherry, S, 'Civic Virtue and the Feminine Voice in Constitutional Adjudication' 72 *Virginia LR* 543 (1986).

25   'Speaking as' is difficult here, both because the role is formally open to all who have attained a certain level of qualification (a screen coarse enough to let some women through) and because given the traditions associated with the judicial role one wonders if woman/judge is not rather like Leon/Wanda: the 'agency' of the latter becoming

'tainted' by its appropriation by the former. Who is it that is entitled to judge the legitimacy of 'speaking as' in this context?

26   I explicitly want to identify the 'audience' for which the judge writes as her constituency, not in the sense that she is chosen by it, not even in the sense that she is somehow a representative of it, but in the sense that she is somehow accountable to that 'audience', both for her judgment and for the justification which she is able to offer.

27   In many ways, as his examples (being a patriarchal family and an army) make clear, his conception might better and more accurately be described as 'neo-feudal', as an attempt to superimpose the bonds of obligation characteristic of feudal communities upon the nation state of late modernity. In this aspect of his work he shares a surprising kinship with Roberto Unger. See Unger, R, *Knowledge and Politics & Passion: An Essay in Personality*, New York, The Free Press, 1984. Both seek to escape the limitations of the liberal vision to which they remain shackled by invoking pre-liberal images, of, in the case of Dworkin, community, and in the case of Unger, personality and epistemology. In both cases, I believe, they cannot escape the darker side of those pre-liberal visions, and the oppression and exclusion which were an inherent part of pre-liberal traditions. See also, MacIntyre, *Whose Justice? Which Rationality?* While both Unger and MacIntyre seem largely unaware of the darker sides of their visions, Dworkin, I think, is uncomfortably aware of the 'dark side' and rather unpleasant ancestry of his obligations of role, newly christened associative obligations in a not altogether successful sanitation exercise.

28   His magnum opus is, after all, *Law's Empire*, and he has described judges as the princes of law's empire. We might do well to ponder the lure of imperial imagery in a work purporting to legitimate law as it is understood in Western constitutional democracies.

29   While I acknowledge Dworkin's attempt to give these 'obligations of role' critical bite, in that, for obligations to be sustained structure of the roles and the relationship between them must be compared to an ideal typical form of the same roles, I have argued at length elsewhere that Dworkin's unexamined notion of the 'group's assumption' and his total failure to acknowledge the issues of voice and silencing implicit in group assumptions makes it clear that this attempt is less than successful. See Berns, 'Integrity & Justice' for a detailed discussion of this issue. See also Berns, *Add Woman and Stir*.

30   A conventional example is the 'new critics'.

31   See West, RL, 'Adjudication is not Interpretation'. While, as I have argued elsewhere, I believe some aspects of West's critique to be somewhat over-stated, the question of how one mounts any challenge to the status quo is left dangling in Fish's work. See Berns, *Concise Jurisprudence*, 60-74.

32   Dworkin's methodology exhorts us to identify 'ideal-typical' forms of these familiar practices and use these ideal-typical forms to criticise existing practices. See *Law's Empire*, 195-206.

33   While he carefully eschews any universal (or even universalisable) claim for his account of equality, he argues at length that he believes equality of resources to be the best account available of the principles which underlie the political economy of the United States.

34   In some ways this notion is disturbingly parallel to Rousseau's much earlier account of the 'general will' and has almost identical totalitarian potential.

35   That this inscription is of both the blood and flesh let there be no mistake. The lines of power and authority are inevitably mapped upon the bodies of those who are, for whatever reason, other.

36   More mysterious still, Dworkin is at pains to insist that his conception of equality is compatible with hierarchy, that a community can be egalitarian in the special sense his thesis requires while still being hierarchically ordered, even quite rigidly hierarchically ordered in the way an army is (or a patriarchal family).

37   Collective assumptions are, it seems to me, fraught with peril. All too often, what any group 'assumes' is determined by the assumptions of its most powerful members. The weak, the marginalised, those who are in certain ways other are more likely to be the 'subject matter' of collective assumptions than they are to be active and equal participants in their construction.

38   It may be that in the notion of a collective assumption Dworkin is attempting to rehabilitate utilitarian insights, and, in particular, those which flowed from a notion of the 'common good'. It is interesting to note that his emphasis upon the need for both equal concern and equal respect, the former being linked to welfare and the latter to autonomy, has been replaced by an expanded notion of equal concern which downplays the place of autonomy within the communities which collectively comprise the nation state. It is but a small step from this notion of equality of concern to a reimagined utilitarianism.

39   See Berns, SS, 'Integrity and Justice or When is Injustice Mandated by Integrity?' (1991) 18 *Melb Univ LR* 258. Reliance upon community to stabilise language and obligation is a profoundly conservative move, and one which denies the impulse to justice. His other examples are an army and an orchestra (in which the group exceeds the sum of its parts but lacks a conductor).

40   No contractarian, Dworkin does not concern himself with consent.

41   Fish, S, 'Change' in Fish, S, *Doing What Comes Naturally: Change, Rhetoric and the Practice of Theory in Literary and Legal Studies*, Oxford, Clarendon, 1989, 141, 153.

42   They could hardly be otherwise, given that they are determinative of both.

43   And here, it seems to me we are truly bound to what is. Institutional practices have a life of their own. I do not deny that they can and do change, sometimes with surprising vigour and speed. Many of these changes, even those which appear most radical, do more to shore up the status quo than to lead to real change. In this context I cannot help but heed the sombre warning implicit in Derrick Bell's analysis of *Brown v Board of Education* and of the civil rights movement to which it gave birth. If, as Bell suggests, the 'impetus towards justice' was, in fact an impetus towards redressing a negative image which was damaging American prospects in an international order increasingly unsympathetic to American apartheid, it was simply another version of shoring up the status quo. See Bell, D, Chapter 2: 'The Benefits to Whites of Civil Rights Litigation', *And We are Not Saved*, New York, Basic Books, 1987, 51-74.

44   Fish, 'Change', 153.

45   *Mabo and Ors v Queensland (No 2)*.

46   *Wik Peoples v Queensland, Thayorre Peoples v Queensland*.

47   *Brown v Board of Education* 347 US 483 (1954); *Roe v Wade* 410 US 113 (1973).

48   Rousseau, *The Social Contract*.
49   I am haunted by Chief Justice Rhenquist's description of the world of a severely battered child as 'the free world'. If what Joshua found was freedom, for many of us there is no alternative to meekly accepting our chains. *DeShaney v Winnebago Soc Serv* 489 US 103 Led 2d 249 (1989).
50   Cover, 'Violence and the Word', 213-214.
51   Jacques Derrida's comments on the death penalty are significant. According to Derrida:

> Well, when one tackles the death penalty, one doesn't dispute one penalty among others but law itself in its origin, in its very order. If the origin of law is a violent positioning, the latter manifests itself in the purest fashion when violence is absolute... If the legal system fully manifests itself in the possibility of the death penalty, to abolish the penalty is not to touch upon one dispositif among others, it is to disavow the very principle of law. And that is to confirm, says Benjamin, that there is something "rotten" at the heart of law. The death penalty bears witness, it must bear witness, to the fact that law is a violence contrary to nature.

Derrida, J, 'Force of Law: The "Mystical Foundation of Authority"', 42.
52   Cover, 'Violence and the Word', 216, n 24.
53   Sir Owen Dixon, considered one of the greatest of the High Court judges, insisted that the only appropriate form of judicial interpretation had its roots in 'the safe harbour' of a 'strict legalism'. The beauty of formalism was, of course, not that the decisions it legitimated were any less interpretations or, indeed, any less political, but that this fact about them was concealed by the rhetoric of rule application.
54   The *Courier Mail*, Saturday, Feb 8, 1997, 8.
55   The *Courier Mail*, Saturday, Feb 8, 1997, 8. The alternative to high principle was, perhaps fortunately, not spelled out.
56   Dworkin, RM, *Law's Empire*, 402. See Berns, SS, 'Integrity and Justice'.
57   Those scary 'collective assumptions' again... assumptions rooted in tradition and in a desire to recapture a but lately vanished sense of belonging, of rootedness. We must, it seems to me, be permanently on our guard against the power of assumptions of this kind, a power born out of fear of the unknown and a desire to ensure against it.
58   How best, one wishes to ask:– truest, or most accurate, or most consonant with the judge's understandings of justice, or ...
59   Perhaps she is, perhaps it is this sense of being taken aback, which marks the relationship between the judge and the judgment which she finds herself offering and calls forth the demand for justification. Today the judge feels compelled to offer a written judgment in only a minority of cases. For the rest, justification is assumed, not attempted.
60   Berns, SS, 'Hercules, Hermes and Senator Smith: The Symbolic Structure of Law's Empire' (1988) 12 *Bulletin of the Australian Society of Legal Philosophy* 35 talks about the 'subject position' of Hercules and about the symbolic structure of Dworkin's work.
61   A community remarkably close, one might think, to that of Fishian pragmatics.
62   It is, I believe, not only our right but also our obligation to judge them. This as well is part of the meaning of accountability. Surely for legitimation to be possible this kind of accountability most become real.

63   White, JB, 'The Ethics of Meaning' in Turner, JN & P Williams (eds) *The Happy Couple: Law and Literature*, Sydney, Federation Press, 1994, 269, 270.

64   White, 'The Ethics of Meaning', 271.

65   This is another aspect of the separation of word and deed to which Cover alludes in 'Violence and the Word', 216-217. Cover insists at 222 that within the act of interpretation itself, attention is necessarily paid to the conditions of effective domination.

66   I note a profound similarity to Martha Minow's insistence that the written judgment ought (surely an 'ethical ought') to explain how and why that decision was reached.

67   In a number of respects, they represented a halfway house between embryonic legal texts for the training of new recruits and judgments in the modern sense. According to Goodman the Yearbooks

> consisted of short verbatim reports of significant arguments and rulings in recent court cases noted by those who were present and grouped by year or session. Initially they were personal; compiled by individual lawyers who wished to have a record of recent pleadings. By 1400 personal compilations gave way to uniform, practical collections of recent pleadings and by 1520 they began to appear in print.

Goodman, E, *The Origins of the Western Legal Tradition: From Thales to the Tudors*, Sydney, The Federation Press, 1995, 244. See Berman, HJ, *Law & Revolution: The Formation of the Western Legal Tradition*, Cambridge, Harvard University Press, 1983, 149. Berman suggests that the style of the Yearbooks 'was probably derived from student notes of arguments in cases in the king's courts'.

68   These are more commonly termed the 'nominate' reports, each bearing, for convenience, the name of its chief compiler.

69   Goodman, *Western Legal Tradition*, notes at 244-5 that it was not until Sir Edward Coke's reports began to appear in 1600 that the 'mystique' of the common law began to emerge, and with it the notion of 'artificial reason' as opposed to natural reason.

70   Goodman, 245.

71   In Australia, unlike the United States, in civil proceedings it is typically the judge sitting both as trier of fact and trier of law.

72 ' The point at which that emerges perhaps marks the full replacement of custom by common law.

73   I do not dispute its importance in some circumstances. Some judicial texts lay bare an entire way of looking at the world and the relationships within that world view.

74   It may be that it comes to the same thing, that the sort of text which he suggests has the capacity to establish community with different constituencies is also that text whose rhetorical capacity is most fully developed, but I do not think that this is necessarily the case.

75   In Australia, it is unusual for Family Court judges to hand down written judgments, and some judges prefer not to do so unless compelled by the nature of the matter before them.

8   Judgment as Rhetoric

Introduction

My insistence upon the rhetoricity[1] of law, and my belief that whatever legitimacy is possible for adjudication as process lies in its success or failure specifically as rhetoric I understand to be unfashionable, at least in comparison to accounts offering an ostensibly more 'principled' foundation for the judicial enterprise. Rhetoric has had a bad press lately. Either it is thought of as a poor (and somewhat shady) cousin to the noble enterprise of philosophy, or, worse yet, it is deemed to be an unprincipled form of casuistry in which the form is routinely mistaken for the substance. The bad press which rhetoric has received only deepens my belief that it is central to the legitimacy of the judicial process and, even more, central to coming to terms with what it means to speak as a judge.[2] Stanley Fish speaks of the symbiotic relationship between rhetoric's bad press and its 'negative polarity'. Fish emphasises:

> the binary oppositions in relation to which rhetoric has received its definition... Underlying this... are three basic oppositions: first, between a truth that exists independently of all perspectives and points of view and the many truths that emerge and seem perspicuous when a particular perspective or point of view has been established and is in force; second, an opposition between true knowledge, which is knowledge as it exists apart from any and all systems of belief, and the knowledge, which because it flows from some or other system of belief, is incomplete and partial (in the sense of biased); and third, an opposition between a self or consciousness that is turned outward in an effort to apprehend and attach itself to truth and true knowledge and a self or consciousness that is turned inward in the direction of its own prejudices, which, far from being transcended, continue to inform its every work and action. Each of these oppositions is attached in turn to an opposition between two kinds of language: on the one hand, language that faithfully reflects or reports on matters of fact ... and on the other hand, language that is infected by partisan agendas and desires, and therefore colors and distorts the facts which it purports to reflect. It is use of the second kind of language that makes one a rhetorician, while adherence to the first kind makes one a seeker after truth and an objective observer of the way things are. It is this distinction that

157

... underwrites the claims of science to be a privileged form of discourse because it has recourse to a "neutral observation language", a language uninflected by any mediating discourse or preconceptions; and it is the same distinction that informs Aristotle's observation... that "nobody uses fine language when teaching geometry." The language of geometry – of formal rules with no substantive content – is contrasted by Aristotle to all those languages that are intended only to "charm the hearer", the languages of manipulation, deception, and self consciously deployed strategy.[3]

In earlier chapters, the force and the violence inescapable in law were emphasised. Yet even if, as Cover insists, judges ultimately *deal* in pain and death, the manner of that dealing both begins and ends in rhetoric. The link between violence and rhetoric, and in particular the way in which rhetoric is called upon to provide both the justification for violence and the warrant to commit it under colour of right, holds the key to legitimation. In what follows, I seek to establish that, to the extent that justification is possible, the process of law becomes its own justification.

More conventional (and possibly more palatable) views seek either to legitimate the process of law by something external to its own workings, or to demonstrate that legitimation as such is neither possible nor necessary.[4] If one accepts, as do Hart and others, a model of rules and of rule application as the key to law, whatever need for legitimation may arise, it arises not at the level of law but at the level of the social/political structures which law sustains.[5] On this account, with rule application the order of the day, questions of legitimacy are always placed just outside the frame of legal discourse.[6]

Rights based accounts, such as that of Ronald Dworkin, only partially abandon this self-referentiality. Of the nature of law Dworkin says:

Our concept of law ties law to the present justification of coercive force and so ties law to adjudication: law is a matter of rights tenable in court. This makes the content of law sensitive to different kinds of institutional constraints, special to judges, that are not necessarily constraints for other officials or institutions. When judges interpret legal practice as a whole, they find reasons of different sorts, specifically applying to judges, why they should *not* declare as present law the most coherent account of the substantive decisions of that practice...[7]

A little later he offers an explanation of the nature of some of those reasons and of the relationship between the various components of 'law-as-integrity': justice, fairness, and procedural due process.

> Justice... is a matter of the right outcome of the political system: the right distribution of goods, opportunities, and other resources. Fairness is a matter of the right structure for that system, the structure that distributes influence over political decisions in the right way. Procedural due process is a matter of the right procedures for enforcing rules and regulations the system has produced. Legislative supremacy, which obliges Hercules to give effect to statutes even when these produce substantive incoherence, is a matter of fairness because it protects the power of the majority to make the law it wants. Strict doctrines of precedent, the practices of legislative history, and local priority are largely, though in different ways, matters of procedural due process because they encourage citizens to rely on doctrinal pronouncements and assumptions that it would be wrong to betray in judging them after the fact.[8]

The structures of legality coalesce to trump any latent impulse towards justice that might linger within law-as-it-is. Always, the pressure is towards the status quo, towards the reinforcement of what is. The 'right' outcome, the 'right' distribution of the basic social goods made available by the political system, lies beyond law.[9] If, from time to time, questions of justice breach the walls of law's empire,[10] most of the time they are repelled by the forces of legality that sustain the status quo. For Dworkin, as for Hart, while questions of justice form part of the background to law and to the institutions of legality, they are relevant at the level of the social and political background to the legal regime and not specifically within the context of the regime itself.

Unlike Hart, however, Dworkin does not believe that remitting questions of justice to the background structure also remits the necessity for justification. While the call to justice is trumped by the rituals of legality, and while the pull of the status quo ensures that law-as-it-is can only be challenged interstitially, legality has its own tests for legitimacy.[11] Dworkin insists that questions of fairness and of procedural due process, questions that are internal to law rather than external to it, provide a very different basis for justification. Law-as-integrity is, therefore, concerned to strike the 'right' balance between justice, fairness and procedural due process. Because the latter two are (at least in the particular context in which they are used) distinctively legal virtues[12] while the former is a political rather than a legal virtue, that balance is one in which the latter two must be given priority.

I, however, want to approach the question of legitimation through the rhetoricity of law. Law's legitimacy can neither be remitted to the processes through which it is generated, as Hart would have it, nor be romanticised as an imperial juggling act in which the 'right balance' between justice, fairness and procedural due process is somehow, and for the present moment, struck.[13] In earlier chapters I emphasised the phases through which this rhetoricity moves. The movement from being, by definition, open to persuasion by others to being, by definition, required to give reasons (and therefore, by implication, to give such reasons as are capable of persuading others) constitutes law's rhetorical shift.

Within the rhetorical shift, the art of interpretation is paramount, and paramount in a way that we have yet to explore in any detail. The literature on the interpretive moment in adjudication focuses, perhaps understandably, upon the written judgment and upon the interpretation of past judicial texts and the way in which these are woven together to answer the needs of the moment and in the process to create a new judicial text.[14] Yet this is to disregard the hearing itself, and, in particular, to disregard the fact that there is no moment within the rhetorical structure of the trial[15] which does not involve interpretation. It is also to disregard the fact that the trial is an essentially oral and visual event, a performance whose meaning is written both in the souls and upon the flesh of those who come before the law. The trial constitutes a text in the process of becoming. Our understanding of the words that are spoken is altered by the visual context in which those words are embedded. How that text subsequently, and through the intervention of multiple interpreters, becomes the appellate decision beloved of jurisprudence, is another and very different story.

During the balance of this chapter, I will attempt to make out three distinct claims about the nature of law and the nature of legal interpretation. The first is my general claim for the rhetoricity of law and the reasons I believe this fact about law to be central to our understandings of legality. The second is constituted by a set of understandings concerning interpretation and concerning the role of interpretation in constituting legality. The third, and most important, is the moral claim to which I alluded in earlier chapters. Whatever legitimacy and majesty our legal system possesses is to be found specifically in its rhetoricity, in the Janus faced obligation of the judge to both be open to persuasion by others and to seek to persuade others. It is this second claim that, intuitively, seems most likely to be imperilled by the debates over meaning and textuality central to post-structuralist thought. I would insist, however, that in reality, it is this context which most fully realises the importance of rhetoric as a source of meaning and authority.[16] I shall begin by addressing my general claim for the rhetoricity of law.

The Rhetoricity of Law

In a work which is largely about adjudication and about the role of the trial in constituting our understandings of legality,[17] an emphasis upon those features of the legal landscape, such as rhetoric, which seem matters of the lawyer's craft rather than of any more exalted realm of legality or morality may seem banal. Some might suggest that is even perverse, particularly given the bad press rhetoric typically enjoys. It is not. I am, in this claim at least, certain of my ground. I want, at the outset, to make it very clear what I am doing in making this claim and to demonstrate precisely how I seek to reposition the debates over legal interpretation.

Jurisprudence has, for some time now, been bewitched by the written judicial text.[18] Since the emergence of the chain novel[19] as a surrogate for the process of judicial interpretation, concern has centred upon the ways in which legality maintains its historicity.[20] We need to be reassured that each new interpretation represents a continuation of what has gone before, a new chapter in an ongoing story with each successive author struggling to make it the best story it can be.[21] As a consequence, it sometimes seems as if the ideal-typical form of the judicial text is as an emanation of that past: for Dworkin, the legislative and judicial texts which have become part of the 'chain novel' of law.[22]

I want to redirect focus, invite attention to the trial as process, and specifically, as a process which is designed to produce (and invariably does produce) particular sorts of concrete outcomes in the world.[23] Whereas, for Dworkin, the critical questions seemed to be about the process by which the law of a particular jurisdiction can be made to approximate the ideal-typical form for that culture and jurisdiction, I am interested in a rather different question. I am interested in how all of the different texts that come together to create the event we identify (after the fact) as a particular proceeding attain the collective weight essential to impel the rhetorical shift, the process by which meaning brings forth judgment.[24] As should be clear, I read the term 'text' broadly. Every trial is made up of a multitude of texts. As I understand the idea of text and textuality, the story told by a plaintiff or defendant, the argument put by counsel, are texts in the same way that the written judgment is a text.[25] Like the judgment, they are simultaneously 'products' of interpretation and 'objects' awaiting interpretation by others.[26] Collectively, these 'performance texts' impel the rhetorical shift, force judgment. The moment comes when no testimony remains to be given; no argument remains to be put. All is in the balance, awaiting judgment. If the judge is to be 'properly judicial' she has no alternative but to act.[27]

Yet, as I understand the legal process, neither the texts that come together in every legal proceeding nor the judgment that they call forth could ever be either simple or unitary. First, these texts are of different sorts, weigh in the process of the trial at different levels and for different purposes. Some of them obey the logic of adjectival law;[28] fact cluster tumbling upon fact cluster, as the gates open and then snap shut once again. This can be admitted; that cannot. That is hearsay; this is true evidence,[29] admissible evidence. This story can be told, and heard; that is immaterial.[30] In a civil matter, in Australia, where the judge is simultaneously trier of fact and trier of law, the multiple levels of meaning and truth within the process sometimes seem to collapse into one another. When this occurs, the line between fact and law,[31] ostensibly maintained in a jury trial by the separation of the roles of judge and jury, blurs slightly.

Still more, while these texts obey an interior logic or order of their own, that is not the same as to say that they are ultimately obedient to any set of overarching principles capable of achieving synthesis among contradictory local perspectives. Rather, they are likely at best to achieve a 'for-the-time-being accommodation', and acknowledgment that such an accommodation is the best that can be hoped for (at least for so long as recourse to violence to enforce compliance with one or another set of more local perspectives remains unthinkable).[32] About the nature of this accommodation and about the relationship between the belief structures (together with the truth claims implicit in them) of local communities and those of the contemporary nation state, Robert Cover had this to say:

> The universalist virtues that we have come to identify with modern liberalism, the broad principles of our law, are essentially system-maintaining "weak" forces. They are virtues that are justified by the need to ensure the *coexistence*

of worlds of strong normative meaning. These "strong" forces...*create* the normative worlds in which law is predominantly a system of meaning rather than an imposition of force...

[This] suggest[s] two corresponding ideal-typical patterns of combining corpus, discourse, and interpersonal commitment to form a *nomos*. The first such pattern... I shall call "paideic," because the term suggests: (1) a common body of precept and narrative, (2) a common and personal way of being educated into this corpus, and (3) a sense of direction or growth that is constituted as the individual and his community work out the implications of their law... Discourse is initiatory, celebratory, expressive, and performative, rather than critical and analytic. Interpersonal commitments are characterised by reciprocal acknowledgment, the recognition that individuals have particular needs and strong obligations to render person-specific responses....

The second ideal-typical pattern, which finds its fullest expression in the civil community, is "world maintaining". I shall call it "imperial". In this model, norms are universal and *enforced* by institutions. They need not be taught at all, as long as they are effective. Discourse is premised on objectivity – upon that which is external to the discourse itself. Interpersonal commitments are weak, premised only upon a minimalist obligation to refrain from the coercion and violence that would make possible the objective mode of discourse and the impartial and neutral application of norms.[33]

It is precisely this social condition which Alasdair MacIntyre lamented in *After Virtue*, forgetting perhaps that maintaining the peace is no mean achievement, particularly given the alternatives which continue to present themselves. Barbara Herrnstein Smith notes that:

MacIntyre displays considerable distain for the inauthentic—because merely "expedient" – types of legislative and judicial activity in which we engage in the absence of a genuine *polis*. Because contemporary secular society does not have and cannot hope to achieve consensus, its political processes are, he suggests, a sham. His example is the United States Supreme Court, the major function of which is not, he observes, to invoke a consistent set of principles, but, rather, "to keep the peace between rival social groups adhering to rival and incompatible principles". The observation is illustrated by the court's decision in the *Bakke* case which, he notes, "both forbade precise ethnic quotas for admission to colleges and universities, but allowed discrimination in favor of previously deprived minority groups". It would be "to miss the point", he remarks, even to try to figure out what consistent principles could be behind such a decision; for, in this as in other cases, the Supreme Court "played the role of a peacemaking or truce-keeping body by negotiating its way through an impasse of conflict, not by invoking our shared moral first principles. For our society as a whole has none." The point, it appears, is that genuine justice is not possible after the Fall; or, as MacIntyre goes on to say, "[w]hat this brings out is that modern politics cannot be a matter of genuine moral consensus... Modern politics is civil war carried on by other means..." It would be worthwhile, I think, to consider the distribution of the social/political costs and benefits of the idea that post-lapsarian politics is equivalent to civil warfare, that judicial decisions reached through negotiation and trade-off are inherently contemptible, that laws framed as "expedient[s] accommodated to special circumstances" are hardly less so, and the nature of political obligation "becomes systematically unclear" where a government is "only a set of institutional arrangements for imposing a bureaucratized unity on a society which lacks genuine moral consensus..." Exactly what, we might ask, are the alternative forms of political process for which we should be holding out? And what should we be doing in the meantime?[34]

MacIntyre's excoriation of post-lapsarian politics as 'civil war carried on by other means' closes the circle. To the extent that the nation state of late modernity remains viable, it remains viable because it successfully monopolises the exercise of violence within its boundaries. The military, the police and the courts are collectively charged with the maintenance of order and with enforcing this monopoly.[35] In the past decade, we have borne witness, repeatedly, to the consequences that attend the collapse of these institutional arrangements or their mobilisation in pursuit of a partisan cause. Yes, politics may well be civil war carried out by another means but the institutionalised politics of the United States and Australia, to name but two such nations, is surely preferable to the very real and bloody civil wars which have flared in Bosnia, on the West Bank, and elsewhere. Repeatedly, we see the horrific consequences of the collision of paideic visions, and a subsequent spiral downward into disorder in the absence of any willingness to comply with the minimalist norms of the imperial state. Because of this, we have good reason to fear the failure of the state to maintain its monopoly over violence.[36]

While this brief excursion into competing political and ethical visions may seem puzzling and out of place in a discussion of the rhetoricity of law, the points that emerge from it are critical. Understood as a rhetorical structure, law is central to the maintenance of order in our post-lapsarian world.[37] The rhetorical framework of the trial, its formal re-presentation of one happening in the form of competing visions, speaks precisely of and to a society for which a return to paideic unity is unthinkable and a downward spiral into competing absolutist visions still more terrifying. One way of reading the increasing discontent with the adversarial framework of the common law and the search for alternatives is as nostalgic, as a search for an (always but lately) vanished past in which paideic unity informed the national vision.[38]

As rhetoric, the arguments of counsel **re**-present the stories told by the parties from a range of perspectives. They offer, within the context of the trial, different shards of reality, and, still more important, connect those stories through rhetoric with law's past, its history, its traditions as seen through the eyes of counsel.[39] The traditional or conventional justification for the adversarial structure of common law proceedings affirmed the idea that out of the ritual and strictly governed clash of opposites the truth would emerge.[40] If we have lost faith in the emergence of anything akin to truth from within the rhetorical framework of the trial, we have not, I think, entirely lost our faith in the potency of the image.

Our focus upon rhetoric offers another insight as well. If our legal system has seldom made good upon the potential suggested by its rhetorical structure, its internal structure demands that we respect partial truths, shards of reality. The central claim of the adversary system is that, to the extent that we will be able to reconstruct an authoritative and binding account of the past, that account must be drawn from the clash of partial truths, competing visions.[41]

Let me explain. Earlier chapters emphasised images of storytelling, the process by which human stories became legal stories. Despite the necessity for translation, for a recasting of stories into legal (and therefore foreign) images,[42] the rituals of legality encourage, indeed, mandate, the development of multiple perspectives. Submissions are put in the alternative; competing possibilities explored by counsel; authorities proffered for this vision or that.[43] Almost invariably, at least when matters proceed to the ultimate appellate court for the jurisdiction, the judgments themselves offer multiple perspectives, explore (as we shall see later in this chapter) subtly different narratives and therefore different images of legality. Law speaks in and through alterity.

Other rituals also abound within law. Peter Winn argues that:

No society has a uniform or consistent set of moral ideas; and legal ritual permits social action in the face of ideological contradiction. Society cannot be governed only by legislation enforced by the physical power of the state. Legal ritual makes uniform structure and order possible with minimum exercise of force.

...[G]ifts, deeds, wills, motions and trials do not have independent reality apart from the rituals attendant upon their creation. These rituals are events which mark, define and alter the rights and duties of people within a community – *create* these very institutional facts. In legal ritual, the social facts against which one judges the legitimacy of the ritual are themselves constituted by the ritual. In the words of an anthropologist, Maurice Bloch, "what is being said is the right thing because by the acceptance of the formalization of language it has become the only thing". Through legal ritual, as through religious ritual, the world as lived and the world as imagined are fused through the agency of a single set of symbolic forms.

Ritual is not a politically neutral process; it has an intimate relationship with society's ideology. Not only does ritual limit awareness of the scope of conflict and contradiction, it can transform conflict into a reaffirmation of certain social structures and values.[44]

Winn argues that the rituals of legality humanise what would otherwise appear to be a starkly brutal process, act as a bridge between the violence of law's outcomes and the rhetoric that justifies those same outcomes. He argues further that:

It is a mistake to assume that ritual strengthens any particular ideology, or is necessarily conservative. Sometimes a ritual may be instrumental in challenging or overthrowing a prevailing ideology. Even more important, at times, rituals can be instrumental in transforming and humanizing social conflicts. In this latter role, ritual has a wider purpose – to establish a meaningful relationship between the values a people hold and the general order of existence within which it finds itself. In this latter role, ritual is a means by which human beings construe and construct their world – thus, a form of meaning itself.[45]

Robert Cover spoke of the jurispathic potential of the imperial state. I would put it more bluntly. In everything that leads up to the moment of judgment, laws and interpretations flourish. On every side arguments are offered, this explanation rather than that, these authorities in preference to those, this truth in preference to that. At the moment of judgment, what had been fecund and plural becomes singular, unitary. Only at the moment of judgment (and only where the decision is that of a single judge) can this singularity be sustained, even for a moment. Once the judge must herself justify her decision, construct written arguments which have the potential to persuade her sister judges that her decision is proper[46] fecundity returns as she seeks ways of justifying her decision to others, shapes arguments and reasons which will persuade them.[47]

Generations of law students have embarked upon a quest for the *ratio decidendi*, the reason for judgment, and the single authoritative sentence that epitomises law.[48] Yet reason is seldom, if ever, as perspicacious as this endeavour suggests. Allusion, image, the dense accretion of fact and symbol and argument, the weaving of these into a whole which (if successful) draws the mind irresistibly in a particular direction: all of these highlight the rhetorical structure of the written judgment. Those who attempt to reduce plurality to singularity are likely to be unable to capture the reasons why a particular judgment is, or is not, persuasive. Even more to the point, their efforts are likely to be frustrated by the shade and play of meaning in the judgment, the half formulated second argument, the absence of the kind of precise singularity they are seeking.

In arguing for a poethics of judgment Richard Weisberg held up Benjamin Cardozo as an exemplar of the judicial method, and it is, I think, instructive to look at why this is the case.

> How an opinion means, how a negotiating session or an argument to a jury means, is more important than what it means. And so, when Cardozo wrote in *Meinhard v Salmon* that the fiduciary stands not for the morals of the marketplace but for the "punctilio of an honor the most sensitive", he was replicating the method of the Yeats and the Arnold he loved so much. The formulation of this highest standard of conduct *has become* that standard – no one need even try to paraphrase it, for any rearticulation would be not only an impoverishment *but a change in the standard.*
>
> Cardozo's opinion, all opinions, stand or fall on their language, but also on the appropriateness of the fit – the fluid harmony – between the words used and the aspiration toward justice that every legal pronouncement should embody. In our system, as Cardozo in particular would note, judicial power in the long run is linguistically grounded:
>
>> The opinion will need persuasive force, or the impressive virtue of sincerity and fire, or the mnemonic power of alliteration and antithesis, or the terseness and tang of the proverb, and the maxim. Neglect the help of these allies, and it may never win its way.
>
> At this point, standard legal methodology might still intercede and suggest that the *outcome* in a given Supreme Court case (or other legal situation) surely predominates over the linguistic "form" in which the outcome is justified (or produced). An opinion may be 'well crafted", but what consolation does that

bring if, finally, we feel that the result in the case is somehow wrong, unjust, misguided?

Standard jurisprudence, thus articulated, sharply distinguishes – as Cardozo never did – between the form of a legal utterance and its substance. Difficult though it may be to grasp, however, Cardozo's insistent unification of legal form and substance makes more sense. The poetic method for law challenges the standard bifurcation in the following three ways:

1.   The "holding" in a case cannot without some alteration be abstracted from the words used to express it.

2.   No opinion with misguided outcome has ever in fact been "well-crafted".

3.   Even opinions that have had salutary effects and are widely applauded will lose power as time goes on if they fail to harmonize sound and sense in working their outcome.[49]

Weisberg writes tellingly of the importance of the judge's craft. He speaks of the way in which, in some cases at least, holding and language meld into one another so that one is persuaded of the rightness of the judgment through (in part at least) the power of its language. In so writing, he speaks directly of the rhetoric of judgment, the way in which narrative, argument and figure come together to create a meaning that insistently escapes the merely literal. In chapter 4, we saw something of this power at work when we examined the various judgments in *Mabo v Queensland*.[50]

When Weisberg moves from acknowledging that much of the power of a judgment lies explicitly in its success or failure as rhetoric to insisting that it is impossible for a misguided judgment to be well-crafted, however, he over-extends his argument. So doing, he betrays his reliance on assumptions about truth and about meaning which are awkwardly at variance with much of his methodology. Some of these assumptions are important enough (and disturbing enough) for me to want to spell them out fully.

On the simplest level, as an example of the power of a judicial epigram he gives us Holmes' infamous epigram 'Three generations of idiots are enough'. His failure to attend to the substance of the epigram, and to recognise the human meaning and the shameful history of the American eugenics movement, calls into question the insistence with which he began. Undeniably, that epigram is among the most famous in American legal history. Equally undeniably, it retains its power today. It is also almost invariably misquoted, exactly as Weisberg misquoted it.[51] When the passage is quoted in full, both its evil and its power are undeniable:

We have seen more than once that the public welfare may call upon the best citizens for their lives. It would be strange if it could not call upon those who already sap the strength of the state for these lesser sacrifices... Three generations of *imbeciles* are enough.[52]

Stephen Jay Gould comments:

The law that Holmes upheld had been implemented for forty-eight years, from 1924 to 1972. The operations had been performed in mental health facilities, primarily upon white men and women considered feeble-minded and anti-social – including "unwed mothers, prostitutes, petty criminals and children with disciplinary problems."

Carrie Buck, now seventy-two, lives near Charlottesville. Neither she nor her sister Doris would be considered mentally deficient by today's standards. Doris Buck was sterilized under the same law in 1928. She later married Matthew Figgins, a plumber. But Doris Buck was never informed. "They told me," she recalled, "that the operation was for an appendix and rupture." So she and Matthew Figgins tried to conceive a child. They consulted physicians at three hospitals throughout her child-bearing years; no one recognized that her fallopian tubes had been severed. Last year, Doris Buck Figgins finally discovered the cause of her lifelong sadness.[53]

Holmes' language retains its power today. His readers have changed. If the rhetoric of the eugenics movement sits awkwardly with contemporary sensibilities, that fact is sufficient to remind us that we cannot simply say that no judgment 'with misguided outcome has ever in fact been "well-crafted"'.That Weisberg should cite Holmes' epigram is a measure of its enduring power and Holmes' mastery of the judicial craft. A measure of the gulf between then and now may be found in our reaction to it. In 1927 the eugenics movement commanded, if not universal approbation, widespread acceptance. For many, perhaps most, in Holmes' intended audience, three generations of imbeciles *were* enough, and the rightness of his epigram seemed beyond question. Today, its casual arrogance and certainty are more likely to summon up images of the horrors of Auchwitz and Buchenwald, and of racial cleansing in Bosnia and Ruanda than an intuitive appreciation of the rightness of the sentiments expressed. We read his lines differently and the point made is one that I believe to be of some significance. Meaning is not fixed, but fluid. What yesterday seemed both perspicacious and perceptive, can today be understood as profoundly evil.

Of course, *Buck v Bell* is no longer good law, but perhaps we need to seek the reason for its failure in the profound changes wrought by the World War II and subsequent horrors.[54]

Weisberg blurs the two when he suggests that where the outcome is misguided the judgment cannot be well crafted. Holmes' epigram remains 'well-crafted', I think, terrifyingly so.[55] Its rhetoric fails to move today's audience. It has thus become a failure in a way that Holmes' could not have predicted. It has become a failure because it is no longer persuasive. The audience to which it is addressed no longer entirely believes the 'truth' which it proclaims. Even those who might momentarily sympathise with this particular movement are no longer comfortable for its aims to be so baldly stated. Its failure does not arise from any want of the judicial craft on Holmes' part. It is a measure of his craft that this passage continues to be (mis)quoted and retains the capacity to chill us. That, as rhetoric, it has become a failure speaks, and importantly, about a central feature of rhetoric and of the rhetoricity of law.

The rhetorician's art is the art of persuasion, and persuasion demands a consummate understanding of and willingness to work towards (and almost certainly even with) an intended audience. Arguments are necessarily framed in the consciousness of having an audience, and with an awareness of the likely belief structures of that audience. Holmes' intended audience was one that believed, perhaps passionately, in the need to preserve the purity of the American nation. For Holmes and others who sympathised with the eugenics movement, the United States was in danger of being swamped by immigrants and by the fertility of the feeble-minded.[56] If, in the waning days of the twentieth century, we are no longer persuaded of the rightness of Holmes' position then we have changed. We no longer believe that if 'society' is entitled to demand that its sons risk death in battle it is equally entitled to sterilise the 'genetically unworthy'. Arguments that might have been persuasive 70 years ago are no longer even acceptable. Their unacceptability is not, I think, the consequence of any failure of judicial craft, but of something very different, the removal of the context which rendered them perspicuous and its replacement with very different context within which very different arguments flourish.

The Interpretive Paradox

Once we recognise the rhetoricity of law that recognition leads inexorably to a second, and equally critical, understanding. If we focus upon the construction of the various narratives that collectively make up the trial as rhetorical event, they turn, somewhat which is equalled by no other social practice, upon nuanced interpretation. It is not simply that 'the law' is subject to interpretation in many of the same ways and by the same methods as other texts. That statement does not even begin to capture the degree to which the trial is itself[57] constituted by discrete acts of interpretation. The geography of the courtroom, the positioning of the judge upon a raised dais, the witness box to one side, bar tables in front, is almost invariable. Its invariability provides a visual text which locates the trial itself within set bounds, choreographs its events in predetermined ways, maintains a set and necessary distance between those who come before the law and those who must judge them. This geography becomes part of the trial itself, establishes constraints upon both action and meaning.[58]

The formal processes of the trial, examination in chief and cross examination, summing up and rebuttal are situated physically within that geography and situated intellectually and psychically within a narrative framework.[59] A story is being told, and the manner of its telling and the constraints upon that telling are neither trivial nor banal. It is being told in particular ways because of the geography of the courtroom and because of the formalities of the trial itself. The spatial geography of the courtroom and the intellectual geography of the procedural script collectively define the roles and the moves appropriate to judge and jury, to counsel and bailiff, to plaintiff and defendant. This geography is both physical/temporal and a part of consciousness. Of its limits, Goodrich comments:

> The decision in the case is instituted upon the presupposition of a non-physical geography in which the place and presence of the court extends from Westminster to Fleet Street. The legal presence or aura of law is no longer attached to a specific building but is rather an intensive and internally governed property of those who speak for or work within the Law...
>
> ...In geographical terms, the cartography that would map such presence is initially to be understood as an intensive geography whose object would be not simply the physical or plastic manifestations of law but rather a mental geography, a mapping of inner spaces and qualities which accord or conform quite closely with the canonist rule that the institution, the Church, does not

inhabit a territory – *ecclesia non habet terrorium.* The *lex terrae* or law of the realm takes its hold upon the space of circulation and action, its effects are measured not through any immediate corporeal threat but through a metaphysics of presence or self-presence of the law in all those sites where its officers and representatives, its dignities and honours are to be found. The etymology of territory as legal jurisdiction can remind us usefully that both text and territory as legal concepts have their roots in a terror *(terreo)* mapped upon the order of the soul and only secondarily upon the body, upon the image as that which represents the mere visibility or written memory of law.[60]

Goodrich speaks of a mapping, of a cartography in which the invisible and the visible law fasten upon those over whom its jurisdiction extends. This geography, a geography not of space but of effect, of a kind of enchainment in which we understand ourselves to be before the law and therefore are always already bound, already within its reach, reminds us of the pre-eminence of vision in the carceral order. We turn the gaze of Bentham's panopticon upon ourselves.

The implications of this geography are largely unexplored. By convention, legal interpretation has been confined to the textual, to statute and judgment, facilitating a process of analogy that allows us to understand it as somehow akin to literary interpretation. Questions about the implications of the setting of interpretation for the act of interpretation are largely unasked... buried beneath the surface of thought. Yet interpretation within Goodrich's invisible cartography, interpretation which attaches (he says) first to the soul[61] and only later and secondarily to the bodies of those who are by their calling a part of the carceral order, cannot ever (one feels) be the same as interpretation which is more innocent, more limited and transparent.

Our understanding of what law is, and what it must be if it is to continue to 'maintain the peace in the absence of genuine consensus' emphasise that legal interpretation is never innocent.[62] As an enterprise, law continually shores up the boundaries of the imperial state, at once legitimating the processes by which we conduct our daily affairs and marking the boundaries of legitimacy. David Engle reminds us that:

Law is not a distinctly bounded "thing" that belongs exclusively to the state. It is a continuum of normative orders ranging from the "law" of the super-market check-out line to the constitutional interpretations of the federal courts. Everyday life is pervaded by norms and procedures whose origins are to be bound both in the rules of ordinary human interaction and in the more formal pronouncements issued from the distant centers of "sociocultural production". Norms originating in diverse ways from diverse sources, of greater or lesser formality and official legitimacy, continually merge, clash, overlap, and constitute one another. Everyday life is not opposed to law, nor does it exist merely by insinuating itself into the interstices of the law. Everyday life constitutes law and is constituted by it.[63]

A little later, citing the work of Barbara Yngvesson, he speaks of 'key actors who mediate legal and commonsense concepts of community':[64]

Yngvesson, for example, shows how the clerk magistrate of a criminal court in New England helps to define the community by responding selectively to applications by citizens and police for issuance of criminal complaints. In picking and choosing among the applications, the clerk lectures, admonishes, and praises and makes explicit and implicit pronouncements about the community itself: Who are its "true" members and who are mere "garbage"? What sorts of nonconforming behavior represent movement toward legitimate community change and what sorts represent deviance that should be sanctioned? The clerk is a gatekeeper to the formal legal system, but he is also deeply rooted in the local social order. Through his everyday knowledge of the community and his specialized knowledge of the law, he occupies a key position at the boundary between the two conceptual systems and is able to manipulate both in his efforts to define the community and direct change along paths he considers desirable.[65]

An understanding of law and legal interpretation that excludes the interpretive acts that patrol the parameters of the 'judiciable' is an understanding of law that is incomplete. These interpretive acts form part of the background against which formal proceedings commence. The magistrate proceeds to hear cases on the understanding that the list of cases before her has been screened, either by a magistrate's clerk as in the New England community studied by Yngvesson, or through the decisions of lawyers and clients, prosecutors and police. All interpretation then occurs against the background of decisions that the matter before the court is, somehow, properly judicial, fit to be heard.[66]

Legal interpretation then is unique in a number of ways.[67] Judicial interpretation is bound to the existing order in ways that other interpretive acts do not share. Judicial interpretation occurs against the background of our cultural understandings of litigation as the ritual climax of the carceral order and of an interpretive context which has identified the matter before the court as properly legal. While force is seldom required, it is always available, ready to be invoked.[68] That this is the case is understood by all and is necessarily central to the interpretive process. Every participant, from the moment he or she comes before the law, is aware that the path embarked upon is one that, potentially, leaves her either defenceless before law's violence or responsible at some level for setting it into motion. No one who comes before the law departs unscathed.

Rhetoric and the Imperative of Persuasion

My final claim is this, that whatever majesty and legitimacy our legal system possesses lies in its rhetoricity, in the Janus faced obligation of the judge to both be open to persuasion by others and to seek to persuade others. Both faces of this obligation are essential, neither being complete without the other. To simply be open to persuasion can often to be seduced by the sweetest argument, the most sonorous words, to fall prey, in short, to all those evils of which rhetoric has conventionally been accused, blowing this way or that before a honeyed tongue. To be open to persuasion while being, at every moment, conscious that one must be able to give such reasons as will justify one's decision to others is very different. There is another factor as well. Earlier in this chapter, I spoke of the way in which the rituals of legality mandated the development of multiple perspectives, different shards of reality. These shards of reality are constrained by the very rituals of legality which mandate them. At their most ambitious, they dare not advance too far beyond what is. They embody our acknowledgment that for every cause of action there are innumerable possible narratives, that it is always 'just possible' that necessities will somehow be understood to incorporate the need for 'Sunday shoes'.[69] I know, we all know, that most of the time these dissident voices, vagrant images of reality are not heard (worse still, are not even voiced, too many lawyers seeing the range of possible arguments as givens rather than possibilities). Nonetheless it is in the narrative structure of law and in its rhetoricity that we will find whatever virtue there is in our legal system. Because the judicial role mandates openness to persuasion, because, subject to the strictures of adjectival law, the judge must remain open to the arguments which come before her and remain willing to be persuaded by them, the form and shape of the arguments become all important. Here, of course, we find the practical, as opposed to theoretical flaw in the system. The 'best chance' for reaching, not the truth, but the best explanation, the most persuasive explanation of what happened, in both criminal law and civil law, lies in ensuring both that that counsel for all the parties are equally skilled. Even more, it lies in ensuring that their own skills and those of the other participants run well beyond the narrowly rhetorical. If the system is to work as it should both lawyers and judges must be as skilled at hearing and interpreting narratives as they are at framing arguments and developing the fit between those arguments and 'the law'. Undeniably our legal system is costly and time consuming, and, increasingly under-resourced. Unlike the civil system, however, the paradigm is open textured rather than closed textured and in this lies its merit.

Something else is mandated as well. The judge has no alternative but to decide and to accept responsibility for her decision. Because both decision and responsibility are always present, and because no decision is beyond challenge, the demand for reasons is also always present. What I find interesting in the demand for reasons is its insistent pull towards narration, towards retelling events in the narrative form. Robin West's account of the collapse of the structure of judgment where the need for narrative is ignored highlights the importance of narrative. Most particularly where opinions are likely to be divided, sometimes bitterly so, where even the most persuasive arguments fall short of the mark and leave us wanting more, narrative plays a critical role. Narrative supplements rhetoric with a different kind of rationality, a different fragment of reality.[70] At times, narrative and rhetoric fuse, each completing the other so that stories and their meanings become the only argument which is required.

In this context, a particular practice of Anglo-Australian judges[71] is worth remarking upon, not least because it is in contradistinction to the usual contemporary practice of the United States Supreme Court. Unlike the more common American pattern, in which one judge writes for the majority and one for the dissent, in Australia there are likely to be several full majority judgments in major cases. While some bemoan the proliferation of judgments characteristic of the Australian High Court, what is fascinating in these judgments is the subtle reweaving of the narrative substance of the case before the Court. Inevitably, those narratives differ in emphasis, in structure, so that the stories themselves seem kaleidoscopic, each new judgment revealing some fact clusters and concealing others.

Telling Stories: Of Narrative and Persuasion

Among recent High Court judgments I have chosen that in *Amadio*[72] to expand upon the claims made in the last section about the importance of narrative. While the points I want to make are equally borne out by other recent cases, *Amadio* is a kind of archetype. This is both because of the richness and detail of its narrative structure and because its judgments should be read as a somewhat selective remembering, a **re**-remembering in accord with half-written scripts. If we separate the 'facts' from the narratives through which those facts were recounted, all of the judges were agreed upon the following.[73]

> The respondents were elderly Italian migrants. The wife had never worked outside the home. The husband had been a market gardener and had, from time to time, been involved in commercial dealings with one or another of their four sons. Both were of limited English literacy. His spoken English was reasonably good, hers was limited although her comprehension was said to be adequate. The subject matter of the case before the High Court concerned an 'open-ended' guarantee in respect of the indebtedness of their second son, who, the evidence suggested, had misled them (or been confused himself) in respect of the obligations contained in the guarantee. The guarantee was effected by way of a memorandum of mortgage. The issue was whether the bank, through its manager, conducted itself improperly in obtaining the mortgage. The manager was aware of the state of the son's business and the history of dealings between the bank and one or another of the son's companies.

Despite their agreement on the above facts, the stories developed by their Honours were very different, and this difference is echoed in the law that they deem relevant and in the manner in which it is applied. I have begun with the judgment of Gibbs J for two reasons. His Honour's treatment of the facts comes closest to the neutral account given above, indeed, it adds almost nothing to the 'bare bones' account. Because his Honour's judgment focuses, not upon the Amadios, but upon the conduct of the bank, the lack of verisimilitude in the account of the plaintiffs is almost immaterial.[74] His Honour begins:

> At the time when the memorandum of mortgage was executed, the respondents, Mr and Mrs Amadio, were aged 76 and 71 respectively. They

had both been born in Italy but had lived in Australia for over forty years. Neither had received much formal education. Mr Amadio had a limited grasp of written English but could speak it reasonably well; Mrs Amadio had some understanding of spoken English, but gave evidence through an interpreter. She had had no business experience, but her husband, who had retired after many years work as a market gardener, had engaged in a number of land transactions, in most of which he had received the assistance of their son, Vincenzo Amadio. The respondents were induced to enter into the transaction by the misrepresentations of Vincenzo Amadio.[75]

After describing in some detail the apparent financial position of Vincenzo Amadio and his opulent life style, His Honour reveals the reality. He notes that it had become necessary for the bank to 'selectively dishonour cheques' to ensure that Vincenzo's business could continue to receive supplies[76] and continues:

> The bank had special reasons for maintaining a tolerant attitude towards the company. The bank valued highly its connexion with Vincenzo Amadio, not only because he was himself an important customer, but because of the business which he brought to the bank, and because the company was engaged in building houses in a joint venture with General Credits Ltd, a subsidiary of the bank. The company did the building at cost plus ten per cent which covered no more than administrative charges; it was intended that any profits on the sale of the buildings should be shared between General Credits Ltd and another company which Vincenzo Amadio controlled.[77]

After additional details concerning the precise financial arrangements between the son and the bank, and a summary both of Vincenzo's dealings with his parents and the dealings of the bank in respect of the guarantee His Honour continued.

> However there were other circumstances in the case... First... was the arrangement made between the bank and Vincenzo Amadio... Although pursuant to that arrangement the company was to obtain an immediate overdraft limit of $270,000... it was a condition of the arrangement that the limit would be reduced to $220,000 within a week, with a further reduction to $180,000 within a fortnight. In other words, within three weeks the overdraft limit was to be reduced below the debit balance which already existed. Then it was intended that the entire overdraft should be cleared... I find it impossible to suppose that a surety who undertook to meet the past and future liabilities of the company, and to give substantial security, would have expected that the

arrangement between the bank and the company included such unusual terms, which meant that the company was given merely a temporary respite, whereas the bank improved its existing and inadequate security. Further, there was the circumstances that the bank had not merely dishonoured the cheques, but had made itself a party to their selective dishonour, in an endeavour to maintain the facade of prosperity that the company erected – a facade which, the bank should have expected, may well have deceived the respondents, since, as Mr Virgo knew, Mr Amadio was present at his son's ostentatious Christmas party... These were unusual features of the account that was to be guaranteed, and the bank was, in my opinion, bound to disclose them.[78]

Thus it was that, according to Gibbs J, the bank was profoundly implicated in Vincenzo Amadio's efforts to maintain a facade of prosperity. That facade was far removed from the reality of the matter, a reality which saw the company enter liquidation within nine months and Vincenzo himself bankrupt shortly thereafter.

In dissent, Dawson J told a very different story. The 'neutral' description of the Amadios is replaced by a 'depersonalised' account in which even the details of age and name are absent. A male and a female respondent replace Mr and Mrs Amadio:

The trial judge found that the respondents, who had migrated to Australia in the nineteen-thirties, had a limited grasp of written English but that the female respondent, although not good at expressing herself, had a fair understanding of spoken English. He found that the male respondent understood spoken English quite well and expressed himself with reasonable fluency. He also found that the female respondent knew little, but the male respondent was far from ignorant, of business transactions and the latter had been active in promoting many land transactions before his retirement.[79]

In the retelling, Dawson J transforms a man who had been a market gardener and engaged in other transactions with the assistance of one or another of his sons into a man who was 'far from ignorant' of business transactions. We are also told that he been involved in promoting many land transactions before his retirement. Subsequently we learn that:

[t]he trial judge was unable to find that in March 1977 the male respondent was incapable of sufficiently appreciating the nature and consequence of the document he executed at that time. There was no suggestion that the female respondent would have done other than follow her husband's lead and there is

no basis for treating her position differently for the purpose of the application of the relevant principle.

Those findings offer no foundation for the conclusion that the respondents were in any position of disadvantage which was used by the bank for its benefit. The age of the respondents did not amount to an infirmity and the fact that English was not their first language did not signify any incapacity to understand sufficiently... The respondents had evidently discussed the matter of the guarantee with their son who was fluent in both Italian and English and upon whom they relied for advice. If that reliance was misplaced that does not convert the occasion into one of exploitation on the part of the bank.[80]

For Dawson, the conduct of the bank, conduct of which it might be said that its silence on material matters constituted 'misrepresentation', was unexceptionable. After all, the Amadios entered the contract of their own free will, although in reliance on their son. If that reliance was misplaced, that was unfortunate, but irrelevant to the standing of the transaction. The bank could hardly be blamed for Vincenzo Amadio's duplicity. There were no characteristics *peculiar to the respondents* that were capable of rendering the conduct of the bank unconscionable. A contract of guarantee is hardly a contract *uberrimae fidei*. Given that it could not be said that the bank misrepresented the true position or took advantage of the respondents **in any way that was unfair**, the contract must stand. The respondents did not suffer from any material disadvantage such as to render its conduct unconscionable. The transaction was entered at 'arm's length' and the contractual parties were of formally equal bargaining power.[81]

There we have it. Two narratives, two selective recollections, two slices of reality and, inevitably, the very different legal outcomes dictated by those narratives. In one, independent contractors of approximately equal bar-gaining power enter an agreement that is, legally, unexceptionable. In the other, the problem is one of knowledge. While the parties remain of approximately equal bargaining power, one party both had knowledge of facts material to the transaction which were so extraordinary that they ought to have been disclosed and stood to gain from the transaction to a degree and in a way which likewise compelled disclosure. In both we learn comparatively little about the Amadios and about the circumstances surrounding the impugned transaction. They remain formal characters within formally scripted roles.

The story told by Deane J, and concurred in by both Mason and Wilson JJ is different both in detail and in inflection. The depersonalised respondents have vanished. In their place, we find an elderly Italian couple with limited English who relied upon their apparently successful son to manage their business affairs. We know their full names, Giovanni and Cesira, a detail that somehow humanises them, transforms them from respondents to neighbours. We know that they lived in Campbelltown, and that their material wealth consisted in a home and adjoining orchard, and a block of four shops in Wicks Avenue, Campbelltown which were the subject of the mortgage. We also learn that they have four sons, of whom Vincenzo is the second. In the telling, the Amadios have become real people, located in place, in context, in culture.

We are given other details as well, details which undoubtedly formed a part of the evidence given at the trial. We learn, for example, that Vincenzo Amadio may have left a meeting with the State Manager of the Commercial Bank (in South Australia) 'under a misapprehension' as to the actual terms of the guarantee. Evidence given by the State Manager, Mr Stratton, noted that Vincenzo Amadio was 'under a lot of strain at the time'.[82] A man who may well have panicked when confronted by the immanent collapse of his financial empire replaces the scheming son of the earlier judgments. On this more sympathetic reading, Vincenzo Amadio was desperately trying to stave off a collapse he was not ready to face. Consequently, he may not have grasped the import of the actual contents of the documents presented to his parents, documents that he had neither seen nor read before he persuaded his parents to execute them.[83] According to Deane J:

> [I]t would be difficult to accept as reasonable a belief that Vincenzo had successfully explained to his parents the content and effect of a document which embodied eighteen separate covenants of meticulous and complicated legal wording in circumstances where to Mr Virgo's knowledge, Vincenzo had himself never seen the document at the time when any such suggested explanation must have taken place...
>
> Mr Virgo gave evidence that Vincenzo did not trouble even to read the document before agreeing that Mr Virgo should take it to Mr and Mrs Amadio for execution. He also gave evidence that Mr and Mrs Amadio did not read it...[84]

The impersonal commercial transaction described by Dawson J is replaced, in Deane's telling, by the 'intrusion'[85] of the commercial world into a family scene of comfortable and cosy domesticity. As the scene opens, we find Mr Amadio reading the newspaper while his wife does the luncheon dishes. The bank manager arrives almost immediately thereafter. While they were expecting the manager's visit, Vincenzo having joined them for lunch and spoken to them about the document he wanted them to sign, the image created by the narrative is of a scene of relaxed domesticity. This scene is of substantial rhetorical importance, not least because it is hardly the sort of scene one would expect if the participants were fully cognisant that they were signing a guarantee which was wholly open-ended, both in duration and in amount. Thus:

> In contrast was the position of Mr and Mrs Amadio. Their personal circumstances have already been mentioned. They were advanced in years. Their grasp of written English was limited. They relied on Vincenzo for the management of their business affairs and believed that he and Amadio Builders were prosperous and successful. They were approached in their kitchen by the bank, acting through Mr Virgo, at a time when Mr Amadio was reading the newspaper after lunch and Mrs Amadio was washing dishes. They were presented with a complicated and lengthy document for their immediate signature. They had received no independent advice in relation to the transaction which that document embodied and about which they had learned only hours earlier from Vincenzo who... had misled them as regards the extent and duration of their potential liability under it.[86]

Other fragments of memory also surface in the judgment of Deane J. Perhaps the most telling is embedded in the passage below:

> Mr Amadio, who has suffered severe loss of memory since being involved in an accident in 1978, was unable, at the trial, to recall the circumstances in which he and his wife had signed the guarantee/mortgage. The only direct evidence of what took place was that of Mr Virgo and Mrs Amadio. The latter, by her own admission, had been unable properly to understand the conversation in English that took place between Mr Virgo and her husband prior to execution of the document...[87]

The persistence of memory...,[88] and its failure to persist, are essential elements in the rhetorical structure of Deane's judgment. It is not simply, that, during the period between the signing of the mortgage and foreclosure by the bank, Mr Amadio's memory failed. While that would have had significant impact, its impact would have been limited. It is, far more strikingly, that, by the time of the trial, only one person knew with any degree of certainty what transpired in the kitchen on 25 March 1977. Only one person could possibly have known what was said, and what went unspoken, and what the terms of the admittedly brief discussion were. That person was Mr Virgo.

More strikingly still, Mr and Mrs Amadio were not, we are told a little later, even given a copy of the guarantee/mortgage that they had signed. Not only was memory obliterated, but also until the moment of foreclosure in December of 1978 there was nothing by way of physical documentation to rekindle it. Whatever conversations they may have had with Vincenzo after it had become clear that his companies had collapsed and he himself was bankrupt, neither they nor he possessed any documentation which could have been used to 'refresh'[89] a vanished memory.

At the end, we are left with three versions of reality, three narratives, each narrative evoking a particular legal paradigm. We may call the first of these narratives the narrative of power. In this narrative, while the text concerns the transactionally advantaged position of the bank, the sub-text (never fully delineated but present throughout the judgment) concerns the level of responsibility which the law expects from those who hold positions of power. Power becomes a privilege, and a privilege that imposes a burden upon those who hold it.

If the first of these narratives is the narrative of power, the second may be termed the narrative of equality. Here, the Commercial Bank and the Amadios bargain at arm's length in respect of a commercial transaction. The Bank had no reason to assume that Mr Amadio was unable to understand the nature and quality of the document that he signed. What Mrs Amadio may or may not have understood was irrelevant. She would, in any case, have done as her husband wished, being a 'good wife'.

The final narrative, we may term a narrative of weakness, of disadvantage. In it, the telling pits the power and sophistication of the Commercial Bank against an elderly migrant couple. As Deane J spells out that narrative:

> [T]he combination of their age, their limited grasp of written English, the circumstances in which the bank presented the document to them for their signature, and, most importantly their lack of knowledge and understanding of the contents of the document was that... they lacked assistance and advice where assistance and advice were plainly necessary if there were to be any reasonable degree of equality between themselves and the bank.

Thus it was that equity was compelled to intervene and grant relief in respect of an unconscionable dealing. As James Boyd White tells us:

> The law establishes roles and relations and voices, positions from which and audiences to which one may speak, as it gives us as speakers the materials and methods of a discourse... It is this discourse, working in the social context of its creation, this language in the fullest sense of the terms, that is the law.[90]

Well might we ask what roles and relations and voices are established by the various judgments in *Amadio*, what social context does each invoke? What audience is the silent partner in each vision and what meaning does this audience give to the act of judgment? I will not try to answer these questions here, although my readers may well explore them for themselves. In the next chapter, however, I will begin to look at one particular aspect of the creation of judicial meaning and at the roles involved.

Notes

1   Witteveen, WJ, 'The Rhetorical Labours of Hercules' (1990) 3 *International Journal for the Semiotics of Law* 227 uses rhetoric is something of the way in which I do. He emphasises that legal discourse has, not one, but many audiences, the parties, a lower court, the wider legal community perhaps. Possible judicial audiences can be approached from a number of different perspectives: ranging from a straightforward sociological analysis to an analysis of the textual strategies used and the audiences to which these textual stratagems are directed.

2   My account of adjudication is local, not universal, relevant to courts in the common law tradition. The role of the civil law judge is very different, and the impact of that difference upon judicial speech must be central to any account of adjudication from within that tra-dition. Adjudication is both culturally specific and context laden. Even within common law legal systems local differences exist which are critical.

3   Fish, S, 'Rhetoric', in Fish, *Doing What Comes Naturally*, 474-475, Cover, R, 'Nomos and Narrative' in Minow, M, M Ryan & A Sarat (eds) *Narrative, Violence, and the Law*, Ann Arbor, Univ of Michigan Press, 1992, 95.

4   The essence of an autopoetic system is its self-referentiality, its attempt to confine all questions, including that of legitimation within the frame provided by its own structure.

5   Hart's account of primary rules and secondary rules is designed to foreclose legitimation. While he acknowledges a 'minimum content of natural law', there is, in reality no work for that minimum content to do, all questions of legitimation being extra-legal. Law's fascination with its own nature (we ask 'What is law?' in a way we do not ask 'What is medicine?' or 'What is teaching?') reflects its circularity. The successful realisation of medicine's purpose, or that of teaching provides all the justification which the enterprise requires. Because the successful realisation of law's

purpose involves violence, law's legitimacy is always open to question and the only legitimacy possible must, at least within the positivist paradigm, come from without.

6   The classical legitimation model lay in the originary myth of the social contract. This approach to legitimation simply pushes the question back one step further. If the laws and the institutions of society are legitimated by some form of founding contract, how may that contract itself be legitimated. Of classical social contract theorists, the only one to begin to address this further (and infinitely regressive) need for legitimation was Jean-Jacques Rousseau. The gulf between the (unjust) contract in the 'Discourse on the Origin of Inequality Among Men' and the (just) contract foreshadowed by 'The Social Contract' is immeasurable. As is well known, Rousseau had recourse to the somewhat mysterious concept of the 'general will' to ensure legitimation. The idea of the general will, together with the metaphysical baggage it carries, is only plausible if certain essentialist propositions about the nature of man and about the capacity of society to corrupt man's 'natural goodness' are accepted without question. See Rousseau, J-J, *Social Contract and Discourses*.

7   Dworkin, *Law's Empire*, 400-401. In his earlier work, Dworkin explicitly insisted that the 'rights' pre-existed their formal resolution in court. I do not know whether he would still insist upon this proposition. It was central to the argument put forward in *Taking Rights Seriously*, that there was 'one right answer' to every legal dispute, that answer which reflected the 'pre-existing' rights and duties of the parties before the court. That earlier formulation seems to me to give a higher priority to questions of justice than is present in his later, more pragmatic, work.

8   Dworkin, *Law's Empire*, 404-405. This passage gives one reason why Dworkin may still hold that his 'right answer' thesis offers the best explanation of our understandings of law. The notion that it is unfair to 'change the rules' during the game is, undeniably a core supposition in our legal system. Dworkin's attachment to this supposition sits uneasily with his rejection of the model of law as rules. It also suggests a model of law and language that is fundamentally positivist, despite his denials of this affinity. For a discussion of these and related issues see Fish, S, 'Still Wrong After All These Years' in Fish, S, *Doing What Comes Naturally? Change, Rhetoric and the Practice of Theory in Literary and Legal Studies*, Oxford, Clarendon Press, 1989, 356. The remarks at 365-366 are particularly relevant to the present argument.

9   The judges are, after all, only the princes of law's empire! Questions of justice operate at a very different level and ought to be remitted to seers (and philosophers). Dworkin's 'thin' account of equality, equality of resources, comes close to figuring equality as a negative right.

10 Those who put such questions forward are emboldened by the popular belief the courts dispense justice, rather than legality. This is ironical, given the reluctance of judges to allow 'justice talk' into their proceedings and the even greater reluctance of legal philosophers to allow considerations of justice to trump more procedural aspects of the legal system. Even an apparently radical voice, such as that of Derrida, contents himself with suggesting that justice is what didn't happen when the law has had its way.

11 To this extent, I do agree with him. Our disagreement lies at the level of language and of understandings about how and why constraints operate.

12   As the passage quoted earlier makes clear, fairness defines the process by which laws are enacted, while due process involves adherence to the conventions that ensure that the outcomes that are produced are stable and predictable.

13   Right balance, right answers... where do these images lead us? If the right answer is that answer which best reflects the pre-existing distribution of rights and duties before the court, is the right balance that which best reflects the pre-existing understandings of the community, that which will not 'take the community by surprise'?

14   I do not mean to belittle statutory interpretation, but this is not the time to discuss it at length, or to discuss why accounts of statutory interpretation tend to concentrate upon the 'canons' of interpretation rather than upon what is at stake in interpretation. The canons of statutory interpretation are themselves predicated upon the assumption that meaning operates in a particular way, and that it is in principle determinate, fixed, and ascertainable. We are here concerned with an issue that I conceive to be prior, the issue of meaning itself.

15   If one is honest, there is no moment within law in which interpretation is not of paramount importance. It's interpretation all the way down.

16   The rhetorical structure of law is also, and profoundly, involved with ritual. Indeed, the process of the trial and its the formal stages through which law is realised 'in the flesh' are among the highest 'public rituals' of our culture. For an interesting discussion of legality as ritual see Winn, PA, 'Legal Ritual' (1991) 2 *Law & Critique* 207. Winn comments in this regard:

> A legal ritual on the other hand is a legal *event*. It is something that is *done*. A rule of law can be expressed abstractly, but a legal ritual exists only in the concrete actions of a particular group of human beings. The execution of a will, the conveyance of real property, the execution of a bank's collateral note or agreement, the making of a formal plea in court, are rituals which may or may not express intentions, but if the proper forms are observed, the legal transaction is completed. Technically speaking, legal consequences do not "follow" from the proper execution of the legal ritual. The proper execution of the legal ritual constitutes the legally significant event.

17   Like Dworkin, although for different reasons, I understand the trial to be central to our understandings of legality. Of all the manifestations of law and of legality, the trial is the most significant and the most singular.

18   While one reason for this undoubtedly lies in the doctrine of precedent, and the central role played by judicial texts in maintaining law's continuity, there are other reasons as well. Culturally, we privilege the written over the merely oral.

19   The 'chain novel' metaphor for adjudication first surfaced in the work of Ronald Dworkin in the early nineteen-eighties. See Dworkin, 'Law as Interpretation'. The debate between Ronald Dworkin and Stanley Fish concerning the implications of Dworkin's choice of the 'chain novel' metaphor for the judicial text is extremely well known. An (only slightly) more sceptical reader might wonder at the choice of a literary genre whose best known exemplar is a pornographic novel (*Naked Came the Stranger*) written as a parlour game as a metaphor for what is involved in adjudication.

20   A better description might take the form of insisting that legality and historicity are inseparable, that it is precisely because of what we call historicity that actions are

understood as properly legal, that legality cannot be understood without reference to that notion among others.

21 For an interesting discussion of the debates over interpretation, see West, 'Adjudication is not Interpretation'.

22 The actual language used conveys other images as well. The discourse of constructive interpretation (upon which Dworkin's imperial edifice is itself constructed) is a discourse in which institutions and practices are understood as akin to roughly shaped pots awaiting the attention of master craftspeople. Those institutions and practices are understood as both prior to and independent of the process of interpretation to which they are subjected. The task of the interpreter is to shape the roughly shaped pots which lie before her until they correspond to a somehow independent and prior understanding of the essence of pothood. The violence of the process, and the essentialist claims underlying it, often escape notice.

23 In this respect at least it is utterly unlike a chain novel. In the ordinary course of events, chain novels may violate assorted literary canons but this is the limit of their violence.

24 I am interested, in other words, in the process by which the story of May O'Donoghue became *Donoghue v Stephenson* [1932] AC 562 and ultimately became, not merely a legal text, but a canonical legal text.

25 The question of orality, and the processes (both mechanical and human) by which the oral texts of an adversary proceeding are become a written transcript of the proceeding I shall address subsequently. There are some very interesting questions here which are related to some of the puzzles surrounding adjectival law. See Haldar, 'The Evidencer's Eye', 176. Haldar notes, albeit in the context of the rules of evidence rather than the transition from oral trial to written transcript, comments:

> Documents, fingerprints, D.N.A extractions, photofits, the mortician's camera are all ways of insuring the truth, making a past reality present yet again as a state of affairs. Pragmatism then appears to be an essential "gloss" upon, or variation to, the correspondence theory of truth.

26 I am conscious that in seeking to identify these more fleeting productions as properly textual I risk taking something ephemeral and reifying it, making it fixed, concrete and ultimately positive. That is not my intent. I intend only to insist that unless we understand these as properly textual we cannot understand the process of judgment.

27 Critically, judgment is both a speech act and a performative.

28 While I do not, in this context, intend to discuss adjectival law, it is important to remember that there are times when the admissibility or otherwise of particular evidence becomes critical. That this is more often the case in criminal proceedings has to do with the nature of the proceedings and in particular with the fact that such proceedings are more likely to turn upon details of evidence and their admissibility than upon points of law. Much of the time, the law is quite clear, the only question is whether evidence tending to connect the defendant with the criminal acts in question is admissible or whether some flaw in the evidence itself or in the manner in which it was obtained rules it out.

29 Put slightly differently:

> There are no questions
> in this park

said the captain
of the guard.

There are only true facts
in this park
said the captain
of the guard.

Helen did not go to Troy.
The Red Sea never parted.
Leander wore water wings.
Roland did not blow his horn.
Leonides fled the pass.

True evidence, true facts. Who guards the gates, determines the truth of fact clusters as if no interpretation were needed or possible? The fragments of poetry quoted above are from McCarthy, E, 'Grant Park, Chicago' in *Other Things and the Aardvark*, Garden City, Doubleday, 1968, 24-26.

30   White, LE, 'Subordination, Rhetorical Survival Skills, and Sunday Shoes: Notes on the Hearing of Mrs G'; in Fineman, MA & NW Thomadsen (eds) *At the Boundaries of Law: Feminism and Legal Theory*, New York, Routledge, 1991, 40.

31   The distinction is, in any case, less than fully perspicacious. Both are interpretive constructs, both a product of particular moments, particular (and wholly contingent) understandings. I should, perhaps, simply say that the distinction is itself a matter of interpretation and let the matter rest.

32   John Rawls describes this outcome as an 'overlapping consensus' between more local beliefs. He argues that in a 'free society' we can hope for nothing more. See Rawls, J, 'The Idea of an Overlapping Consensus', (1987) 7 *Oxford J of Leg. Stud* 1 and Rawls, J. 'The Domain of the Political and Overlapping Consensus', 64 *N.Y.U.L.R.* (1989) 233. Rawls elaborates upon these ideas in *Political Liberalism*, New York, Columbia Univ Press, 1993. For Rawls, liberalism dare not hope for more than this system maintaining consensus in which the commitment of local communities is secured by the willingness of the imperial state to exempt their private affairs from its norms. I have analysed (and criticised) this thesis at length elsewhere. See Berns, SS, 'Tolerance and Substantive Equality in Rawls' in Grbich, J (ed) *Feminism Law and Society*, Bundoora, La Trobe University Press, 112 and Berns, SS, *Add Woman and Stir*. I do not mean to belittle the achievement this represents. We have only to look at the West Bank to see the dangers that await us if the consensus fails to hold. This system maintaining discourse (necessary as it is) creates its own hostages to fortune.

33   Cover, R, 'Nomos and Narrative', 105-106. Irene Watson's 'Indigenous Peoples' Law-Ways: Survival Against the Colonial State' (1997) 8 *Australian Feminist Law Journal* 39 spells out what is at stake in the clash of visions:

Colonial powers play with the question of indigenous law-ways. In Australia they play with the idea of incorporating 'customary law', as they call it. They examine which part of indigenous law they can splice and incorporate into the colonial system of law and which unsavoury, uncivilised parts are best left out. In the name of human rights. 'God forbid, spearing and other inhumane acts'. And yet

> we watch as the incarceration levels of indigenous peoples rise and we watch our indigenous children become institutionalised at levels in excess of any peoples on earth...
>
>> And still indigenous peoples question not only by what right the colonial power has come to exist but also to what extent colonial rules and regulations become incorporated into indigenous legal systems. I would say there is nothing or very little of the colonisers "law" that we would seek to incorporate into Indigenous law. The question remains to be answered, how far is the state prepared to go, in peeling away the layers of the imposed colonial legal system?

Watson, 'Indigenous Peoples' Law-Ways', 58.

34   Smith, 'Judgment After the Fall', 225-226.

35   This is a part of the reason that the proliferation of private militias in the United States and more recently in Australia is a profoundly worrying development. It also explains our simultaneous fascination with and distrust of the rent-an-army movement. When Robert Cover noted that for the most part the balance of terror was just as he would wish it, he spoke truly. Cover, 'Violence and the Word', 211. The alternatives to a statist monopoly of violence are, truly, **un**speakable.

36   Perhaps Cover (and John Rawls) are wrong. Perhaps the commitment required to sustain existing institutional arrangements, far from being contingent and minimal, demands a profound commitment to the worth of the individual and the importance of individual autonomy. If so, at least some of the institutional arrangements of modern democracies are constructed upon seriously flawed premises.

37   In Adam's fall we sinnéd all.

38   Given the other evidence of discontent and of the hunger of some for paideic unity, this would be unsurprising. Evidence abounds, in both Australia and the United States, of political movements whose sole reason for existence is to appeal to this kind of nostalgia, a nostalgia which speaks in equal parts of a eulogy to a vanished past in which men were men, women were women, and everyone was... (name your favourite in-group) and of the Third Reich. It is perhaps noteworthy that the civil law has always, or so it seems to me, been bureaucratic in the Weberian sense in a way the common law escapes.

39   The intrusion of a visual image here surprised me even as I wrote the line. It is a reminder perhaps of how much of our understanding of the trial is visual.

40   An ancestral form of Dworkin's 'right answer thesis' has long been part of common law mythology.

41   I note, in passing, that alternatives to the adversary system are again being sought, that, under the banner of reform, the Australian Law Reform Commission is seeking to determine whether it is possible to incorporate some inquisitorial elements and whether this would reduce costs overall. Results to date are not precisely promising. I am of the view that some of the suggested changes are likely to both undermine the value base of the adversary system and offer very little in the way of real economies.

42   What is interesting here is the way plaintiffs and defendants simultaneously lose control of their own stories as those stories are retold in legal terms and gain new stories, new ways of understanding what has happened to them. That they do not

always feel themselves to own those new stories and, in some cases, feel themselves unable to lay claim to them is disturbing.

43 It is significant that, in a closely fought civil trial, authorities can always be found to support more than one vision of reality. In a criminal proceeding it may be that the distinction turns, more often than not, upon the rules of evidence and the multiple possibilities to be found within adjectival law.

44 Winn, 'Legal Ritual', 227.

45 Winn, 'Legal Ritual', 229. The symbolic significance of some trials is truly awesome... in the United States *Brown v Board of Education* served to define a particular cultural moment. That the potency of this moment has now been called into question and that its practical significance is gradually being eroded may be a consequence of a rhetorical failure, as Weisberg argues (*Poethics*, 9-10), or of the pragmatics which drove the decision, as Derrik Bell argues in *And We are Not Saved*, 51-74.

46 I intend this proper to carry full weight.

47 Here it is important to insist that this search and these arguments carry full moral weight. To seek to persuade others, to bring them share ownership of a particular decision, a particular law vision requires a reaching out, a willingness to acknowledge other perspectives. This part of the process also, I believe, both underlies and reinforces calls that the judiciary become more representative.

48 The reader will note that I speak here of a proceeding at first instance. Within the appellate jurisdiction matters are vastly more complex, and joint judgments sometimes bear the scars of their jointure.

49 Weisberg, *Poethics*, 7.

50 *Mabo and Ors v Queensland (No 2)*. Perhaps the most telling example of the ability of language to create meaning came in passage from the joint judgment of Dean and Gaudron at 104 cited in chapter 4 at 71.

51 Stephen Jay Gould comments tellingly upon the frequency with which the epigram is misquoted:

> The line is often miscited as "three generations of idiots..." But Holmes knew the technical jargon of his time, and the Bucks, though not "normal" by the Stanford-Binet, were one grade above idiots.

See Gould, SJ, The Mismeasure of Man, London, Pelican, 1981, 335.

What is noteworthy about the misquotation, and its persistence, is that it transforms a technical term which has largely fallen into desuetude into the vernacular and that vernacular retains its power in full. Indirectly, therefore, by replicating the form in which Holmes' epigram has become part of the legal imagination Weisberg bears testimony to the fact of its continuing hold over the legal imagination.

52 *Buck v Bell* 274 US 200 (1927). It is worth noting that the law upheld in this Supreme Court decision was implemented for some 47 years.

53 Gould, *The Mismeasure of Man*, 335-336.

54 In opting for the latter, I betray, I think, my optimism. If many among us still harbour such sentiments, they are less often publicly expressed and would be unlikely to find their way into judicial argument. That they are on the rise again, at least in Australia is for a majority of us a sign of profound concern.

55   The fact that Weisberg (mis)quoted it is an accurate enough measure of the success of Holmes' craft which remains fresh and vigorous. The problem lies in the fact that the argument Holmes is making is no longer one that we (as his audience) are prepared either to hear or to countenance. Its politics belong to another era.

56   We hear echoes of that rhetoric when we listen to Pauline Hanson and the rhetoric of the One Nation party.

57   When I speak of the trial itself, I speak of it both as a public ritual that symbolises our public commitment to the ideal of justice, and as a rhetorical phenomenon.

58   In this context I remind the reader that actions have meanings... most particularly within the trial context the actions and rituals which form a part of the trial process can be read as texts.

59   I should note in this context that I understand the role of narrative within the process of the trial very much more broadly than does Robin West. In 'Narrative, Responsibility, and Death' she begins by insisting that 'Lawyers are in the business of telling stories and arguing about rights'. To argue about rights is to tell a particular kind of story in a particular way. They are not alternatives. West, RL, 'Narrative, Responsibility, and Death' in West, *Narrative, Authority, and Law*, 419.

60   Goodrich, P, 'Specula Laws: Image, Aesthetic and Common Law' (1991) 2 *Law & Critique* 233. Goodrich's analogy to the canon law is apt enough. The altar of the law provides a (dangerous) supplement to our reading of the sacrificial altar. Unless it is written in blood the covenant remains unwritten.

61   I feel this has to be true, not only does legal interpretation attach first to the soul, it attaches to our souls from the moment we first become aware of the symbolic significance of the legal order.

62   I would carry the point rather further; the notion of 'innocent interpretation' is necessarily an oxymoron. Such an interpretation would be interpretation devoid of soul, of mind, of intelligence, the interpretation of an organism in which perception of the outside world was wholly direct, as unmediated by mind as by passion.

63   Engle, DM, 'Law in the Domains of Everyday Life: The Construction of Community and Difference' in Sarat, A & TR Kearns, *Law in Everyday Life*, Ann Arbor, Michigan Univ Press, 1995, 123, 125-126.

64   Engle, 'Law in the Domains of Everyday Life' 132.

65   Engle, 'Law in the Domains of Everyday Life' 132-133. One might usefully imagine him as a border guard positioned at the intersection of two disciplinary orders, simultaneously mediating the discontinuities between them and ensuring that those discontinuities do not exceed the limits of sociability. It is important that we not forget that law is not the sole relevant disciplinary order. There are numerous others, and each of them has its own characteristic forms of discipline.

66   In *Hegarty v Shine*, the Irish Court of Appeal, seeking refuge from 'moral contagion', declared the matter on appeal before it to be no fit subject matter for a court of law. Its decision remains part of the canon on that aspect of law, just as do the decisions of the two lower courts in the same matter. Each generation will have its own 'improper' cases, cases where the boundary between the legal and the social is contested, perhaps passionately so.

67 I am not denying that the techniques of literary interpretation cannot properly and usefully be employed in the interpretation of legal texts, I could hardly make such a claim without deeming illegitimate my own earlier readings.

68 It is perhaps worth mentioning that when actual force, as opposed to its ever present potential, is required, its use is read as a procedural and ritual failure, not as its climax.

69 White, 'Subordination, Rhetorical Survival Skills, and Sunday Shoes'.

70 See West, *Narrative, Authority, and Law*, 429.

71 The same practice is conventional among Canadian appellate tribunals.

72 *Commercial Bank of Australia Ltd v Amadio* (1983) 151 CLR 447.

73 I know that facts do not exist apart from the narratives in which they are embedded. I have tried to 'neutralise' the facts, remove those details that pull the judgments in one direction or another. The very act of neutralising the facts pulls them closer to an account with which a formalist might feel at home (although never quite reaching such an account).

74 According to Gibbs J the circumstances surrounding the guarantee/mortgage were of so unusual a nature that they ought to have been disclosed to the Amadios by the bank manager. Non-disclosure constituted a misrepresentation. As His Honour noted at 458:
    [T]he failure by the bank to make disclosure of these circumstances amounted to a misrepresentation, (albeit unintended) of a material part of the transaction between the bank and the company, and that the memorandum of mortgage, including the guarantee which it contains, is not binding on the respondents.
    For Gibbs J, the central problem lay in the power of the bank and its abuse of that power. Australian academic, now Federal Court judge, Paul Finn has characterised such a situation as one of 'transactional disadvantage'.

75 *Amadio*, 450-451, per Gibbs J.

76 *Amadio*, 451.

77 *Amadio*, 451-452.

78 *Amadio*, 457-458.

79 *Amadio*, 489, per Dawson J.

80 *Amadio*, 489-490. The selective disappearing of the 'female respondent' is part and parcel of the narrative strategy. While unremarkable in terms of the context in which the decision was handed down and the formalist narrative strategy adopted, it is remarkable in that (as we learn only in the judgment of Deane J) the only evidence available to the court was that of the 'female respondent' (through an interpreter) and the 'bank manager'. The 'male respondent' had lost his memory due to an accident that supervened between the signing of the mortgage and the date of the trial.

81 The fiction of arm's length contractual parties and formal equality of bargaining power overwhelms the reality of the situation. Even the classic market requirement of 'equal knowledge' is explained away. After all, the respondents must have been aware that the requirement for a guarantee was an indication of a parlous financial state. The market fiction becomes the reality.

82 *Amadio*, 471.

83 While Vincenzo Amadio may have had an opportunity to read the documents he did not do so. His parents did not attempt to.

84 *Amadio*, 478-479.

85   The speed of this intrusion is noteworthy. Mr Virgo presented the guarantee to the Amadios the day after Mr Stratton's meeting with Vincenzo Amadio. As Deane J notes, 'The grass was not left to grow'. *Amadio*, 471.

86   *Amadio*, 476, per Deane J. The absence of any sign of tension or concern is telling. Papa Amadio is reading the papers, Mama doing the dishes.

87   *Amadio*, 472.

88   The oblique reference to Salvador Dali's famous surrealist painting is intended. It captures perfectly the frozen imaginary of judgment, the recasting of stories as so many fragments of truth.

89   The reference is deliberate.

90   White, JB, *When Words Lose Their Meaning: Constitutions and Reconstitutions of Language, Character and Community*, Chicago, Univ of Chicago Press, 1984, 266.

9 To Speak as a Judge/Woman: A Different Voice?

Introduction

Towards the end of the last chapter, we began to examine some of the ways in which narrative may itself become a surrogate for rhetoric. As we saw in the various judgments in *Amadio*, the stories told by the judges are both shaped by particular sorts of rhetorical structures and contribute to the continual reshaping of those structures. Central to these rhetorical structures is the role of the judge. To speak as a judge is to participate in the creation of significant cultural scripts, scripts which determine the meanings of particular acts and the consequences which flow from those acts. While the judiciary is by no means the only active agent in the process of cultural scripting, its role is unique. To judge is always to deal with particularities, to be confronted by and to address individual stories and to be charged with forging those stories into universal scripts which can, in their turn, be brought to bear on further particularities. This movement, from the unique and particular to the universal and back once again to participate in the shaping of yet another script which is wholly particular[1] sets the role of the judiciary firmly apart.

Parliaments are charged with lawmaking, but parliamentary lawmaking becomes transgressive at the moment when it abandons the general to fasten upon the particular. Parliamentary stories are stories that reflect the will of the majority, which reject particularity and specificity. Laws must be universal, the stories to which parliaments respond collective stories, stories which allow the framing of broadly based commands. At this level, individualised rules are pernicious, smack of corruption and decay, of favouritism or of the targeting of out of favour individuals.

Not so the judge. To perform her task, the judge must confront a universal script and provide an individual reading, spin a wholly particular narrative out of that script. That narrative links the universal and the particular, tells her (and us) that the case before her is or is not a member of a particular class. Only when that unique and particularised narrative is

193

complete can judgment be given. In this way, the judge both complies with an ancient script that clearly delineates her role and participates in the continual rewriting of that script. Here I am explicitly referring to the ritual aspect of the practices of legality. In earlier chapters I suggested that the 'trial' in our culture, both as reality and, increasingly, as refigured and rescripted by the mass media, serves many of the same purposes as the ritual sacrifice. The 'courtroom drama', so called, whether an American or British import or one scripted in Australia plays a major role in the generation of public understandings of legality and legal process. This ritual component is, I believe, of critical importance. It serves **both** as a form of assurance that we not only have a past but also are true to that past and as a site of potential transgression in which (sometimes quite radical) change begins its journey to legitimation.

The judicial scripts that have become a critical site of change within the common law tradition are unique. As narratives they simultaneously authorise and justify acts of violence, both have and are intended to have particular sorts of consequences in the world. These consequences are wholly particularised: this man rather than that will be deprived of property, this woman rather than that lose her child. The narrative and the violence are linked.

The tension between narrative and violence, the fact that these are not just stories but stories with particular kinds of consequences, has conceptual implications which extend far beyond the ambit of Ronald Dworkin's chain novel analogy. In saying this, I do not deny that it is certainly possible (and perhaps even useful) to see a written judgment as somehow akin to a chapter in a chain novel. Very little imagination is required to read the judgments in *Amadio* as three plausible continuations of just such a novel. All this is simple, even banal. But even if we elect to read them in this way,[2] it does not follow that the questions Dworkin directs us to ask about these scripts are an appropriate response. If among our cultural scripts are the script of power, the script of (formal) equality, and the script of inequality and overreaching, other questions are possible, and more telling. We may wish to ask, not simply which script makes the story of the law the most coherent story it can be, but which script speaks most clearly of and to the kind of society we hope to become. Such a question recognises that judicial stories are never simply stories. They are stories with particular kinds of outcomes, and those outcomes are critical as the stories that seek to justify them. Seen in this way, some judgments at least can (and should) be read as alternative imaginings of social relations. On this reading, the proliferation of judgments, something to be denigrated by those who persist in a reading of adjudication that likens it to rule application, becomes a cause for celebration of cultural and legal possibility. To the extent that these alternative imaginings make their way from the law reports into more popular fora, they do become alternative readings of the kind of society we want ourselves to be. In this way, those quite rare cases that capture the popular imagination have the potential to become sites of change. This potential suggests that current moves to make the judiciary more representative may be critical, not because outcomes would be different, but because different kinds of stories would be heard. As the process continues, those differences in the hearing become differences in the telling. The stories told by a more representative judiciary would in this way reflect different perspectives, different windows on reality and those stories in turn will generate possibilities and influence future stories and their telling. This understanding of the role of judicial narratives emphasises that, important as outcomes are to the parties before the court and to the law itself, they are only part of the law.

> In every opinion a court not only resolves a particular dispute one way or another, it validates or authorizes one form of life – one kind of reasoning, one kind of response to argument, one way of looking at the world and its own authority – or another. Whether or not the process is conscious, the judge seeks to persuade her reader not only to the rightness of the result reached and the propriety of the analysis used, but to her understanding of what the judge – and the law, the lawyer, and the citizen – are and should be, in short, to her conception of the kind of conversation that does and should constitute us. In rhetorical terms, the court gives itself an ethos, or character, and does the same both for the parties to a case and for the larger audience it addresses – the lawyers, the public, and the other agencies in government. It creates by performance its own character and role and establishes a community with others. I think this is in fact the most important part of the meaning of what a court does: what it actually becomes, independently and in relation to others.
>
> The life of the law is in large part a life of response to these judicial texts. They invite some kinds of response and preclude others; as we deal with these invitations, both as individuals and as a community, we define our own characters, our own minds and values, not by abstract elaboration but in performance and action. Much of the life and meaning of an opinion (or a set of opinions) thus lies in the activities it invites or makes possible for judges, for lawyers, and for citizens; in the way it seeks to constitute the citizen, the

lawyer, and the judge, and the relations among them; and in the kind of discoursing community it helps to create.

When we turn to a judicial opinion then, we can ask not only how we evaluate its "result" but, more importantly, how and what it makes that result mean, not only for the parties in that case, and for the contemporary public, but for the future: for each case is an invitation to lawyers and judges to talk one way rather than another, to constitute themselves in language one way rather than another, to give one kind of meaning rather than another to what they do, and this invitation can itself be analysed. Is this an invitation to a conversation in which democracy begins (or flourishes)? Or to one in which it ends?[3]

In this chapter I shall be asking what (if anything) is likely to happen to this conversation when difference and judgment meet. The narratives in *Amadio* were all, although in different ways, androcentric narratives, specifically, narratives in which Mrs Amadio's understanding of the financial arrangements was understood by all concerned to be inconsequential in the overall scheme of things. Only Deane J even bothered to tell us that Mrs Amadio was not a party to the conversation concerning the guarantee but 'doing the dishes' while the guarantee was discussed.[4] As we interrogate narratives such as those in *Amadio* it is tempting to wonder whether, in such a case, a woman's voice would have made a difference. If a 'woman's voice' would have offered us a different narrative, a different shard of reality, what facts, what images might have been thought relevant? What (if anything) might this particular difference have come to mean? What, if anything, would it signify for law if we could identify such a voice as 'different'?

Meaning and Difference

I am not making any overarching claim for a 'different voice', at least not in the sense that such a claim was made by the well known arguments of Carol Gilligan and those who have followed her. Their arguments suggest that women speak with a moral voice that is somehow different, in which the dominant mode of reasoning reflects an ethic of care.[5] Gilligan argued that women engage in moral reasoning in a distinctive way, one that tended to favour an ethic of care above an ethic of justice. While she emphasised that both men and women could reason in both care based and justice based paradigms, her work has often been used to support essentialist arguments for women's moral superiority. Quite apart from whether this kind of generalisation is sustainable more broadly, I do not believe that it 'works' within the context of adjudication. The language of law is explicitly the language of justice rather than care.6 To the extent that the narratives of women judges are lawlike, I believe that those narratives will be written in legally cognisable ways, explicitly making use of rhetorical positions that are likely to carry persuasive force. These rhetorical positions or devices will almost invariably be justice based rather than care based. I am concerned, not with differences in moral reasoning, nor with the possibility of a distinction between an 'ethic of care' and an 'ethic of justice',7 but with differences in narrative voice. I want to ask instead whether women's judicial narratives are likely to be, for that reason (and in some as yet unspecified way), different. In that respect, my own position is far closer to that of Martha Fineman than Carol Gilligan. Fineman notes:

> Women's gendered existence is constituted by a variety of experiences – material, psychological, physical, social and cultural. Some of these experiences may be described as biologically based, while others seem more rooted in culture and custom. The actual *or* potential experiences of rape, sexual harassment, pornography and other sexualized violence women may suffer in our culture also shape individual experiences. So, too, the potential for reproductive events such as pregnancy, breast-feeding and abortion has an impact on women's constructions of their gendered lives. Further some gendered experiences are events which are shared with men. For example, a life event such as ageing falls in this category. But, there is often a unique way in which these events are generally or typically lived or experienced by women as contrasted with men in our culture. Thus, while both men and women age, the implications of ageing from both a social and economic perspective for the genders are different.
>
> Human beings are products of their experiences. There is little or no independent 'essence' to an organism, distinct from its experiences. Of course, certain physical and chemical components or characteristics of human beings both provoke experiences and act as filters through which such experiences are processed. A person, therefore, is the sum of these physical attributes as acted upon, by and through his or her lived or social and cultural experiences. What we call knowledge, what we value and label virtuous, grows out of these experiences. The very questions we ask along with the answers we fashion express these differences. It follows that from this assertion of fundamental

non-objectivity or non-essentialism that, if women collectively have different actual *and* potential experiences from men, they are likely to have different perspectives – different sets of values, beliefs and concerns as a group.[8]

Fineman argues that to suggest that women (as a group) have perspectives that in some ways are materially different from those of men simply emphasises that women have had different experiences by virtue of being women. Those experiences will, in turn, have a direct bearing upon the narratives that persuade them and upon the narratives upon which they believe are likely to persuade others. With this I substantially agree. In the course of arguing for affirmative action in academia, Duncan Kennedy made a similar point. Some of the moves in his argument are both appropriate and useful in the present context. According to Kennedy:

> First, both the choice and the application of academic standards have strikingly contingent and ideological dimensions. Law faculties distribute political resources (jobs) through a process that is political in fact, if not in name. One group (white males of the dominant culture) largely monopolizes this distribution process and, perhaps not so surprisingly, also largely monopolises the benefits (jobs). Second, anybody who disagrees with what I have just said, and maintains instead that standards are and should be apolitical, holds a position that is itself ideological. Law faculties shouldn't make the ideological choice between color-blind meritocracy and some form of race-conscious power-sharing without substantial participation of minorities in the decision...[9]

Kennedy suggests that arguments about the merits of academic work (and I believe that the argument can be extended much more broadly) can be positioned along two very different continuums. The first continuum is characterised by judgments of truth and falsity and about this kind of judgment Kennedy notes that once these are argued through to the end there is likely to be widespread consensus.[10] The second continuum touches more directly and obviously upon judgments concerning 'originality, interest, and value'. Here, disagreements are likely to be endemic and intensely politicised. Of those involved in these debates Kennedy suggests:

> More important for our purposes, they will generally concede that interest or value can be judged only by reference to a particular research tradition or scholarly paradigm, usually one among many that might have won dominance

in the field. Yet conclusions at the level of what is valuable or interesting are very often dispositive in deciding which of two articles[11] is better.

Once we acknowledge the possible existence of different research traditions, or collectively scholarly projects, we have to acknowledge that the white male occupants of faculty positions have more than the power to decide which performances are better. They have also had the power to create the traditions or projects within which they will make these judgments. It seems obvious that these traditions or projects are culturally and ideologically specific projects.

The projects themselves, as well as the judgments of originality, interest, and value they ground (not the narrow judgments of truth and falsity) would almost certainly change if people of excluded cultures and excluded ideologies were allocated power and opportunity to create research traditions and scholarly projects of their own, or to participate in those ongoing... There are no metacriteria of merit that determine which among culturally and ideologically specific research traditions or scholarly paradigms is "better" or "truer". Judgments of merit are inevitably culturally and ideologically contingent because they are inevitably paradigm dependent.[12]

Judgments of merit are invariably (and necessarily) situated, made from within specific paradigms and according to the patterns of value judgment which are characteristic of those particular paradigms. Within this context, the 'who' of judgment matters, and matters profoundly. In remarks following her inauguration as an associate justice of the United States Supreme Court, Ruth Bader Ginsburg spoke of the importance of ensuring that differing perspectives were woven into the tapestry of justice. According to Her Honour:

Justice Sandra Day O'Connor recently quoted Minnesota Supreme Court Justice Jeanne Coyne, who was asked: Do women judges decide cases differently by virtue of being women? Justice Coyne replied that in her experience, "a wise old man and a wise old woman reach the same conclusion".

I agree, but I also have no doubt that women, like persons of different racial groups and ethnic origins, contribute what a fine jurist, the late Fifth Circuit Judge Alvin Rubin, described as "a distinctive medley of view influenced by differences in biology, cultural impact, and life experience".

A system of justice will be the richer for diversity of background and experience. It will be the poorer, in terms of appreciating what is at stake and the impact of its judgments, if all of its members are cast from the same mold.[13]

While a wise old man and a wise old woman may reach the same decision, the stories told by a wise old man and a wise old woman about that decision and its meaning are likely to be very different. It is this difference which is likely to become critical in setting the parameters for further cultural scripts. Something else is likely to become critical as well. It is deeply connected with language and narrative and with the fact that every narrative is profoundly dependent upon its audience. In judicial narratives, as in academic narratives, not only is the positionality, the context, of the narrator profoundly important, so to, is the positionality, the context of the narratee.[14] We pay too little attention, I believe, to the audiences for whom judgments are given (and written).

On an immediate and inescapable level, the act of judgment is the culmination of the trial. Judgment is oral, and the spoken word is immediately directed to the parties and their counsel. It is also directed to all of those whose role it is to ensure that judgment is carried out. At this level, the audience is pre-determined, known to the judge from the outset and an integral part of the trial as process. In this context the giving of reasons for judgment and the act of judgment are linked, the roles tightly scripted, the connections formal and ritualised.

Where, however, there is to be a formal written judgment and that judgment is to be published, the connections are more tenuous. Because there are many potential audiences, we need to ask for whom it is written, and in what voice. Whom does the judge see as her audience? On what level ought her judgment to be read? Is she writing for a majority or in dissent? What impact will these differences have upon the language and structure of her judgment? We cannot assume a common language, a common narrative vocabulary.[15] When, earlier, we looked at the structure of the judgments in *Mabo*, the differences in narrative voice were even more striking than the structural and doctrinal differences. Differences in narrative voice do more than simply mirror individual differences in temperament and style. Because judgments are written in the consciousness of multiple audiences, because they consciously and deliberately create sites for future debate,[16] they operate on multiple levels. They both acknowledge the commonality engendered by a language shared and the differences of tone and voice that are an inevitable part of diversity. Thus, even if, on one level, narrator and narratee share a common language, on another this commonality is itself a site of diversity, a diversity that is both informed and mediated by the existence of a variety of linguistic markers.

Among the most straightforward of these linguistic markers is gender. In English, in contradistinction to many languages, most nouns are not syntactically gendered. Consequently their form is not differentiated by gender, rendering English grammar rather less complex than the grammar of a language such as French or Latin in which noun forms are almost invariably differentiated by gender. Despite the lack of formal gender markers, however, as a matter of cultural and linguistic fact, many English nouns are tacitly understood 'as if' they were gendered. Thus it is, for example, that where it is necessary to use a pronoun to refer to a ship that pronoun will almost invariably be female. In the case of other nouns, especially those that refer to particular prestigious occupations, the pronominal association is characteristically male.

In linguistics, the male gender is known as the 'unmarked term'. It identifies the norm. Thus, when we hear the (putatively) gender neutral nouns 'lawyer', or 'judge', we assume that the 'lawyer' or 'judge' referred to is male because such nouns carry invisible 'gender' markers. They are also implicit in some terms that refer to general categories of productive activities. Worker and homemaker are obvious examples.

Shelina Neallani[17] reminds us that even putatively universal nouns carry 'markers', for example, those of race and sexuality. This cognitive baggage determines the way in which such nouns are structured in our imaginations and thus influences our reactions. In societies such as Australia, Canada, and the United States, the 'cognitive baggage' carried by 'universal' nouns such as man and woman constitutes a complete set of coded meanings. Thus, unless qualifiers are added, woman is understood as white heterosexual woman, man is understood as white heterosexual man. Buried within these sets of coded meanings are the further assumptions that these individuals are middle class, able bodied, and (usually) of Anglo-Celtic ethnic origin. Words such as 'woman' and 'man' lost their innocence long ago. Other markers may figure as well, depending upon the particular context. These markers may include physical characteristics such as weight or cultural practices such as religion. They frequently include the dress codes associated with membership in certain religious groups as well as the dress codes associated with gender norms. Accent is another important marker, one that functions as a surrogate for both ethnic origin and class position.[18] The interaction of these 'markers' is complex and never more complex than when the role to which they attach is of profound symbolic importance within the culture. Sometimes, the impact of these

202 To Speak as a Judge

'markers' can be so profound as to submerge individual identity in role structure. Shelina Neallani speaks of the way in which some women of colour adopt a raceless persona, thus minimising the perceived difference experienced by members of the dominant group.[19]

> One's position in the class structure is an aid to racelessness. It may overcome race as a negative factor in the dominant society. Class has the power to minimize internalized oppression and to reduce domination. When members of the dominant group perceive that they are of the same class as a person who would normally be oppressed on the basis of race or sex, this oppression may be lessened because belonging to the monied class means having power in the form of access to education, the legal system, and the political process. If a Woman of Colour belongs to a wealthy class, she appears more raceless; the stereotypes about her are not as prevalent, and she receives better treatment.
>
> As a Woman of Colour, I believe that racelessness is produced by the understanding that our success depends not only on our abilities, but also on White Mainstream People feeling comfortable with us, by perceiving a 'likeness' with us. While it is one way of diminishing our oppression, the strategy of racelessness can be seen as accommodating behaviour which has its own costs.[20]

The trappings of the judicial role, the stigmata of wig and gown, superimpose[21] something very close to a raceless and genderless persona upon the judge. Despite this, despite the fact that, axiomatically, her place in the class structure plays as critical a role in the construction of her perceived identity as do the 'wildcards' of gender and race, the category judge is, definitionally, linguistically unmarked. Because it is linguistically (and culturally unmarked), not only is judgment male, it is also and explicitly 'white' and in colonial outposts such as Canada, Australia and the United States,[22] Anglo-Saxon. The reality of many judges is simultaneously genderless and raceless and irrevocably marked by the spectral indicia of gender, of race, and of ethnicity that proscribes the desired collapse into a universal persona.

In this chapter, I want to call attention to the subtle and powerful interaction of linguistic and positional markers with a reality that violates those markers.[23] This interaction is not the product of a simple dualism but of the jostling of a multiplicity of potential personas, both within the rhetorical structure of the trial and outside it. I spoke earlier of the role of the judge as a surrogate for a kind of high priest, and of a very particular authority attached to that role. The vestments in which the judge is customarily attired simultaneously obliterate and highlight her otherness. To her audience she appears at once indistinguishable from her brothers and marked, perhaps only by her speech, perhaps by other indicia of gender. Within the dynamics of the trial gender[24] slides repeatedly between foreground and shadows, impaling itself upon consciousness anew with every fresh utterance. The sign of differánce becomes the word. The judge speaks, as judge, and yet is inevitably heard as woman. The orality of the trial can, therefore, never be entirely authentic, the voice of the woman/judge, within the rhetorical context of adjudication, becoming its own dangerous supplement (woman/judge). In the end, the problem is not that she speaks with a different voice, but that her voice embodies differánce. However successful the stigmata of wig and gown, at the moment of judgment, her voice gives the game away,[25] undermining the promised finality. Within the essentially oral medium of the trial the sought after genderless persona remains tantalisingly out of reach.

The law has spoken, but its speech is not as had been hoped. The matter is somehow not at an end. The issue is not one of outcome but of voice. Inevitably, as the trial recedes, the written judgment remains, triumphant in its textuality, destined, if successful, to find its place as another chapter in a Herculean chain novel. Earlier I spoke of the ways in which still powerful conventions of judicial attire superficially impose a genderless and raceless persona upon the judge.[26] This persona, destabilised during the trial by the persistence of the feminine voice, is immediately and profoundly reinstated by the conventions of the written judgment. Within the frame of reference of the law report the judge becomes (except to those who are aware of the reality of the matter) simply the judge. Because the writing of judges is 'always already there'[27] 'there is always another precedent, another interpretation, another possibility'.[28] Like the theatrical trappings of wig and gown, the conventions of judgment obliterate the stigmata of race and of gender. We are left to seek otherness in the interstices of judgment. The question remains. How will we, indeed **will** we, know it when we see it?

Repetitions and Reiterations

The rhetorical movement of the trial iterates endlessly, moving from rhetoric and persuasion to judgment and returning once again to rhetoric to explain and justify the outcome. The sign of otherness is at first muted. Sometimes it appears to be masked by the conventions associated with judging, foregrounded in the act of judgment, only to be submerged beneath the surface of the judicial text and perhaps forgotten. These iterations reinstate the promise of a blind and universal judgment at every juncture. If we seek a different voice in judgment, unless we constantly rehearse the lineage of difference, keep the sign of otherness fixed before us, all that will remain are the conventions of judging. In the rituals of dissent, of concurrence, of a joint judgment, of a leading judgment and the single honorific 'J' what is relevant is that she was a judge. Most particularly in the written judgment, to speak as a judge is to speak in a way which cannot be bracketed. Convention dictates that Mme Berthe Wilson becomes, in the law reports, Wilson J, Mary Gaudron, Gaudron J, Sandra Day O'Connor, O'Connor J, Ruth Bader Ginzberg, Ginzberg J.[29] On the face of the text, all that matters is the status of the judgment, whether she spoke for or with a majority or in dissent.

On one level, of course, this is precisely how it should and must be if the word is to function as judgment. On another level, it reminds us forcefully and brutally that the grammar of judgment excludes differánce. To the extent that the written text is to perform the role we have assigned it, to the extent that the writing of judges becomes law, it is because it contains its own mechanisms for subverting and neutralising difference. The law, as Stanley Fish has observed, wishes to have an independent existence, and that independent existence has become a fundamental part of the grammar of judgment. As narrative structure, judgment demands of its author an understanding of her audience. To the extent that the written judgment seeks simultaneously to justify what has been done and to persuade others, it must adhere to a pre-determined grammar of judgment, respect the insistence of legality that it have an independent existence.

In this way, the grammar of judgment signals the judge's adherence to the predetermined structures of legality. Given the conventions that surround the production, in writing, of authoritative texts, the extent to which these conventions reinforce the eradication of differánce is both remarkable and unremarked. Elsewhere, even in the law, outsider voices are heard, sometimes explicitly, as outsider voices.[30] To some extent at least, conventions of scholarship are shifting, if only slightly. From time to time, on the face of scholarly texts, an attempt is made to foreground differánce, to acknowledge the perils implicit in 'speaking as'. These changing conventions, perhaps no more than ripples on the surface of academia, are not foreshadowed as possibilities within the unwritten conventions governing the publication of judgments. Indeed, it might be thought that even to admit of them as possibilities, as subversive counter-texts, is to destabilise legality by particularising judgment, rendering it defective as law.

Judicial texts, as texts, are governed by very different conventions. Here, the distinctions between unreported judgment and reported judgment, the symbolic importance given to the authorised report, are critical indicia of authority, measures of the weight to be assigned to a particular judgment in the hierarchies of legality.[31] Legality colludes as well in the convention that the particularities of the judge are irrelevant to the status of the judgment. What matters is not the persona of the judge, but the status of the court and of the judgment: whether it speaks for a majority of the court, or is a concurring judgment, or a lone dissenting judgment. Conventions of legality such as these, largely unwritten but carefully inculcated[32] in those who would take their places before the law contribute to the eradication of individuality. That there are exceptions, that certain judges and certain landmark judgments assume an iconic status,[33] only serves to highlight the extent to which legal conventions eradicate (and are intended to eradicate) the particularity of the judge.

One consequence of these conventions is that judgment becomes most completely successful (and most completely lawlike) when particularity is completely eradicated.[34] To the extent that particularity cannot be expunged, the authority of the judgment is open to question and to compromise. Doubt emerges as to whether it is the law that has spoken or the individual judge.[35] Against this background, the suggestion that as a judge a woman would, by virtue of that fact, speak with different voice is profoundly subversive of fundamental conventions of legality. For the judge herself, to self consciously speak with a different voice is to abrogate responsibility, to fail to justify what one has done in the most appropriate and compelling way possible. For the written judgment to persuade, to fulfil the purpose for which it was written, it must be consonant with the conventions of legality. Particularity must be vanquished, the judge must speak simply as a judge.

While my understanding of the operation of these conventions has much in common with Stanley Fish's notion of an interpretive community, it goes well beyond the relatively benign assumptions that Fish makes concerning meaning and authority. For Fish, such a community simply provides the context within which interpretation takes place and without which interpretation is impossible, sets the normative conventions and moves which count as legitimate interpretations within that community. My understandings of these conventions suggest that, from the perspective of the judge, the decision to comply with them or to abrogate them is non-trivial. At the point at which the judge forsakes the conventions and moves of legality and speaks with a different voice, allows her particularity to appear on the face of the judgment, she has abandoned not one, but two central obligations. She has, to some extent at least, stepped outside of the moves within which justification is possible. Because her judgment fails to achieve universality, whatever justification is proffered is incomplete, a failed attempt.

As rhetoric as well such a judgment is, for the present at least, likely to be a failure. Persuasion depends upon a kind of rightness in the individual judgment. The arguments put must be not simply well formed but recognisable as a compelling continuation of an ongoing story, a story and a continuation to which the particularity of the judge is wholly irrelevant. To the extent that she speaks with a 'different voice', universality collapses into particularity. Judgment ceases to be a plausible continuation of an authoritative legal narrative and becomes a break with tradition. As rhetoric it may serve to challenge long standing traditions and in that way have persuasive force, but within law, as the continuation of an ongoing legal story it is likely to be a failure.

Layers of Difference/Differánce

In this way, paradoxically, an impasse is reached. Within the trial itself (as within the written judgment) the rituals of legality coalesce to eradicate difference and particularity. Inevitably, they are less than completely successful. As judge, her 'different voice' unsettles the accustomed rhythms of the trial, reaffirming particularity despite the universal trappings of judgment. Even where she does not speak in a different voice, the difference in her voice makes the trial mean differently.

Within the trial, the subjectivity of the judge resists mapping onto any straightforward model. Even when her role demands that she be open to persuasion, it demands equally that she orchestrates proceedings, establish limits, determine what may be said and what must remain unspoken. The inherent contradictions in the judicial role are insufficiently remarked. Her voice is never unitary, never uncomplicated, perhaps never truly her own. Her role demands that she speak as a judge, yet the precise nature of judicial speech is difficult to delineate. It is not simply that she fills the role of the judge. We expect more of our judges than that. She must be a judge, and in everything that she does be and remain truly judicial.

If within the cartography of the trial, difference potentially destabilises legality, the written judgment is very different. Here, the conventions of judgment obliterate difference, submerge it beneath predetermined forms. If the majority delivers a joint judgment, even the identity of its principal author is obliterated by these conventions. What is important is not who the author is, but that the judgment speaks for a majority of the court. All of this is in keeping with the ways the law wishes to be understood. It wishes to have an independent existence, wishes to insist that individuality and identity are unjudicial, too easily mistaken for bias, for a decision reflecting the personal whim of the judge and not the law.

Yet despite this conventional eradication of identity, in Australia, as in the United States and England, the individual persona and character of certain judges has stamped their courts and their judgments. In Australia we speak of Dixon and of Evatt and more recently of Brennan, as such judges. Their identity stamped the courts they sat upon and hangs as a sign over our conceptions of legality. When Dixon spoke of the safe harbour of a certain kind of legalism, his understanding of the demands of that legalism stamped a very particular ethos upon the High Court upon which he sat. Much the same can be said of the greatest American judges: Marshall, and Learned Hand, and Holmes and Warren. Judges like these become lightening rods for legality, their decisions always already more than simply decisions. It is not necessarily that they are the greatest judges of their generations, indeed they may not be. For whatever reason, they come to symbolise the judicial role, both in their own time and for the future.

Our understandings of legality pull in two directions. On the one hand, the conventions of judgment erase the identity of the judge. Within the court, the stigmata of wig and gown[36] are intended to eradicate identity and reinforce the ritual character of the trial. Within the written judgment the forms specifying the hierarchical position of the court, the status of the judgment, whether majority, concurring, or dissenting have the same effect.

Just as the trial is set apart firmly from daily life, so too every written judgment is set apart from writings that are more ordinary. The judge becomes, simply, a judge. Both distance and authority are reinforced. These conventions are most readily maintained when judges are not individuals, but repeated iterations of an archetypical judge. The threat of difference is precisely that it disrupts these conventions, breaks the chain of iterations and forces us to confront individuality in an institutional setting designed to eliminate it. Difference forces us to confront the fact that the judge is a person, both unique and particular.

There are dangers here of course. In Australia in the one court where robing was abandoned for a time at least, it has been reinstated. The naked humanity of an unrobed judge, revealed as an ordinary human being, can and did become a lightening rod for the anger and frustration of many of those before the court. The threat of repeated violence, the fact that, without wig and gown, the judge became simply an ordinary person, and by extension, one who is not entitled to call down violence upon others had done its work. The experiment, one designed to minimise the distance between court and litigant, and thus to 'humanise' the court was abandoned. Its success, and not its failure, necessitated its abandonment.

On a lesser scale, something similar can happen when difference becomes visible. When, despite wig and gown, despite forms of dress designed to eradicate identity and individuality, difference becomes visible, potentially at least, it undercuts the authority of the court. Judges become simply ordinary individuals, people both like and unlike you and I. To an extent, at least, for judgment to be properly judicial the distance between the bench and the dock must be maintained. It is not simply that this distance is part of the ritual geography of the trial. It is central to the authority of the court.

If the difference between sacrifice and slaughter lies in the distinction between altar and slaughterhouse, between priest and butcher, the difference between legality and summary justice lies, at least in part, in the distance between judge and subject. Ordinariness overwhelms that distance. If the judge is simply an ordinary woman, her ordinariness undercuts the authority of her judgment. We do not want our judges to be simply members of the community. That is at once too little and too much. Even those of us who argue from time to time that the judiciary must become more representative mean something very different by the representativeness we advocate. Those who perceive the unrepresentative character of the judiciary as profoundly problematical argue that by drawing its membership from a narrow and limited base certain potential sources of bias are build in. According to Madame Justice Bertha Wilson, the demand for a more representative judiciary rests upon two basic propositions:

> one, that women view the world and what goes on in it from a different perspective from men; and two, that women judges, by bringing that perspective to bear on the cases they hear, can play a major role in introducing judicial neutrality and impartiality into the justice system.[37]

Yet, this perception reverses understandings that have become conventional in a way that can be profoundly threatening. Most particularly in law, traditional patterns of thought retain their power. At a fundamental level, we justify the power and authority of the courts through the proposition that legal principles apply universal (or nearly universal) values to the concrete situation before the court. Against this background, the insistence that a more representative judiciary is essential in order to ensure that the legal system is neutral and impartial destabilises conventional understandings of the relationship between universality and particularity. Iris Young contrasts the public realm with private particularity. According to Young:

> The public realm of citizens achieves unity and universality only by defining the civil individual in opposition to the disorder of womanly nature, which embraces feeling, sexuality, birth and death, the attributes that concretely distinguish persons from one another. The universal citizen is disembodied dispassionate (male) reason... Precisely because the virtues of impartiality and universality define the civic public, that public must exclude human particularity.[38]

The conventions of judging: the ritual geography of the court, the power of the traditions that insist that judges remain gowned (and, until recently, wigged) emphasise that the judge is the embodiment of reason. Collectively they reject the particularity of the judge, struggle to disembody her. Corporeality unsettles these conventions, and by unsettling them, destabilises our confidence in the universality of justice. If it matters that the judiciary is unrepresentative, if that fact has implications for the justice and impartiality of the legal system, a great deal more is called into question than simply whether judges from different backgrounds bring different experiences.

Within this context above all, the liberal values of neutrality and impartiality collide with understandings which remind us that experiences, understandings and perspectives are quite fundamentally dependant upon who, in particular, one is. Inadvertently then, and in ways which have yet to be acknowledged in the various debates concerning adjudication, the insistence that a more representative judiciary is essential has the potential to destabilise conventional liberal understandings concerning law. In fundamental ways, our explanations of why a more representative judiciary is essential destabilise liberal understandings of equality, and indeed, of justice. If our particularity counts, it counts in ways that demolish traditional vocabularies of justice. If who we are as men and women of different racial and ethnic backgrounds, different religious traditions, different class backgrounds matters, conventional understandings of neutrality and impartiality are hopelessly inadequate. We need a new vocabulary of justice, and a new understanding of what it means to judge.

Notes

1   This movement has been tacitly acknowledged throughout common law history, as the familiar designation of the particular case as *res judicata* suggests. The official story of each legal decision is both final and particular, not in the ordinary order of things to be reopened and universal, ready as law to become an integral part of further narratives.

2   By saying 'choose' I am insisting that alternative readings are equally legitimate and mean to signal that fact.

3   White, JB, 'The Judicial Opinion as a Form of Life' in White, JB, *Justice as Translation*, Chicago, Univ of Chicago Press,1990, 89, 101-102.

4   'Doing the dishes' may be read as metaphor for an entire way of life so that in the end it is immaterial whether Cesira Amadio was 'doing the dishes' (as a matter of fact) or not. That was her role.

5   Gilligan, Carol, *In a Different Voice*.

6   This comment is obvious, but necessary. A care perspective would find the common law failure to acknowledge a duty to rescue almost unintelligible.

7   Still less am I concerned with Robin West's image of an act of power which is loving. I find the idea unpalatable and its potential paternalism disturbing. See West, RL, 'Adjudication is not Interpretation' 278:

> In public life, no less than in private life, I believe we should criticize acts of power not be reference to their rationality, or their coherence, or their "integrity", but by reference to their motivation and their effects. An act of power in public life as well as in private life that is praiseworthy is an act of power which, in short, is loving: it is the act that originates in the heart and is prompted by our sympathy for the needs of others and empathy for their situation.

8   Fineman, MA, 'Feminist Legal Scholarship and Women's Gendered Lives', in Cain M & CB Harrington (eds) *Lawyers in a Postmodern World: Translation and Transgression*, New York, New York Univ Press, 1994, 229, 239-240.

9   Kennedy, D, 'A Cultural Pluralist Case for Affirmative Action in Legal Academia' in Kennedy, D, *Sexy Dressing Etc.*, Cambridge, Harvard University Press, 1993, 34, 58.

10 What he does not go on to say, but what I think he would be unlikely to deny, is that this kind of question (at least in law) touches upon aspects of our belief system which are so deep rooted as to be wholly beyond question. An obvious and simplistic example of this kind of question would be whether or not 'murder' is 'wrong'.

11 In this context it is important to note that precisely the same point is perspicacious with respect to judicial narratives. Such narratives (addressed – it goes without saying – to particular audiences) are more or less persuasive according to the frame of reference from which they are understood.

12 Kennedy, 'Affirmative Action', 59.

13 Martin, E, 'Women on the bench: a different voice? 77 *Judicature* 126 (1993) quoting Justice Ruth Bader Ginsberg.

14 Kennedy, 'Affirmative Action', 80-81 argues:
    The individual in his or her culture, the individual as a practitioner of an ideology, the individual in relation to his or her own neurotic structures is always somewhere, has always just been somewhere else, and is empowered and limited by being in that spot on the way from some other spot. Communities are like that too, though in a complicated way.

15 American research has examined the role orientations of women state Supreme Court judges, identified four role orientations: the representative role, the token role, the outsider role, and the different voice role. Overall, there was evidence that a substantial proportion of women Supreme Court judges behaved as representatives, that is, they were inclined to vote in an identifiably pro-woman way on cases involving women's issues. The token and the outsider role are mirror images. They are used as analytical tools to examine voting behaviour on issues such as criminal rights and economic liberties that do not immediately impact upon women. Token behaviour is evidenced by conforming to the dominant majority and adopting largely centrist positions while outsiders tend to address audiences outside the institution and exhibit comparatively extreme voting behaviour. Female Supreme Court judges in the United States are more likely to adopt outsider roles than to exhibit token behaviour. Evidence of a different voice in the sense in which that phrase is used by Carol Gilligan is, at best, equivocal. See Allen, DW & DE Wall 'Role Orientations and Women State Supreme Court Justices' 77 *Judicature* 156 (1993).

16 The propensity of women judges to adopt the outsider role in contradistinction to the token role is particularly interesting in the context of the definition of 'outsider role behaviour'. Allen & Wall (158-159) argue that 'Rather than attempt to moderate conflict, persuade colleagues to adopt centrist positions, and compromise away differences, outsiders address audiences outside the institution'.

17 Neallani, S, 'Women of Colour in the Legal Profession: Facing the Familiar Barriers of Race and Sex' 5 *Canadian Journal of Women & the Law* 148 (1992).

18 Matsuda, 'When the First Quail Calls' provides an interesting discussion of the way in which voice and accent may vary according to setting and role. She speaks of her own

Hawaiian 'creole' dialect that she uses in informal settings and the 'standard English' which demarcates her professional role. In this way, voice becomes an ally in creating a raceless persona. In 'Voices of America' she also spoke of her first visit to Australia some years ago, and of the fact that even her best professional accent did not enable her to avoid the suspicion and abuse of taxi drivers. Her perceived difference overwhelmed the raceless persona she adopted.

19   Members of minority ethnic often make use of two distinct dialects, one characteristic of standard English and one reflecting the patois of the 'private community' to which they belong. In 'Voices of America' Mari Matsuda speaks of her own ability to shift between the Creole patois of her Hawaiian-Asian ancestry and standard English.

20   Neallani, 'Women of Colour in the Legal Profession' 158-159.

21   They are intended to do just that, remind us of the universal and ritualised aspects of judging.

22   It should go without saying that in other locations the particular reading given 'judge' would be different, both because of the background context and because the judicial role may be different. The specificity of context is critical to meaning.

23   Perhaps we should see the call, in Australia and elsewhere, for a more representative judiciary as an attempt to destabilise these associations.

24   Race, as marker of difference, functions somewhat differently. Here speech is less likely to signal difference if only because those who are sufficiently senior to be acceptable candidates are likely, at least in their professional lives, to speak in a manner which is indistinguishable from that of their colleagues. The sign of gender is oral, that of race visual. Within the structure of the trial, which seems the greater violation, the more inescapable. Douzinas et al (153) remind us that 'the growth of literacy moved the trial from oracular and divine manifestation, to oral and finally written processes of judgment'.

25   I want to suggest a parallel here with the Sartrean phrase *le jeux sont fait...* conventionally translated 'the game is up'.

26   While these conventions are weaker in the United States where there is no equivalent to the regalia of a British or Australian appellate tribunal, they persist in the judicial robe. In Australia, the first court to abandon them for normal business attire (which is, of course, radically gendered) has abandoned the experiment. Without the distance thus created, law's monopoly upon violence might seemed likely to break down.

27   Douzinas et al, 155

28   Douzinas et al, 157.

29   The traditions and conventions of adjudication move rather more slowly than do the conventions of academia!

30   This kind of construction is not without its problematical aspect. Those who position themselves on the margins within the academy are insiders from an external point of view. That they 'self-consciously' foreground their positions as women, as indigenous people, is one of the moves that is available within the academy. It is not a move that is possible within the conventions which govern 'speaking as' in adjudication, at least not in the case of a formal written judgment, an authorised text.

31   A longitudinal study of the impact of electronic publication of judgments might well provide a fascinating way to document how, in the electronic era, these patterns of authority are being reconfigured.

32 As a law student I carefully memorised the appropriate formula for citing a case in an oral argument, and the need for an apology to the bench if unable to procure the authorised version. Today, my own students are being inducted into the same rituals.

33 In Anglo-Australian law, two figures that come immediately to mind are the former Master of the Rolls in the English Court of Appeal, Lord Denning, and the Chief Justice Barwick of the High Court of Australia. In both cases, their iconic status has served to diminish rather than reinforce the 'weight' attached to their judgments.

34 If, as many believe, the voice of law is an explicitly masculine voice, a kind of perfection has been achieved in universalising that voice.

35 Lord Denning (in England) and Lionel Murphy (in Australia) come instantly to mind as judges whose persona overshadowed almost completely their judicial role, in the end, subverting the authority of their judgments.

36 As Australian judges at last put aside their wigs, they have also put aside their immunity from public criticism. An angry and abusive public is targeting them and their decisions in a new and different way.

37 Wilson, Madam Justice B, 'Will Women Judges Really Make a Difference' (1990) 28 *Osgoode Hall LJ* 507, 515. The difference lies, not in our voices, but in our experiences.

38 Young, IM, *Justice and the Politics of Difference*, Princeton, Princeton Univ Press, 1990, 110-111.

10   Justice, Finally

Introduction

Stories and storytelling have brought us a very long way. As a metaphor for adjudication, the conventions of storytelling remind us that legal stories are never accidental.[1] While this may sound brutally deterministic, that is not my meaning. When I say that legal stories are never accidental, my meaning sounds on two distinctive levels. First, our democratic conventions insist that we do not come before the law accidentally. Whether we are brought before the law because others have decided that it is meet and proper that this should be done, or whether we so will it, a conscious act is required. Second, the decision to go before the law compels the creation of a 'legal story'. No other story will do. Once that decision has been made, the process of translating a human story into a legal story begins.

A legal story is a very special kind of narrative.[2] It extracts deeply embedded facts from their natural setting, and relocates them within established legal paradigms. For this to happen, the human story must be fractured,[3] broken down into its constituent elements so that each element can be made 'legally relevant', assume its proper place in the drama which is about to unfold. Even if every element in the human story has a legal analogue, so that the fit seems perfect, complete, the stories are not the same, cannot be the same. The logic, the focus, the structure of the 'human story' is not that of the legal story. Its characters are different as well, obedient to different conventions.

Through the conventions of legal storytelling: the writs, the interrogatories, the depositions, and through the lens provided by the requirements of adjectival law, the legal story unfolds. These provide the filters through which a polyvocal performance is distilled, reduced to comprehensible dimensions. They are essential in another way as well, as building blocks which ensure that this story can take its place among other legal stories. Once we have mastered the conventions of legal storytelling, they enable us understand the trial both as process and as ritual.

The demands of legality simultaneously strip events of their human meaning and supplement reality in particular ways.[4] No one comes before the law lightly. Whether legality is ardently pursued, or whether it forces itself upon an unwilling party, the decision to come before the law is one of moment. So powerful are its conventions, we often forget that they bring with them their own repertoire of characters. Wherever the story began, whatever meanings it may have held for those intimately involved in its unfolding, these are not the meanings of the courtroom. Only characters familiar to the law can speak the meanings of the courtroom.

This process of characterisation is easiest to discern in cases a little distant from us in both time and place. *Hegarty v Shine* provides an excellent example.[5] When we are told that the plaintiff's 'circumstances are so pitiable that they must necessarily excite compassion in the breast of every man'[6] we know at once that we must read this story against a particular set of understandings. Its central trope, that of the 'fallen woman' and the price that she must pay for having strayed, establishes both the genre and the characters. While the theme of the fallen woman remains a well-known cultural construct, the social and economic meaning of her falling is situated. For a Victorian audience, and even more for a Victorian court of law, the presence of this character means that the legal story becomes a classic morality play. Whether its central character, the plaintiff, has succumbed to the blandishments of the defendant and allowed herself to be seduced by him or has allowed passion to overcome her, her departure from feminine virtue dooms her from the outset. Both her agency and her responsibility for her own condition are beyond question. She has, as the court self-righteously notes, led an immoral life and contracted a 'loathsome disease'.[7]

During the Victorian era, the core elements in this drama were stock ingredients in art, in literature and in the theatre. While they differed slightly depending upon the venue, they were invariably recognisable. More contemporaneously, they survive in classical melodramas and morality plays. Legally, the extent to which they were woven through Victorian law reminds us that while the positivist reading of law common in that period steadfastly rejected any necessary connection between law and morality, legal conventions assimilated the characters of these morality plays into judicial precedent. Moralistic readings were the rule rather than the exception. The allegedly meretricious conduct of the prostitute, the paramour and the fallen women were invariably used to deny them legal remedies to which they would otherwise be entitled. More recently, of course, we are routinely told that the rape of a street worker is less serious and less traumatic than that of a nun. The texts remain striking similar, an eradication of male sexual responsibility accompanied by a reaffirmation of the inevitability of the madonna/whore dichotomy.

Yet, as it is well to recall, there is another way of understanding these conventions. Susan Currie reminds us that:

> The stories women tell have not been treated with respect by our society. When women have passed on their stories from generation to generation, these stories have been called old wives' tales... Because the right story is *his* story – the story of our society, our history (his story) is about men's lives and not about women's lives...
>
> ...the common law developed on a case by case basis. As different men in different situations told their stories to the common law courts, the common law courts started to build up a coherent body of rules to resolve men's disputes. The disputes the courts would listen to were about property. Under the feudal system it was men who were the property owners, so the views of women were not heard in the courts. When the courts started to hear disputes that were not related to property, they decided that not all disputes were worthy of regulation by the law.[8]

The gulf between the human story and the legal story has already been noted. Insufficiently noted, perhaps, are particular ways in which the themes of legal stories are gendered, and the stories told about these themes are stories developed to resolve disputes among men. As summed up for the jury by the trial judge, the story is one of fraud and concealment, of the defendant's wilful concealment of a material fact, one that sufficed to transform an act of consensual sexual congress into a civil assault. One way of reading the (rather strained) language of fraud and concealment is as an attempt by her counsel to render a story of lust and betrayal in a language that met the needs of the law.

When Ball J in the Court of Appeal derides the charge given to the jury by the trial judge, what he is deriding is the possibility that the discourse of fraud might be appropriate in these circumstances. The contents of a share prospectus might be fraudulent, as might representations in respect of goods or services. More problematically, representations by a physician in respect of the character of a purported treatment might be fraudulent as where, in *De May v Roberts*,[9] sexual intercourse was represented to be appropriate treatment for a medical condition. Here, however, the master discourse of lust and seduction overwhelmed the human story of innocence and betrayal.[10] Once the possibility of fraud in this context has been deemed 'absurd', the story moves along predictable lines. Fraud, innocence, and betrayal: all are irrelevant. Because they are irrelevant, they can be replaced with questions of contract, of immorality, of *contra bones mores*. We are told that only a pre-existing contract can generate an obligation that is enforceable by a court of law. Here, of course, there can be no contract that the law will acknowledge. Where her story might have been, there is only silence, a silence underscored by the appellate court's insistence that it is unnecessary to canvass the facts. The victim has become something very different: an immoral seductress, one undone by her own depraved passions.

The Limits of Narrative

Yet stories, even legal stories, always share another feature. Because they are stories, they exist only in the telling, only through the eyes of the narrator or narrators and those for whom the stories are told. There is no point-of-viewless paradise from which legal stories emerge, unscarred by the human voices of those who have created them. Indeed, the point of focusing upon narrative, upon the construction of legal stories and the voices of those who contribute to those stories is to insist upon the one feature that is, at once, the greatest strength of common law traditions and their greatest weakness.

The metaphors of classical jurisprudence conceal the voices that have created legal narratives, giving those narratives pseudo-inevitability. It is not that they are anonymous, or that pseudonyms are involved. They are quite literally narratives whose social and legal power comes from the fact that the narrator ultimately disclaims responsibility for the outcomes they prescribe. These metaphors are themselves revealing enough: images of the 'law working itself pure' through the agency of the 'princes of law's empire', of the 'golden thread' beloved of British and Australian jurists. Collectively they set the law above the jockeying for position characteristic of partisan politics. Because our traditions uniformly insist that that it is the law to which we are subject, and not the judges who declare it, that we live under the rule of law, and not men, questions of power and authority disappear from view. The only authority that is visible becomes that of the law.

It is paradoxical, I think, that the death of the author has long been a central conceit of jurisprudence, although classical jurisprudence would not have described it in anything like those terms. The insistence both of legal positivism and of the jurisprudence of rights which now seeks to replace it that it is the law which is central and not the persona of the individual judge signals the eradication of the author from the judicial text. In a particularly vivid illustration, Ronald Dworkin's chain novel metaphor for adjudication decentres the author and replaces the concept of authorship with a quasi-autonomous text, one that in some way controls successive authors and depersonalises them.

Despite this, everything we know about narrative, about storytelling and the ways in which stories persuade us and become believable, reminds us that power and authority are central to legal narratives. They are never innocent; indeed the history of the common law precisely signifies the struggle for power and authority between the monarch and the nobility as the 'king's law' gradually supplanted the customary jurisdiction of the manor courts.

Up to this point, I have focused upon the telling of the legal story, of the ways in which narrative and argument fuse, so that often the narrative assumes a primacy which displaces (unintentionally) the figure of the narrator. In speaking of the way in which a polyvocal story is necessarily transformed into a 'seamless web' through the medium of the trial, I have primarily been concerned with the process by which this occurs: the rhetorical movement from persuasion, through judgment, to persuasion once again. Yet, as readers will already have noticed, in each legal story there are many narrators. Some of these speak with authority and others do not. That is a fact, both of life and of law.

In some cases, this is a commonplace. No one really doubts that a respected businessman is more likely to command the respect of the court than a prostitute or a street kid. Neither does anyone doubt that an experienced senior barrister is likely to be more persuasive, and in the setting of the trial, more powerful than a duty solicitor. These sources of potential injustice are frequently cited, the subject of voluminous reports and studies on access to justice. Within the court, then, some narrators are – because of experience, because of position, because of who and what they are – more powerful than others are. Their stories in turn are more likely to be persuasive, more likely to move the judge. All of this has become, as I have said, commonplace.

Yet it is not only narrators who differ in power, in authority, in their persuasiveness. Narratives as well may become powerful, sanctified by long usage and by custom. Their authority is conferred upon those who speak them, the story told already familiar, well rehearsed. We might call these narratives 'master narratives'. Property stories were among the most potent of early common law stories. The most powerful of these stories pertained to legal rights, such as the right to the possession of real or personal property. These stories followed a predictable pattern. In them, the plaintiff alleged that the defendant had infringed his legal rights and demanded that they be restored. Because these stories and the writs which developed around them protected rights, they automatically qualified for a hearing in the royal courts. Thus, as the new jurisdiction of the king's court became powerful, its justice came to be associated with the protection of proprietary rights of various kinds.[11]

Stories about misdeeds were more ambiguous. In these stories, the plaintiff did not demand the restoration of that which was rightfully his, but compensation for misconduct by the defendant. Originally, these stories were remaindered to local manor courts and were not deemed worthy of the king's justice. Some of these stories were, however, special. These special stories were originally supposed to be about the kind of violence that might foreshadow public disorder, a breach of the king's peace, or lead to private vengeance or an ongoing feud. In their telling, a formula developed, one that recited that the trespass had been done 'with force and arms and against the king's peace'.[12] A plaintiff who told such a story was able to purchase a writ of trespass entitling him to be heard in the king's court. Like the stories about property, these stories were also, typically, stories told by men about men, although upon occasion they might be stories told by men about women.

Not all legal stories were about men. Women had appeared and argued in the manor and local courts and continued to do so. Legislation protecting women's economic interests was occasionally enacted, sometimes at the behest of women's gilds in the great cities of London and York. The developing common law jurisdiction, the king's court, was more restrictive, perhaps because its development coincided with a gradual diminution in women's rights more generally as the feudal system attained hegemony throughout England and Wales. Even in the king's court, however, single or widowed women were sometimes allowed to tell their stories, if they were the right kind of stories, stories about property and economic rights.[13] Married women were excluded, being *femme covert*.[14]

Access to the king's court, unlike the local or manor court, was not as of right.[15] Rather, a plaintiff had to consciously frame his case so as to bring his cause of action within its jurisdiction and the records of these early cases suggest that this jurisdiction was actively sought. During this developmental period, written reports of cases were little more than summaries of the claims and counter-claims argued before the court. Among the earliest of these reports are those to be found in the compilation known as the Year Book Cases.[16] These early reports are fascinating. They are almost pure narrative, a recounting of the allegations made by the plaintiff and of any counter claim which was raised. As we read them we begin to develop a clear picture of the stories that the king's court was willing to hear. While originally quarrels over property had been the *liet motif* of the emerging common law, its ambit gradually widened. Among the stories in the Year Book cases are stories of a dispute over a woman,[17] of wine drawn off from a cask and replaced with salt water, rendering the wine that remained undrinkable,[18] of a horse improperly shod so that it became lame.[19] In each of these stories, the litany of violence is invariable, recited almost as an incantation. Thus we read that the defendants 'with force and arms to wit with swords and bows and arrows' drew off much of the wine belonging to the plaintiff, replacing it with salt water so that the wine remaining was wholly spoilt.[20] At the dawn of the procedural republic we find the legal fictions needful to serve it. Conflict and violence fuse, so that disputes involving seduction, theft, and/or carelessness are all assimilated to the ritual incantation of force and arms. The invariability of this litany of violence, its immunity to context, alerts us to its real function – a jurisdictional manoeuvre.

If the rhetoric of ritualised violence chronicled in the Year Book cases seems foreign to contemporary readers, it is because the violence of law's underbelly had not yet been filtered through the conventions of judgment. The alternative to formal, litigious resolution of disputes was self-help, and self-help remedies almost inevitably carried the risk of violence. The focus of these early cases upon allegation and counter allegation, emphasise that the legal narratives in the Year Book cases were naive procedural narratives. Their almost total inattention to the elucidation of principles, to accuracy as to the identity of the parties[21] and even to the ultimate outcome, underscores their naivety. It also highlights something else of profound importance. From the perspective of the law, and its wish to have an independent existence, and from that of the developing ranks of sergeants-at-law, these niceties were relatively unimportant, however important they may seem to later day observers. Rather, these narratives were hornbooks, instructional manuals about forms and procedures, not about principles and outcomes. At its inception, the common law can be found busily at work laying the cornerstone of the procedural republic. At this time, doctrinal categories were still fluid and under-determined. Because it was necessary for a prospective plaintiff to purchase a writ, there was, in fact, no real niche for doctrine to fill. The writ said all that was needful, and if the plaintiff could not find one that was appropriate, or bring his story within the confines of the action on the case, he was nonsuited.

But there is something else as well going on here. Because conflict and violence are often understood as bound together we ought not to be too surprised at the routine incantation of violent events. Pierre Schlag notes that:

> Lawyers understand the violent, instrumental, and performative potentials of any given law while legal academics strive mightily – whether they are doing "theory" or "doctrine" – to avoid such recognition. A lawyer looks at doctrine and sees a tool, a vehicle, an opportunity, a threat, a guarantee. A legal academic typically sees only a propositional statement.[22]

What we do not find is almost as astonishing to the contemporary mind as what we do find. Much of the time, all we are given is the allegation as contained in the writ. We are not given the detail of the arguments put by the serjeants-at-law, although we can surmise them. We are typically not even told whether the plaintiff's action succeeded or failed (although this can be discovered from the plea rolls).[23] It is not until the nominate reports appear that these (now essential) elements of the common law make an appearance in case reports.

What, then, we might well ask, was the function of these very early legal narratives? If they were not precedents, if they did not give reasons for judgment, why were they recorded and by whom? What did they contain? We have glimpses of some of the answers and those glimpses indicate something of the process by which causes of action took shape. They seem, in part, to have been notes taken by students attending courts as apprentices-at-law, in short by 'wanna be lawyers'. Initially, they served as guides or templates for complying with the various causes of action available before modern doctrinal categories such as contract, tort (and even equity) assumed anything like their contemporary shape. They were not authoritative in the way we now understand precedents to be, indeed, were not even written by the judges themselves. Instead of recording outcomes, they recorded inputs, writs and allegations that yielded legal causes of action. They were, in short, a record of the kind of stories that enabled one party to invoke state violence against another party rather than having to resort to self help remedies or seek redress in the local courts.[24] They were also, and more importantly, a record of the way in which these stories must be told for the desired relief to be forthcoming. In all the ways that matter, they were far more akin to a library of precedents than to case reports. If we think of these early compilations as case reports, in the modern sense, we misconceive the mechanisms through which the common law developed. The Year Book cases provide insights into the development of the jurisdiction of the 'king's bench', as the king's court came to be known, and the society in which it evolved.

In this context, the insignificance of what is later to become the towering edifice of precedent is remarkable. Writs there are in abundance, and forms of pleadings, and should the available writs fail to encompass the facts the possibility of bringing an action on the (special) case, but no overarching conception of precedent. While the elaborate systems of writs and pleadings characterising medieval law are long gone, the legal snippets in the Year Book cases exemplify one aspect of the common law method, the machinery involved in the translation of human stories into legal stories. The process of translation is obvious in the following extract:

Simon of Paris brought a writ of trespass against Walter Page, bailiff of Sir Robert Tony, and divers others, and complained that on a certain day they took and imprisoned him etc. wrongfully and against the peace etc. *Passeley* for all, except [Walter] the bailiff, answered that they had done nothing against the peace. And for the bailiff he avowed the arrest for the reason that [the aforesaid] Simon is the villein of [the aforesaid] Robert, whose bailiff Walter is, and was found at Necton in his nest, and Walter tendered to him the office of reeve and he refused and would not submit to justice etc. *Toudeby* rehearsed the avowry and said that to this avowry he ought now to be answered, for that Simon is a free citizen of London and such has been these ten years and has been the King's sheriff in the said city and has rendered

account at the Exchequer; and this (said he) we will aver by record; and to this
very day he is an alderman of the town, and we demand judgment whether
they can allege villeinage in his person. *Herle.* With what they say about his
being a citizen of London we have nothing to do; but we tell you that from
granddam and granddam's granddam he is the villein of Robert, and he and all
his ancestors, grandsire and grandsire's grandsire, and all those who held his
lands in the manor of Necton; and Robert's ancestors were seised of the villein
services of Simon's ancestors, such as ransom of flesh and blood, marriage of
their daughters, tallaging them high and low, and Robert is still seised of
Simon's brothers by the same father and same mother. And we demand
judgment whether Robert cannot make avowry upon him as upon his villein
found in his nest. *Toudeby.* We are ready to aver that he is a free man and of
free estate, and they are not seised of him as their villein. Beresford, J. I have
heard tell that a man was taken in a brothel and hanged, and if he had stayed at
home no ill would have befallen him. So here. If he was a free citizen, why
did he not remain in the city? *At another day Toudeby* held to the assertion
"not seised of him as of his villein nor of his villein services". *Passeley.*
Whereas he says that we were not seised of him as of our villein, he was born
in our villeinage, and there our seisin began, and we found him in his nest, and
so our seisin is continued. We demand judgment. Bereford, J. One side pleads
on the seisin, and the other side pleads on the right: In that way you will never
have an issue. *Herle.* Seised in the manner that we have alleged. Bereford, J.
The court will not receive such a traverse. You must say that you are seised of
him as your villein and of his villein services. *And so [the defendant's
counsel] did. Issue joined.*[25]

What are we, almost 700 years later, to make of such a story? In
simplest terms, Simon has returned to his birthplace to visit his family after
establishing himself as a freeman (apparently quite prosperous as he was
both a sheriff and an alderman) in London. An attempt is made to reclaim
his services. In the end, because the plaintiff (through his counsel)
successfully holds his ground and insists that Robert is 'not [presently]
seised of him as of his villein nor of his villein services' the court holds
that the only traverse it will accept is a direct counter-claim. The
defendant's counsel must, therefore, insist that Robert is (presently) seised
of him as his villein. Allegations in respect of Simon's birth do not make a
good answer. That story (which was also true) is inadmissible and cannot
be put to the jury. While this story must be understood in the context of the
gradual breakup of the feudal system and the first of the great modern mass
movements of people, what is critical is that the truth of the matter is
immaterial. The difficulty for the court, and it is worth noting that four

years elapsed between the issuance of writs and the verdict, is that it is true both that Robert is not presently seised of Simon *and* that Simon was born a villein.[26] Simon prevails and is awarded £100 damages, a substantial sum in fourteenth century terms.

How should the court insist that such a cause of action be framed, given that no legal principles govern the matter? If the defendant is allowed to assert that the facts of Simon's birth are sufficient in themselves to establish his villeinage, the defendant will surely prevail before a local jury who would be well aware of those facts. If the reverse is true, the plaintiff will likely prevail, both because documents detailing Simon's service as sheriff in London and subsequently as alderman should suffice for proof and because there is no evidence that Robert is presently seised of him and of his labour. The form of the question to be put to the jury is critical. The court is clearly making a choice here, and it is a choice about outcomes, not simply about the form which pleadings should take. It is also a choice about values, one made against the background of rapid social change and legislative attempts to stem the flow of migrants from village to city.[27]

Even at this very early stage, certain critical elements of common law method are present, and it is those elements that are of importance in this context. The adversarial character of the proceedings, the jockeying for position, the way in which form takes precedence over substance, the partiality of the stories: all of these are as much a part of the common law now as they were in the fourteenth century. If the multiplicity of writs and associated pleadings characteristic of the Year Book cases have been replaced by a blank form, and the ubiquitous jury of the medieval period largely restricted (in Australia at least) to criminal matters, the critical importance of the stories and their telling has not changed.

Much is currently made of the 'deficiencies' of the common law, in particular the absence of any duty upon the court to seek out the truth. These early snippets of legality with their emphasis upon the precise formulation of the question (of fact) which should be put to the jury remind us that it is not always the case that there is one 'truth'. Surely, in *Paris v Page* the problem is precisely that there are two truths. The decision to admit one narrative and to exclude another is, ultimately, a policy decision. In the eyes of the king's court, what is relevant is not the status Simon enjoyed at his birth, but his present status and that is beyond doubt, free. Read against the background of chronic labour shortages in medieval England, a consequence both of the periodic plagues sweeping Europe and the increasing mobility of the labouring population, the court seems to be acknowledging the first stirrings of the liberal capitalist order and the gradual decay of the feudal system. Against the background of contemporaneous legislation[28] attempting to curtail precisely this sort of movement and ensure a continuous supply of labour on the estates of feudal England this is significant.

We see something else here as well, the (almost absolute) importance of procedures. While the procedural fanaticism of the system of writs with which the common law began is well known, the Year Book cases highlight another aspect of this proceduralism. The endless debates about the form of the question to be put to the jury, the nexus between the form and the outcome is precisely about proceduralism. When Bereford J says: 'One side pleads on the seisin, and the other side pleads on the right', it is the 'right' which prevails. The claim of an infringement of the plaintiff's legal rights as a freeman of the city of London, prevails over the defendant's attempt to regain possession of the plaintiff's services. In this way, a record such as this foreshadows countless others, cases in which the battle is precisely about the procedures essential to safeguard legal (and more recently, political) rights against other sorts of claims.

Speaking Judgment and the 'Procedural Republic'

If the truth is simultaneously material and immaterial, perhaps we should ask what roles values such as truth and justice play in our understandings of legality. Perhaps, indeed, we should inquire more deeply into the role of the courts as the centrepiece of what has been styled the 'procedural republic'.[29] If, within our understandings of legality, justice is no more and no less than adherence to appropriate procedures for regulating conflict, it is a justice at variance with ordinary understandings, and one in which difference must, ultimately, make no difference. For difference to count, for a different voice to be heard, even if its difference is the product of different life experiences becomes, within the procedural republic, a symptom of failure. The precise point of the jurisprudence of rights, as of the jurisprudence of rules that preceded it, is not the protection of difference but its flattening, its privitisation, and ultimately its eradication. The hegemony of the liberal citizen signals the true meaning of law's violence. It is not simply that, as Robert Cover insisted, 'judges deal in pain and death'. Of course they do. We all know that, and the more thoughtful among us know as well that that there is no realistic alternative. Were it to be otherwise, it would be a law without effect, without consequences and thus no law at all worth having. Cover spoke, however, of the outcomes inherent in conflict resolution, of the inevitability of loss in an adversarial system, indeed, in any system that resolves rather than mediating conflicts.[30] I am speaking of something very different and more deeply embedded, the eradication of the legitimacy of difference.

Formal and substantive equality collude in the eradication of difference. Both carry with them rules and procedures for managing conflicts among citizens and both insist that it is as citizens that we are equal and entitled to standing before the courts of a liberal society. In this way, our differences (and the attendant inequalities and hierarchies) are privatised. Once hidden, and therefore excluded from our personae as citizens, they become lifestyle choices rather than core elements of our being. Publicly, and necessarily, the proceduralism at the core of our legal system carries with it its own mandate.

Yet what this means, more or less inevitably, is that our public speech is necessarily the speech of citizens. Difference is unacceptable within this frame of reference. If we are to speak as judges, then we must do just that, speak as judges. To ask about the possibility of a different voice in judgment is to try to deny that the courts form the apex of the procedural republic. It is to threaten to collapse one of the walls of which Michael Walzer spoke when he suggested that we should

> think of liberalism as a certain way of drawing the map of the social and political world. The ... preliberal map showed a largely undifferentiated land mass, with rivers and mountains, cities and towns, but no borders... Society was conceived as an organic and integrated whole... Confronting this world, liberal theorists preached and practiced the art of separation. They drew lines, marked of different realms, and created the socio-political map with which we are still familiar... Liberalism is a world of walls, and each one creates a new liberty.[31]

Of these divisions the most important is that between the 'political' and the 'affectional'.[32] If, as citizens, we are indistinguishable and the speech and thoughts appropriate to us are simply those of citizens, difference is, at the outset, inaudible. Within the liberal political, the question with which I began this book, whether it is possible to speak simultaneously as a judge and as a woman, is symptomatic of disorder, of a deep and abiding potential for injustice. The difficulty in the end is not simply authority but difference. Within the political, and the courts belong, irrevocably to the political, difference is inadmissible, unacceptable, even unrecognisable as political speech and as judicial speech. Within the political we are only citizens. Speech that is not the speech of citizens is excluded. To the extent that we rupture of the mask of the liberal citizen, we disrupt the political, threaten to fracture[33] it, break open the liberal order at a fundamental level. Here, what is relevant is the nature of the liberal political. I believe that it is Rawls who has sketched its parameters most fully. Chantal Mouffe describes his central arguments in these terms:

> The way he envisages the nature of the overlapping consensus clearly indicates that, for Rawls, a well-ordered society is a society from which politics has been eliminated. A conception of justice is mutually recognized by reasonable and rational citizens who act according to its injunctions. They probably have very different and even conflicting conceptions of the good, but those are strictly private matters and do not interfere with their public life. Conflicts of interests about economic and social issues – if they still arise – are resolved smoothly through discussions within the framework of public reason, by invoking the principles of justice that everybody endorses. If an unreasonable or irrational person happens to disagree with that state of affairs and intends to disrupt that nice consensus, she must be forced, through coercion, to submit to the principles of justice. Such a coercion, however, has nothing to do with oppression, for it is justified by the exercise of reason...
>
> ... What "political liberalism" is at pains to eliminate is the element of "undecidability" that is present in human relations. It offers us a picture of the well-ordered society as one from which – through rational agreement on justice – antagonism, violence, power, and repression have disappeared. But it is only because they have been made invisible through a clever strategem: the distinction between "simple" and "reasonable pluralism". In that way, exclusions can be denied by declaring that they are the product of the "free exercise of practical reason" that establish the limits of possible consensus. When a point of view is excluded it is because this is required by the exercise of reason; therefore the frontiers between what is legitimate and what is not legitimate appear as independent of power relations. Thanks to this legerdemain, rationality and morality provide the key to solving the "paradox of liberalism": how to eliminate its adversaries while remaining neutral.[34]

The Rawlsian conception of the political tracks precisely our cultural understandings of what it means to speak as a judge. While I would argue, and have in fact argued elsewhere,[35] that it is an impoverished conception of justice and of political society, as a metaphor for much of what happens in our courts (at least at the appellate level) it is remarkably astute.

To speak simultaneously as a judge and as a woman denies the principle upon which the liberal edifice is constructed: that what is relevant in the political is our identity as equal citizens. The role of judge is one archetype of the political, the sign and symbol of one of its two essential axes. Within the liberal social and political order[36] one either speaks as a judge or one does not.

The central insight of liberalism, and of the courts that have come to epitomise the liberal order and the insight that gradually led to the eradication of status was the threat posed by difference. As contract replaced status as the 'political' mode of ordering relationships, thus implicating the courts in the construction of the social order in a new way, contract and obligation became synonymous. Difference became, not a natural part of social, economic and political life, but a precursor of conflict.

To insist upon difference, and upon the possibility that one may simultaneously speak as a judge and as a woman, is to threaten the disintegration of the liberal order precisely because any politics that recognises and affirms difference and diversity is a politics of ongoing and endemic conflict. We the people are different; our differences are of critical importance in the ways in which they make us who and what we are. A politics of difference cannot be confined. Its public sphere is neither the sanitised marketplace of the liberal vision nor the oppressive unity of the republican vision. Its central metaphor is conflict, not unity. It is a place in which differences are fought out and temporary coalitions formed. Such conflicts and differences are central to the polity and lie at the core of a vibrant public sphere. If we are to develop a politics of difference, we need ground rules for managing conflict, not for curtailing the agenda until consensus is reached.[37] We need courts, and judges, who are at home with difference, who recognise that that wisdom comes in many different forms. What is critical in adjudication is not simply the procedures and the rituals, but the hearing and retelling of stories, the engagement between past and future, between what we are and what we hope to become.

Notes

1   These conventions include those that are determinative of genre, as well as those that locate particular stories irrevocably in time or place.

2   In the detail and specificity of its conventions, it is akin to a Mills and Boon novel.

3   This fracturing, an inevitable part of translating a human story into a legal story, is law's 'dangerous supplement'. The metaphor of fracturing, as an emblem of the process by which human story becomes legal story recalls the 'skeletal principles' of the common law. Law fractures human stories, some human stories fracture law.

4   Whether this is a 'dangerous supplement' remains to be seen.

5   See the analysis of *Hegarty v Shine* in chapter 6. The iterations of morality and immorality illustrate how 'stock characters' become part of the law.

6   *Hegarty v Shine*, per Deasy LJA at 148. The Victorian fascination with images of dead and dying women particularly where the subject is a 'fallen woman' is worth reflecting upon as is the undertone of sexual excitement in the judgment.

7   The subtext is obvious, if deeply rooted in assumptions concerning gender and class.

8   Currie, S, 'Validating women in the legal system: An analysis of the invisibility of women's perspectives in the law' (1995) 14 (1) *Social Alternatives* 14.

9   9 NW 146 (Mich 1881). See also *Bolduc v Reg* [1967] SCR 677.

10   The abandoned suit for breach of promise of marriage hints at this second story.

11   Such stories were enforced by *praecipe* writs in which the defendant was commanded to do some act. They protected legal rights such as the right to land or other property.

12   These stories are often called legal fictions, both because of their formulaic character and because the allegation of force and arms was often clearly false.

13   Two such early cases were *La Rivere v Abbot of Abingdon* (1318) YB Hilary 11Edw II, fol 340 and *Arderne v Moraunt* (1315) YB Pasch 8 Edw II, fol 272. In both, the dispute was over property. In the former, the plaintiff was a widow, in the latter, apparently, unmarried. These customary common law rights were gradually diminished. During the reign of Henry VII and Henry VIII, new legislation deprived widows of the capacity to alienate any lands which they had inherited from their husbands.

14   In England coverture first emerges in the common law.

15   Here we see the birth of the 'procedural republic'. A would be plaintiff's story must be brought within a pre-determined writ, formulaic and precise.

16   To ascertain details such as the outcome of the trial, critical to contemporary lawyers, critical, it is necessary to repair to the plea rolls.

17   *Gyse v Baudewyne* (1310) YB Hilary 3 Edw II.

18   Milsom, SFC, *Historical Foundations of the Common Law* 2 ed, London, Butterworths, 1981, 289) tells us that:

> In 1317 a plaintiff counted that he had bought a tun of wine from the defendants, and had left it with them until he could arrange for its transportation; the defendants however, with force and arms to wit with swords and bows and arrows, drew off much of the wine and replaced it with salt water, so that the wine was wholly spoilt, to the plaintiff's great damage and against the king's peace.

19   *The Farrier's Case* (1371) YB Trinity 46 Edw III, fol 19, pl 19 is one of many cases taking this form. Here the report is unclear as to whether the action was brought in trespass or in case, the defendant asserting that the writ could not be upheld as it did

not refer to *vi et armis*. In the end, the writ (presumably in case rather than trespass) was upheld and the matter allowed to proceed.

20   The report makes it clear that the wine had been left with the defendant by way of bailment. Force and arms would have been superfluous to say the least.

21   In *La Rivere v Abbot of Abingdon* (1318) YB Hilary 11 Edw II fol 340 the law French of the report identifies the plaintiff as one Steven (Esteven). Only when we match the report in the Year Book with the plea rolls do we discover that the plaintiff was in fact Denise, the wife of the late John de la Rivere.

22   Schlag, 'Clerks in the Maze', 221.

23   Since these trials were invariably jury trials, the outcomes were determined by jurors and were not understood to be of precedential value.

24   Because this was the king's court and the king's justice, rules effectively excluding women from property ownership also came to exclude them from access to law. There are two assumptions here: first that if you do not own property you have no need of law, and second that the king's court is for those who, through feudal hierarchies, come under the king's protection. Women failed to qualify under either category in the countryside of England and Wales although the situation was much more fluid in the great cities of London and York where women retained legal capacity until much later. See Berns, SS, 'Women in English Legal History: Subject (almost), Object (irrevocably), Person (not quite)' (1993) 12 *Univ. Tas. L.R.*, 26.

25   *Paris v Page* (1308) YB Pasch 1 Edw II, fol 4.

26   Battles over status recur. In *Roys v Abbot of St Benet of Holme* (1313) YB Mich 7 Edw II, fol 214 while the ostensible cause of action is in respect of a trespass to land (*vi et armis*) and wrongful taking and destruction of chattels, the underlying issue is whether John Roys is, as the Abbot claims, his villein, or whether he had been, as he claimed, freed and given ownership of certain lands. After skirmishing over the wording of the pleadings, and over whether, given that the Abbot or his men had allegedly destroyed the charters establishing his enfeoffment of two parcels of free land, the Abbot could avoid the suit on the grounds that the plaintiff is unfree, the issue is finally joined. Finally, the Abbot is successful: the court will not hear the allegations of trespass (since a villein lacks standing to sue) until the status of the plaintiff has been determined. This was what the plaintiff wished to avoid, since the Abbot or his men allegedly destroyed the document establishing his freedom.

27   Among these legislative instruments we find the *Statute of Labourers* and the *Statute of Apprentices*. Both had, as their primary reason for existence, an attempt to stem the migration from country to city, and, in turn, the transformation from villein to citizen. It is instructive to contrast this social vignette with the much more recent 'fugitive slave cases' in the United States. In the fugitive slave cases, the 'seisin' was all that mattered, the alleged slave could not obtain a writ of trespass and so assert his free status. In nineteenth century America, a 'new' proceduralism, held sway. For an alleged slave to establish his freedom it was necessary for him to prove that he had been born free or legally freed. That he was now free was no answer to an allegation of unfree status. See Cover, R, *Justice Accused*, for a perceptive account of this 'new proceduralism' and its roots in the emerging procedural republic.

28   Among the enactments with this purpose are the *Statute of Apprentices* and the *Statute of Labourers*.

29 Sandel, M, 'The Procedural Republic and the Unencumbered Self' (1984) 12 *Political Theory* 81-96.
30 I do not suggest that mediation and conciliation are, as alternatives to litigation, more sensitive to difference. The themes of loss and violence in Cover's work are characteristic of conflict resolution in our legal system.
31 Walzer, M, 'Liberalism and the Art of Separation' (1984) 12 (3) *Political Theory* 315.
32 In recent writings Rawls emphasises the distinction between the political and the personal and familial, which, he notes, 'are affectional domains, again in ways which the political is not'. Rawls, 'The Domain of the Political and Overlapping Consensus', 242. Rawls conceives of his view of the political as free standing and insists that his 'aim is to specify the special domain of the political in such a way that its main institutions can gain the support of an overlapping consensus'.
33 Liberal principles, like legal principles, remain skeletal, brittle, susceptible to fracture.
34 Mouffe, C, 'Democracy, Power, and the "Political"' in Benhabib, S, *Princeton Univ Press*, Princeton, NJ (1996), 245, 252-253.
35 Berns, SS, *Add Woman and Stir*.
36 This is, without doubt, a liberal order. What I am coming to question is whether it is possible to escape the flattening of difference and the denial of violence and power characteristic of liberal social and political orders whilst maintaining any of its apparent virtues, most particularly tolerance and respect for the liberty of the individual. Equality is, I believe, less a virtue than a precondition for a liberal order.
37 That approach can safely be left to malestream models. Within malestream theorising, conflict becomes indistinguishable from violence and a downward spiral into the Hobbesian. Women, perhaps, are better able to understand conflict in positive terms and to recognise that it offers the potential for growth as well as destruction. Pregnancy is the archetype of positive, as opposed to destructive, conflict, and that fact, more than any other, emphasises that conflict is essential to growth and to renewal.

Bibliography

Allen, DW & DE Wall, 'Role Orientations and Women State Supreme Court Justices' 77 *Judicature* 156 (1993)

Barker, F, *The Tremulous Private Body: Essays on Subjection'*, London, Methuen, 1984

Barthes, R, *Image-Music-Text,* trans. Stephen Heath, New York, 1977

Behrendt, L, 'Black Women and the Feminist Movement: Implications for Aboriginal Women in Rights Discourse' (1993) 1 *Australian Feminist Law Journal* 7

Bell, D, *And We are Not Saved*, New York, Basic Books, 1987

Benhabib, S, *Democracy and Difference: Contesting the Boundaries of the Political*, Princeton, NJ, Princeton Univ Press, 1996

Berman, HJ, *Law & Revolution: The Formation of the Western Legal Tradition*, Cambridge, Harvard University Press, 1983

Berns, SS, 'Hercules, Hermes and Senator Smith: The Symbolic Structure of Law's Empire' (1988) 12 *Bulletin of the Australian Society of Legal Philosophy* 35

Berns, SS, 'Tolerance and Substantive Equality in Rawls' in Grbich, J (ed) *Feminism Law and* Society, Bundoora, La Trobe University Press, 1990, 112

Berns, SS, *Add Woman and Stir,* 1990, unpublished doctoral thesis on file at the University of Tasmania

Berns, SS, 'Integrity and Justice or When is Injustice Mandated by Integrity?' (1991) 18 *Melb Univ LR* 258

Berns, SS, 'Women in English Legal History: Subject (almost), Object (irrevocably), Person (not quite)' (1993) 12 *Univ. Tas. L.R.,* 26

Berns, SS, *Concise Jurisprudence*, Sydney, Federation Press, 1993

Berns, SS & P Baron, 'Bloody Bones - A Legal Ghost Story: To Speak as a Judge' (1994) 2 *Australian Feminist Law Journal* 125

Cavell, S, *The Claim of Reason,* Oxford, OUP, 1979

Cavell, S, *Disowning Knowledge in Six Plays of Shakespeare*, New York, Cambridge Univ Press, 1987

Charvet, J, *The Social Problem in the Philosophy of Rousseau*, London, Cambridge Univ. Press, 1974

Cornell, D, 'The Violence of the Masquerade: Law Dressed up as Justice' 11 *Cardozo LR* 1047, 1051 (1990)

Cornell, D, M Rosenfeld & DG Carlson, *Deconstruction and the Possibility of Justice*, New York, Routledge, 1992

Cover, R, *Justice Accused*, New Haven, Yale University Press, 1975

Cover, R, 'The Folktales of Justice: Tales of Jurisdiction' 14 *Capital Univ. LR* 179 (1985)

Cover, R, 'Nomos and Narrative' in Minow, M, M Ryan & A Sarat (eds) *Narrative, Violence, and the Law*, Ann Arbor, Univ of Michigan Press, 1992, 95

Cover, R, 'Violence and the Word' in Minow, M, M Ryan & A Sarat (eds) *Narrative, Violence, and the Law*, Ann Arbor, Univ of Michigan Press, 1992, 203

Currie, S, 'Validating women in the legal system: An analysis of the invisibility of women's perspectives in the law' (1995) 14 (1) *Social Alternatives* 14

de Tocqueville, A, *de la democratie en Amerique* 167 (1981)

Delgado, R, 'Critical Legal Studies and the Realities of Race – Does the Fundamental Contradiction have a Corollary' 23 *Harv CR-CL LR* 407 (1988)

Delgado, R, 'Norms and Normal Science: Towards a Critique of Normativity in Legal Thought' 139 *Univ. Penn. L.R.* 933, 942 (1991)

Derrida, J 'Force of Law: The "Mystical Foundation of Authority"' in Cornell, D, Rosenfeld, M & DG Carlson *Deconstruction and the Possibility of Justice*, London, Routledge, 1992, 3

Douzinas, C & R Warrington, "A Well-Founded Fear of Justice": Law and Ethics in Postmodernity, (1991) 2 *Law & Critique* 115

Douzinas, C, R Warrington & S McVeigh, *Postmodern Jurisprudence: The Law of Text in the Tests of Law*, London, Routledge, 1991

Dworkin, RM, 'Law as Interpretation' 60 *Texas LR* 527 (1982)

Dworkin, RM, 'How Law is Like Literature' in Dworkin, RM, *A Matter of Principle*, Cambridge, Harv Univ Press, 1985

Dworkin, RM, *Law's Empire*, Cambridge, The Belknap Press, 1986

Engle, DM, 'Law in the Domains of Everyday Life: The Construction of Community and Difference' in Sarat, A & TR Kearns, *Law in Everyday Life*, Ann Arbor, Michigan Univ Press, 1995

Fineman, MA, 'Feminist Legal Scholarship and Women's Gendered Lives, in Cain M & CB Harrington (eds) *Lawyers in a Postmodern World: Translation and Transgression*, New York, New York Univ Press, 1994, 229

Fish, S, *Doing What Comes Naturally: Change, Rhetoric, and the Practice of Theory in Literary and Legal Studies*, Oxford, Clarendon Press, 1989

Fish, S 'Change' in Fish, S *Doing What Comes Naturally: Change, Rhetoric, and the Practice of Theory in Literary and Legal Studies*, Oxford, Clarendon Press, 1989, 141

Fish, S 'Force' in Fish, S *Doing What Comes Naturally: Change, Rhetoric, and the Practice of Theory in Literary and Legal Studies*, Oxford, Clarendon Press, 1989, 503

Fish, S, 'Dennis Martinez and the Uses of Theory' in Fish, S, *Doing What Comes Naturally: Change, Rhetoric, and the Practice of Theory in Literary and Legal Studies*, Oxford, Clarendon Press, 1989, 372

Fish, S, 'Going Down the Anti-Formalist Road' in Fish, S *Doing What Comes Naturally: Change, Rhetoric, and the Practice of Theory in Literary and Legal Studies*, Oxford, Clarendon Press, 1989, 1

Fish, S, 'Rhetoric', in Fish, S *Doing What Comes Naturally: Change, Rhetoric, and the Practice of Theory in Literary and Legal Studies*, Oxford, Clarendon Press, 1989, 471

Fish, S, 'Still Wrong After All These Years' in Fish, S *Doing What Comes Naturally: Change, Rhetoric, and the Practice of Theory in Literary and Legal Studies*, Oxford, Clarendon Press, 1989, 356

Fish, S, 'Working on the Chain Gang: Interpretation in Law and Literature' in Fish, S, *Doing What Comes Naturally: Change, Rhetoric, and the Practice of Theory in Literary and Legal Studies*, Oxford, Clarendon Press, 1989, 87

Frost, R, 'Mending Wall' in McKenzie, JA & JK, *The World's Contracted Thus: Major Poetry from Chaucer to Plath*, Melbourne, Heineman Educational Australia, 1975, 226-227

Gatens, M, *Feminism and Philosophy: Perspectives on Difference and Equality*, Cambridge, Polity Press, 1991

Gilligan, C, *In a Different Voice: Psychological Theory and Women's Development*, Cambridge, Harv Univ Press, 1982

Goodman, E, *The Origins of the Western Legal Tradition: From Thales to the Tudors*, Sydney, The Federation Press, 1995

Goodrich, P, 'Specula Laws: Image, Aesthetic and Common Law' (1991) 2 *Law & Critique* 233

Gould, SJ, *The Mismeasure of Man*, London, Pelican, 1981

Haldar, P, 'The Evidencer's Eye: Representations of Truth in the Laws of Evidence', (1991) 2 *Law & Critique* 171-186

Hesse, H, *Demian, The Story of Emil Sinclair's Life*, trans. by M. Roloff & M. Lebeck, Harper & Row, New York, 1965

Hunter, R, 'Deconstructing the Subjects of Feminism: The Essentialism Debate in Feminist Theory and Practice' (1996) 6 *Australian Feminist Law Journal* 135

Jay, M, *Downcast Eyes: The Denigration of Vision in Twentieth-Century French Thought*, Berkeley, Univ. of Calif. Press, 1994

Jones, KB, *Compassionate Authority: Democracy and the Representation of Women*, London, Routledge, 1993

Kafka, F, 'In the Penal Colony' in *The Transformation and Other Stories: Works Published during Kafka's Lifetime*, translated from the German and edited by Malcolm Pasley, London, Penguin, 1992

Kennedy, D, 'Freedom and Constraint in Adjudication: A Critical Phenomenology' 36 *J Legal Education* 518 (1986)

Kennedy, D, 'A Cultural Pluralist Case for Affirmative Action in Legal Academia' in Duncan Kennedy, *Sexy Dressing Etc.*, Cambridge, Harv Univ Press, 1993, 34

Leff, AA, 'Unspeakable Ethics, Unnatural Law' 1979 *Duke LJ* 1229

MacIntyre, A, *After Virtue*, 2nd ed, London, Duckworth, 1985

MacIntyre, A, *Whose Justice? Which Rationality?* Notre Dame, Univ of Notre Dame Press, 1988

Martin, E, 'Women on the bench: a different voice? 77 *Judicature* 126 (1993)

Matsuda, MJ, 'When the First Quail Calls: Multiple Consciousness as Jurisprudential Method', 11 *Women's Rights LR* 7 (1989)

Matsuda, MJ, 'Voices of America: Accent, Anti-Discrimination Law, and a Jurisprudence for the Last Reconstruction', 100 *Yale LJ* 1334 (1990)

McCarthy, E, 'Grant Park, Chicago' in *Other Things and the Ardvark*, Garden City, Doubleday, 1968

McHugh, P, *Prostitution and Victorian Social Reform*, London, Croom Helm, 1980

Michaelman, FI, 'Foreword: Traces of Self-Government' 100 *Harv LR* 4 (1986)

Michaelman, FI, 'Law's Republic' 97 *Yale LJ* 1493 (1988)

Millay, E St Vincent, 'Renascence' in *Collected Poems of Edna St Vincent Millay*, New York, Harper & Row, 1956, 3

Milsom, SFC, *Historical Foundations of the Common Law* 2nd ed, London, Butterworths, 1981

Minow M & E Spelman, 'Passion for Justice' in JT Noonan Jr and KI Winston, *The Responsible Judge: Readings in Judicial Ethics*, Westport, Praeger, 1993

Mouffe, C, 'Democracy, Power, and the "Political"' in Benhabib, S, *Democracy and Difference: Contesting the Boundaries of the Political*, Princeton, NJ, Princeton Univ Press, 1996, 245

Neallani, S, 'Women of Colour in the Legal Profession: Facing the Familiar Barriers of Race and Sex' 5 *Canadian Journal of Women and the Law* 148 (1992)

O'Shane, P, 'Launch of the Australian Feminist Law Journal, August 29 1993 The University of Melbourne' (1994) 2 *Australian Feminist LJ* 3

Parashar, A, 'Essentialism or Pluralism: The Future of Legal Feminism' (1993) 6 *Canadian Journal of Women and the Law* 328

Posner, R, 'Legal Reasoning From the Top Down and From the Bottom Up: The Question of Unenumerated Constitutional Rights' 59 *Univ of Chicago Law Review* 433 (1992)

Rawls, J, *A Theory of Justice*, Oxford, Oxford Univ Press, 1972

Rawls, J, 'The Idea of an Overlapping Consensus', (1987) 7 *Oxf J of Leg Stud* 1

Rawls, J, 'The Domain of the Political and Overlapping Consensus', 64 *N.Y.U.L.R.* (1989) 233

Rawls, J, *Political Liberalism*, New York, Columbia Univ Press, 1993

Rousseau, J-J, *The Emile*, trans by B Foxley, Melbourne, Everyman's Library, 1911

Sandel, M, 'The Procedural Republic and the Unencumbered Self' (1984) 12 *Political Theory* 81-96.

Sandel, M, *Liberalism and the Limits of Justice*, Cambridge, Cambridge University Press, 1982

Schlag, P, 'Normative and Nowhere to Go' 43 *Stanford LR* 167 (1990)

Schlag, P, 'Clerks in the Maze' in Campos, PF, P Schlag & SD Smith, eds, *Against the Law*, Durham & London, Duke University Press, 1996, 218

Serat, A, & TR Kearns 'A Journey Through Forgetting: Toward a Jurisprudence of Violence' in A Serat & T Kearns, *The Fate of Law*, Ann Arbor, Univ. of Mich Press (1991) 209

Sherry, S, 'Civic Virtue and the Feminine Voice in Constitutional Adjudication' 72 *Virginia LR* 543 (1986)

Stacy, H, 'Legal Discourse and the Feminist Political Economy: Moving Beyond Sameness/Difference' (1996) 6 *Australian Feminist Law Journal* 115

Unger, R, *Knowledge and Politics & Passion: An Essay in Personality*, New York, The Free Press, 1984

Walzer, M, 'Liberalism and the Art of Separation' (1984) 12 (3) *Political Theory* 315

Watson, I, 'Indigenous Peoples' Law-Ways: Survival Against the Colonial State' (1997) 8 *Australian Feminist Law Journal* 3

Weber, S, 'In the Name of the Law' in Cornell, D, M Rosenfeld & DG Carlson, *Deconstruction and the Possibility of Justice*, New York, Routledge, 1992, 232

Weisberg, R, *Poethics and Other Strategies of Law and Literature*, New York, Columbia Univ. Press, 1984

West, RL, 'Adjudication is not Interpretation: Some Reservations about the Law-as-Literature Movement' 54 *Tenn. L.R.* 203-278 (1987)

West, RL, *Narrative, Authority, and Law*, Ann Arbor, Univ of Mich Press, 1993

West, RL, 'Narrative, Responsibility, and Death' in West, *Narrative, Authority, and Law*, Ann Arbor, Univ of Mich Press, 1993, 419

West, RL, *Caring For Justice*, New York, New York Univ Press, 1997

White, JB, 'The Judicial Opinion as a Form of Life' in White, JB, *Justice as Translation*, Chicago, Univ of Chicago Press, 1990, 89

White, JB, *When Words Lose Their Meaning: Constitutions and Reconstitutions of Language, Character and Community*, Chicago, Univ of Chicago Press, 1984

White, JB, 'The Ethics of Meaning' in Turner, J Neville & Pamela Williams (eds) *The Happy Couple: Law and Literature*, Sydney, Federation Press, 1994, 269

White, LE, 'Subordination, Rhetorical Survival Skills, and Sunday Shoes: Notes on the Hearing of Mrs G'; in Fineman, MA & NW Thomadsen (eds) *At the Boundaries of Law: Feminism and Legal Theory*, New York, Routledge, 1991

Williams, P, *The Alchemy of Race and Rights: Diary of a Law Professor*, Cambridge, Harv Univ Press, 1991

Wilson, Madam Justice B, 'Will Women Judges Really Make a Difference' (1990) 28 *Osgoode Hall LJ* 507

Winn, PA, 'Legal Ritual' (1991) 2 *Law & Critique* 207

Witteveen, WJ, 'The Rhetorical Labours of Hercules' (1990) 3 *International Journal for the Semiotics of Law* 227

Yablon, CM, 'Forms' in Cornell, D, M Rosenfeld & DG Carlson, *Deconstruction and the Possibility of Justice*, New York, Routledge, 1992, 258

Yeats, WB, 'The Second Coming', Colmer, J & D, *Mainly Modern,* Adelaide, Rigby, 1969, 185

Young, IM, *Justice and the Politics of Difference*, Princeton, Princeton Univ Press, 1990

Index

act of judgment, 9–10, 18, 27–30, 37, 40, 42–44, 76, 145–149, 183, 200, 204
  as clôture, 193–96
  as institutional violence, 53–54
adjectival law as theory of knowledge, 39–40
Allen, DW, 211
authority
  and difference, 196–203
  and legitimation, 21–26
  and the speech of women, 1–2, 21–22, 32–34
  as conferred by interpretive community, 141–44
autopoetic dimension of law, 149

Ball C, 109, 110
Barker, F, 99
Barthes, R, 100
Behrendt, L, 150
Bell, D, 154, 189
Berman, HJ, 156
blind justice as anomalous within the visual frame of the trial, 34, 95, 150
Brennan, CJ, 64–75, 80, 89, 90, 98–99 136, 207
Brown v Board of Education, 10, 100, 143, 154, 189

Cavell, S, 78, 84, 97, 101
chain novel in Dworkin, 47, 161, 185–186, 194, 218
Charvet, J, 152
clôture, law as, 24, 28–29, 95
Commercial Bank of Australia Ltd v Amadio, 176–83, 193–196
contract as dependent upon law, 55–57
Cornell, D, 34, 35, 80, 125
Cory J, 119

courts as jurispathic, 6, 87, 133, 144, 151, 166
Cover, R, 16, 34, 40, 44, 46–50, 51, 53, 77–78, 87, 98–100, 133–134, 144, 146, 151, 155–158, 162, 166, 187–188, 225, 230–231
Currie, S, 216, 229

Dawson, J, 72–81, 89, 178–180, 191
de Tocqueville, A, 22, 25, 34
Deane, J, 67–75, 100, 179, 180–182, 191–192, 196
death of the author, 138–139, 218
Delgado, R, 17, 36
Demian, 36
Derrida, J, 28, 35, 49, 54–56, 77–81, 146, 155, 184
Descartes, 87, 135
difference
  and judgment, 225–28
  as precursor of conflict in liberalism, 228
  as threat to legality, 228
different voice, 2, 12–15, 19, 29–31, 84, 88, 196, 203–206, 211, 225–226
  as narrative voice, 225–28
Douzinas and Warrington, 16, 47, 49, 81– 82
Douzinas, Warrington and McVeigh, 23, 35, 38, 47, 68, 82, 212
Dworkin, RM, 16, 35–36, 47–50, 59, 79, 80, 97, 135–44, 158–161, 184–188, 194, 218
  community and authority in, 158–60
  law as integrity in, 158–60

Engle, DM, 172, 190
ethical tort, 1, 40, 68, 76

Fineman, MA, 187, 197–198, 211
Fish, S, 45, 47, 92, 100, 135–44, 151, 157, 183–185, 204–205

238

community and authority in, 142–43, 142

interpretive community as a model for law, 143

force legitimated by authority, 1

gap between process and persuasion, 37–38

Gatens, M, 98

Gaudron, J, 67–75, 100, 189, 204

genderless persona, 202

Gibbs, J, 176–178, 191

Gilligan, C, 2, 12–19, 29–31, 84, 88, 196, 203–206, 210–211, 225–226

Ginsburg, Justice, 199

Gonthier J, 119

Goodman, E, 148, 156

Goodrich, P, 171–172, 190

Gould, SJ, 169, 189

Haldar, P, 16–18, 39, 47, 81–82, 186

Hawkins J, 117, 127

Hegarty v Shine, 107–11, 118, 122, 215

Hercules, 16, 29, 35–36, 42, 59, 79, 97, 146, 155, 159, 183

Hesse, H, 36

Hobbes, T, 19, 34, 43, 49, 54, 78, 91

Hunter, 150

intent to enter legal relations, 55

as acknowledgement that an agreement would be enforced by law, 116, 126

interpretation

and the geography of legality, 171–73

interpretive community, 13–14, 129, 138, 140, 205

Irigaray, 2

J

Jay, M, 97, 169, 189

Jones, KB, 16, 91, 99, 101, 129–130, 134, 150

judge

as subject, 15, 83–84

judgment

and choice, 47

and difference, 32

and responsibility, 2

as alternative imagining of social relations, 193–96

as insulated from execution, 58–59

as simultaneously particular and universal, 193–96

judicial conscience, as an artful dodger, 16, 53, 151

justice and difference, 15

Kafka, F, 35, 55, 78

Kennedy, D, 11, 19, 41, 47–48, 198, 211

La Forest J, 118–123, 127

law

as storytelling, 4–7, 214–25, 217–25

as the modern religion, 200–203, 208

as written text, 208

Le Bel J, 123

Leff, AA, 34, 98

linguistic markers, 200–202

Locke, J, 19, 78, 85

Lyotard, 1, 40, 68

Mabo & Ors v Queensland (No 2), 63–76, 89, 143, 168, 200

MacIntyre, A, 49, 80, 151–153, 163–164

Martin, E, 211

Mason, J, 179

Matsuda, MJ, 5, 17, 36, 211–212

McCarthy, E, 187

McHugh, 126

McLachlin J, 122–123

Michaelman, FI, 152

Milsom, SFC, 229

Minow, M, 34, 52, 57, 76–77, 79, 151, 156

moral/formal dilemma, in Cover, 51

Mouffe, C, 227, 231

Norberg v Wynrib, 118–24

orality

as central to the trial process, 23–24

ordinary stories

as distinct from legal narratives, 4–5

paideic community
in Cover, 163
Parashar, A, 150
persuasion
as central to narrative, 11
as key to legitimacy, 149–50
philosopher's stone, 135
philosophical scepticism, as a
specifically masculine intellectual
position, 95, 101
polyvocality, 8, 39, 214, 218
and bias, 8–9
Posner, R, 135, 151
procedural republic, 220–230

raceless persona, 202
Rawls, J, 15, 19, 48, 99, 187–188, 227,
231
relationship
between textuality and power, 27
representative voice, 131–33
rhetoric
as a source of meaning and authority
in law, 161
as inherently polyvocal, 174–75
as seduction, 37–39
written judgment as, 10, 27–30, 33,
42–43, 47, 49, 60–63, 65–67, 71,
75, 80, 115, 118, 147–50, 155,
157–158, 161, 165–166, 168–170,
174–175, 183, 190, 193, 203, 206,
220
rights
as linked to responsibilities, 12
Roe v Wade, 143
Rousseau, JJ, 19, 55, 78, 88, 98, 100,
137, 138, 143, 152, 154, 184

Sandel, M, 138, 152, 231
scepticism
and interpretation, 87–88
as a specifically masculine intellectual
position, 84–88
Schlag, P, 16, 81, 221–230

seamless web, 8, 11, 12, 16, 24, 29–30,
35, 59, 77, 79, 102, 107, 124, 218
Serat, A, 50
Sherry, S, 138, 152
skeletal principles, as essential to law,
65, 90, 92, 98–100, 117, 229
Smith, BH, 16, 80, 125, 155, 163, 188
social contract, 21, 54–56, 78–79, 85,
93, 100, 137, 184
Sopinka J, 120–122
Spelman, E, 57, 76–77, 79
Stacy, H, 130, 150–151
Stephen J, 114–117
subversive moment, in law, 51–53, 57–
58, 76
as fundamental, 57–58

tangled web, law as, 2, 11, 29–30, 39,
42, 44, 53–54, 143
terra nullius, 64–65, 70, 74–75, 117
texts
as gendered, 128–29
The Queen v Clarence, 111–18, 120,
122–123
theory and practice, dichotomy between,
67, 69
Toohey, J, 71–74, 76, 81
as rhetorical process, 161–62
as visual spectacle, 95–96

Unger, R, 153
unmarked term, 13, 201

veil of ignorance, 15, 19, 48
violence
as central to law, 54, 144–46
voices of the ancients, 11, 41

Walzer, M, 226, 231
Watson, I, 187–188
Weber, S, 25, 34–35
Weisberg, R, 10, 18, 77, 80, 189
and the poethics of judgment, 167–70
West, RL, 12, 19, 34, 60–63, 77–78,
153, 175, 186, 190–191, 210
White, JB, 146, 183
and the ethics of judgment, 146–47

White, Justice Margaret, 46
Wik Peoples v Queensland, Thayorre Peoples v Queensland, 143
Williams, P, 57, 79, 99, 156
Wills J, 111–113
Wilson, Justice, 179, 204, 209, 213
Wilson, Madam Justice Berthe, 204, 209, 213

Winn, PA, 165–166, 185, 189
Witteveen, WJ, 183
woman as the never to be of justice, 2–3

Yablon CM, 125
Year Book cases, 108, 147, 220, 222, 224–225
Young, IM, 209, 213